Study Guide

CONTEMPORARY LINGUISTICS

AN INTRODUCTION

Seventh Edition

Teresa Merrells
Mount Royal College

U.S. edition prepared by

Janie Rees-Miller
Marietta College

Mark Aronoff
State University of New York at Stony Brook

 bedford/st.martin's
Macmillan Learning
Boston | New York

Manufactured in the United States of America.

2 1 0 9 8 7
f e d c b a

For information, write: Bedford/St. Martin's, 75 Arlington Street, Boston, MA 02116 (617-399-4000)

978-1-319-04089-5

PREFACE FOR INSTRUCTORS

The *Study Guide* that accompanies *Contemporary Linguistics* is designed to be more comprehensive than a simple workbook, and as such it includes summaries and reviews of important concepts found in Chapters 1 through 8 of the textbook as well as extensive supplementary practice exercises. It is particularly well suited to those undergraduate and graduate students with no prior knowledge of linguistics; it may also be profitably used by students who need additional self-study material, by professors who need supplementary lecture material, and by teaching assistants who need to organize recitation sections. Thus we are once again pleased that the Canadian editors of *Contemporary Linguistic Analysis*, upon which this U.S. book, *Contemporary Linguistics*, is based, have reissued the *Study Guide* to accompany the text.

Student-friendly features that distinguished the previous editions of the *Study Guide* have been retained in this edition and expanded:

- **Practice exercises** cover the major topics in each chapter and provide an intermediate step between explanation of linguistic processes and their application to more challenging problems. A number of new exercises in this edition reflect a wide variety of world languages.

- **Charts** summarize important concepts graphically and guide students through the process of problem-solving.

- **Cross-references** refer students to the appropriate sections and pages in the main text and to relevant sections on the companion website. This edition also includes cross-references to figures and tables in the main text.

- **Reminder boxes** give helpful hints for understanding concepts and solving problems.

- **Review exercises** for each chapter consolidate skills acquired throughout the chapter. New problems have been added to the review exercises in the chapters on phonology, morphology, semantics, and historical linguistics.

- **Recap boxes** at the end of each chapter list important concepts covered in the chapter and have been fully updated.

- The **Answer Key** at the back of the book enables students to check their own work.

- Each chapter ends with a space for students to jot down **questions** or **problems** that they want to ask their professor or teaching assistant about.

This new edition of the *Study Guide* has been thoroughly revised to reflect the contents and order of presentation in the seventh edition of *Contemporary Linguistics*. In all chapters of the *Study Guide*, explanations have been revised for clarity where necessary, and practice exercises have been revised or added where appropriate to suit students' needs and to reflect the contents of the book's new edition.

As with the previous edition, this *Study Guide* closely follows its Canadian precursor in its organization and layout. Each chapter begins with an overview of material and ends with a review list of concepts and skills. Chapters comprise summaries of important concepts and processes and include numerous practice exercises and reminder boxes. Some practice exercises have been specially written for the U.S. edition of the *Study Guide*, and sources for these exercises are listed in the back of the guide.

We are grateful for the assistance we have received in preparing the *Study Guide*. We would like to acknowledge reviewers who gave feedback on the *Study Guide*: Barbara Bevington, Janet Cowal, Andrea Dallas, Hana Filip, Paul Franckowiak, Rachel Hansen, Brent Henderson, Sarah Hulsey, James Hunter, Kyle Johnson, Yong Lang, Vivian Lin, Monica Macaulay, Tim Pulju, Sarah Tully Marks, Sheri Wells-Jensen, and Chris Wen-Chao Li. We would particularly like to thank Carson Schutze, who has again provided us with helpful suggestions for this revision of the *Study Guide*. Our gratitude is also extended to the staff at Bedford/St. Martin's. Editor Joelle Hann kept us on our timetable and coordinated the various stages of production. Harold Chester checked data and assured accuracy in the final stages of production. Finally, we acknowledge the feedback from students, for whom the *Study Guide* is intended.

Janie Rees-Miller
Mark Aronoff

PREFACE TO THE CANADIAN EDITION

This study guide is intended to accompany the eighth edition of *Contemporary Linguistic Analysis: An Introduction*. It began as a series of worksheets distributed to students in class and gradually expanded to include brief explanations of course content and additional practice exercises. This material was eventually linked together with reminders and review sheets. As the study guide evolved, it became more generic and all-encompassing. As a result, the study guide is of potential use to any instructor of introductory linguistics using *Contemporary Linguistic Analysis: An Introduction*.

The study guide contains a preview of major concepts followed by chapters on the core components of theoretical linguistics: phonetics, phonology, morphology, syntax, and semantics. The study guide focuses on these aspects of theoretical linguistics, since these are areas of introductory linguistics in which students typically require a great deal of practice to better understand the methods of analysis used within each of these branches of linguistics. The study guide also allows students practice using these methods of analysis in other branches of linguistics, including language classification, historical linguistics, language acquisition, neurolinguistics, psycholinguistics, sociolinguistics, and writing systems.

Each chapter in the study guide begins with a list of the main topics found in that chapter. Each of these topics is expanded on within a section of the chapter. Each section of the chapter contains brief explanations of important concepts, questions for students about these concepts, and numerous exercises. Each chapter is closely linked to the text through references to tables, figures, examples, and diagrams of linguistic structure (e.g., syllable, word, and sentence representations). Each chapter also includes general questions aimed at getting students to actively think about the concepts presented in the text. This feature is designed to complement the text's ability to engage students with the material. All chapters include reminders of important concepts and conclude with a review checklist that students can use to prepare for exams. Students who wish to work and study independently will find an answer key to this study guide on the Companion Website at **www.pearsoncanada.ca/ogrady** (access code protected).

I gratefully acknowledge Anna Moro's extensive contributions to the material found in Chapters 9, 12, 14, and 15 of the study guide. Without her, these chapters would not have the depth that they do. I also acknowledge contributions made by Carrie Dyck, Elaine Sorensen, Leone Sveinson, Joyce Hildebrand, and Lorna Rowsell to Chapters 1 through 6 and Chapter 8. I would like to thank all the reviewers for their comments, especially Carrie Dyck and William O'Grady for their invaluable suggestions and advice, which have improved the overall quality of the study guide. Thanks also go to Elizabeth Ritter for using an earlier version of the study guide with her students and providing valuable feedback, and to John Archibald for his continued support. Finally, I extend my gratitude in memoriam to Michael Dobrovolsky for his inspiration and for encouraging me as an undergraduate to pursue linguistics.

Teresa Merrells

CONTENTS

NOTE TO STUDENTS:
HOW TO USE THIS STUDY GUIDE

Welcome to the study of linguistics! For many of you using *Contemporary Linguistics* this is your first experience with the field of linguistics. Everyone speaks a language and has ideas about language, but using the analytical tools for the scientific study of language can at first seem daunting. However, with study and practice, you can discover beauty in the systematic ways in which human language behaves and be fascinated by the ways in which languages differ.

This *Study Guide* is designed to help you accomplish that goal. Since each section of the *Study Guide* is keyed to pages and sections of *Contemporary Linguistics*, you can use the relevant sections of the guide to review some of the important concepts and practice skills that you have read about in the text. For greatest benefit, we suggest the following procedure:

1. Read the appropriate section in *Contemporary Linguistics*.

2. Recall important concepts and terms, and try to explain them in your own words.

3. Read the review explanations in the *Study Guide*.

4. Work the practice problems.

5. Check your answers using the Answer Key in the back of the *Study Guide*.

6. List questions or problems on the last page of the chapter in the *Study Guide*.

7. Ask your instructor or teaching assistant for help with any difficulties and for explanations of concepts that are not clear.

This may seem like a lot of work, and it may indeed be time-consuming. However, learning the concepts and skills of a new discipline is a step-by-step process, and each step builds on the preceding one. We are confident that *Contemporary Linguistics,* complemented by this *Study Guide,* will give you the necessary foundation for understanding the principles and methods of linguistics.

one

Language: A Preview

The following are some of the important concepts found in this chapter. Make sure you are familiar with them.

Specialization
Creativity
Linguistic competence
Grammar

Specialization (Section 1)

Humans are specialized for language. The characteristics below illustrate some of the aspects of our special capacity for language.

- *Speech Organs*

    Our lungs, larynx, tongue, teeth, lips, soft palate, and nasal passages are used both for survival (i.e., breathing, eating, etc.) and for producing the sounds of our language.

- *Speech Perception*

    We are also equipped for speech perception, and we have the ability at birth. Studies have shown that newborns are able to perceive subtle differences between sounds and are even able to perceive differences between sounds they have never heard before.

- *The Human Mind*

    Our minds form words, build sentences, and interpret meanings in ways not found in other species.

This specialization for language sets us apart from all other creatures.

Creativity (Section 2)

Human language is creative. That is, language does not provide us with a set of prepackaged messages. Rather, it allows us to produce and understand new words and sentences whenever needed. However, there are limitations on both the form and interpretation of new words and sentences. Linguists attempt to identify and understand these limitations.

PRACTICE 1.1: Creativity

1. Arrange the words *bird*, *worm*, *catches*, *early*, *every*, and *the* into an English sentence.

_____

_____

_____

2. Write two other sentences using the same words. _____

_____

_____

_____

_____

_____

3. Use the same words to create a "sentence" that is not an acceptable English sentence.

_____

_____

_____

4. Compare the sentences you wrote in 1 and 2 with the sentence in 3. Why is the sentence in 3 unacceptable in English?

_____

_____

_____

_____

Linguistic Competence (Section 3)

Linguistic competence can be defined as subconscious knowledge that enables the native speakers of a language to produce and understand an unlimited number of both familiar and novel utterances. The **native speakers** of a language are those who have acquired it as children in a natural setting like the home rather than in a classroom.

Linguists divide the subconscious knowledge that the native speakers of a language share into the following fields of study:

1. Phonetics: the study of the sounds found in language, including the articulation and perception of speech sounds

2. Phonology: the study of how speech sounds pattern in language

3. Morphology: the study of word structure and word formation

4. Syntax: the study of sentence structure

5. Semantics: the study of the meaning of words and sentences

This subconscious knowledge allows the speakers of a language to produce an infinite number of sentences, many of which we have never uttered or heard before. This is often referred to as language **creativity**. We don't memorize language; we create it.

While we all have this unconscious knowledge of our native language, we often make mistakes when we talk. That is, our actual use of language does not always reflect our linguistic competence.

PRACTICE 1.2: Linguistic competence

Your linguistic competence allows you to decide whether new words and novel sentences are acceptable or not. Test your linguistic competence by answering the following questions.

1. Put a check mark beside those words that are possible English words.

   a. tlim _____   e. plog _____

   b. stuken _____   f. skpit _____

   c. tseg _____   g. ngan _____

   d. fomp _____   h. breb _____

   Why are some of the above not possible English words? (Hint: Think about the combination of sounds.)

2. Put a check mark beside those words that are possible English words.

   a. speakless _____   d. reglorify _____

   b. beautifulness _____   e. horseable _____

   c. unrug _____   f. weedic _____

   Why are some of the above not possible English words? (Hint: Think about the prefix or suffix and its contribution to the meaning of the word.)

3. Put a check mark beside those sentences that are possible English sentences.

    a. The building was tossed yesterday away.   _____

    b. The building is swept every morning.   _____

    c. Every child should obey parents his.   _____

    d. Somebody left their gloves in the theater.   _____

    e. George surprised Mary with a party.   _____

    f. Joe surprised the stone.   _____

    Why are some of the above not possible English sentences?

Grammar (Section 3)

Grammar, to a linguist, refers to all the elements of our linguistic competence: phonetics, phonology, morphology, syntax, and semantics. In very general terms, grammar can be defined as the system of mental rules and elements needed to form and interpret the sentences of a language. The study of grammar is central to understanding language and to what it means to know a language. This is because:

- All languages have sounds, words, and sentences.
- All grammars allow for the expression of any thought.
- All grammars share common principles and tendencies called universals.
- All grammars are equal.
- All grammars change over time.

However, our grammatical knowledge is subconscious: we can decide what sounds right and what does not even though we may not be sure about why this is so.

There are two different perspectives on grammar: prescriptive and descriptive. A **prescriptive grammar** gives the socially accepted rules within a language, while a **descriptive grammar** is an objective description of the knowledge that the native speakers of a language share.

PRACTICE 1.3: Distinguishing prescriptive and descriptive grammar

1. Examine the boxes below (based on "The Verbal Edge," *Readers Digest*, August 1994), and see if you can tell which type of grammar is being exemplified.

   a. Which is correct: "Between you and I" or "Between you and me"?

"Between you and I" is **WRONG**.	You might say, "Many believe that there's an enormous rivalry between you and I." That may sound correct, but the pronoun *I* is wrong here.
"Between you and me" is **RIGHT**.	*Between* is a preposition, and prepositions are followed by objects. *I* is a subject or nominative pronoun. Objective pronouns that follow a preposition are *me, you, him, her, us,* and *them*.

   b. Which is correct: "She is older than me" or "She is older than I"?

"She is older than me" is **WRONG**.	The word *than* is a conjunction. It joins two sentences, words, or phrases. There are *two* sentences here: (1) "She is older" and (2) "I am."
"She is older than I" is **RIGHT**.	In a comparison joined by *than* or *as*, you need to complete the sentence. You wouldn't say "She is older than me am," so it must be "She is older than I."

   c. Which is correct: "Who do I ask" or "Whom do I ask"?

"Who do I ask?" is **WRONG**.	*Who* is generally appropriate whenever you use *he, she,* or *they*, and *whom* acts as a substitute for *him, her,* or *them*.
"Whom do I ask?" is **RIGHT**.	You would not say "I ask he," so the correct wording is "Whom do I ask?" (It sounds formal—which is why the incorrect "Who do I ask?" is usually used in informal speech.)

   d. Which is correct: "The list of upgrades are the same" or "The list of upgrades is the same"?

"The list of upgrades are the same" is **WRONG**.	The subject of a sentence must agree with the verb with respect to person (first, second, or third) and number (singular or plural).
"The list of upgrades is the same" is **RIGHT**.	The subject of this sentence is *list*, which is third-person singular. The verb *be* therefore must be in the third person, singular (present tense) form *is* and not *are*, which is plural.

The above are all examples of a prescriptivist view on language. While a prescriptivist grammar is useful in helping people learn a foreign language in that it contains the socially accepted rules for language use, linguists are more interested in descriptive grammar.

2. Each of the following aspects of linguistic competence contains two statements. See if you can identify which statement is prescriptivist and which is descriptivist. Do this by writing either P.G. (prescriptive grammar) or D.G. (descriptive grammar) beside each statement.

    a. Sounds

       _____ The English words *Mary*, *merry*, and *marry* should be pronounced differently because they are spelled differently.

       _____ English contains over twenty different consonant sounds.

    How many different vowel sounds are found in English?

    Do all languages have the same consonant and/or vowel sounds? Think of a language that has different consonant or vowel sounds.

    b. Words

       _____ The use of *has went* instead of *has gone* is an example of how change is causing the English language to deteriorate.

       _____ Many nouns in English are formed by adding the suffix *-ment* to words (e.g., *achievement, government, judgment*).

    Why would no English speaker construct the word *chairment*?

    c. Sentences

       _____ There are at least two ways in English to make a sentence refer to the future.

       _____ The auxiliary *shall* should be used with first person (i.e., *I, we*), whereas *will* should be used for second and third persons (e.g., *He will go, but we shall stay*).

Revise the following sentence in two different ways to make it refer to the future: *The horses eat hay.*

How do other languages make statements refer to future time?

d. Meaning

_____ The word *cool* should only be used to refer to temperature.

_____ Words often come in pairs of opposites (e.g., *hot/cold, light/dark*).

How is the meaning of a sentence different from the meaning of the words that compose it?

REMINDER

Linguistics is the study of the structure of human language. Linguists attempt to describe in an objective and nonjudgmental fashion the internalized and unconscious knowledge that the native speakers of a language share, which allows them to both speak and understand their language. While the primary focus of this guide is on English, many of the principles and theories discussed apply to all other languages as well.

Review Exercise

Each of the following statements illustrates a concept covered in Chapter 1. For each statement, determine which concept is being illustrated. Do this by writing the number of the concept beside each statement. The first one is done for you.

Concepts:
1. Linguistic competence
2. Prescriptive grammar
3. Descriptive grammar
4. Universality

Statements:

a. _____4_____   All languages have a way of making negatives.

b. _____   Speakers of American English know that one way to make questions is to move an auxiliary verb ahead of the subject noun phrase.

c. _____   Many nouns in English are formed by adding -*ness* to an adjective, for example: *sadness*, *silliness*, and *happiness*.

d. _____   *Brung* should never be used as the past tense of *bring*.

e. _____   Every language has a set of vowels and consonants.

f. _____   Speakers of any language are capable of producing an unlimited number of novel sentences.

g. _____   In English, there is no theoretical limit on the number of adjectives that can occur before a noun.

h. _____   In the sentence *My friend is smarter than me*, *me* is incorrect because it is an object pronoun and this comparative construction requires the subject pronoun *I*.

i. _____   In English, the plural is formed by adding [-s], [-z], or [-əz] to the end of nouns.

j. _____   Every language has a way of forming questions.

k. _____   Speakers of American English know that the different vowel sounds in the words *bat*, *bet*, *but*, and *bit* are crucial to their meanings.

☑ **RECAP**

Make sure you understand these terms. (See also the Key Terms at the end of Chapter 1 of the main text.)

- creativity
- descriptive grammar
- generality
- grammar
- inaccessibility
- linguistic competence
- mutability

- native speaker
- parity
- prescriptive grammar
- speech organs
- speech perception
- universality

Questions? Problems?

_____

_____

_____

_____

_____

_____

_____

_____

_____

_____

_____

_____

_____

_____

_____

_____

_____

_____

two

Phonetics: The Sounds of Language

Phonetics is the study of the articulation and perception of speech sounds. Following are some of the important topics and concepts covered in this chapter. Make sure you are familiar with them.

International Phonetic Alphabet	Vowel articulation
Segments	Phonetic transcription
Sound producing system	Suprasegmentals
Consonant articulation	Processes

Phonetic Transcription (Section 1)

Human language contains a finite number of speech sounds, or **phones**. The speech sounds found in language are transcribed using the symbols found in the **International Phonetic Alphabet (IPA):**

- Each symbol in this alphabet represents one and only one speech sound.

- Each speech sound in language corresponds to one and only one IPA symbol.

- Since symbols represent sounds, the same symbols can be used in whatever language that sound occurs.

- It is important to remember that IPA symbols represent sounds and not spelling in a particular langauge. To indicate this difference, symbols are enclosed in [ ] brackets. Don't forget to use them.

REMINDER

The focus in this chapter is on learning the IPA symbols corresponding to the vowel and consonant sounds of English. Many, but not all, of these sounds are found in other languages. In addition, there are many sounds that do not occur in English but that are found in other languages. For more information on some of these sounds, their descriptions, and their IPA symbols, please refer to Table 2.28 and Table 2.29 in the text.

Segments (Section 1.2)

An individual speech sound (or phone) is called a **segment**, and each segment is represented by a symbol in the phonetic alphabet. Words typically consist of a number of different speech sounds. To transcribe, you need to determine not only the number of speech sounds in a word but also what those speech sounds are. But don't be fooled by spelling. Each of the following boxes illustrates a reason why we can't rely on spelling to determine the number of speech sounds in an English word.

Some letters or combinations of letters have more than one speech sound associated with them. In each of the following example sets, determine if the underlined letter(s) are pronounced the same way for all the words presented.

1.	'o'	as in	h<u>o</u>t	ech<u>o</u>	w<u>o</u>man
2.	'c'	as in	<u>c</u>areful	<u>c</u>entury	<u>c</u>ello
3.	'ou'	as in	sh<u>ou</u>ld	t<u>ou</u>gh	s<u>ou</u>nd

Sometimes one speech sound can be represented using different letters or combinations of letters. In each of the following example sets, determine if the underlined letter(s) have the same or different speech sounds.

1.	thr<u>ou</u>gh	cl<u>ue</u>	sh<u>oe</u>	t<u>oo</u>
2.	r<u>ea</u>l	s<u>ee</u>	sorr<u>y</u>	Sh<u>ei</u>la
3.	str<u>aw</u>	t<u>a</u>lk	f<u>ou</u>ght	l<u>o</u>st

Many words in English contain double letters. Double letters do not necessarily mean that there are two speech sounds. Say each of the following words and determine if the doubled letter is pronounced twice.

str<u>ee</u>t   b<u>oo</u>k   mi<u>tt</u>en   ki<u>ll</u>er

Finally, many words in English contain silent letters. These are letters that are not pronounced and that therefore do not correspond to a speech sound. Say each of the following words and determine if all of the letters are pronounced.

knife   leave   pneumonia   thumb

The above points also illustrate some of the reasons for using IPA rather than conventional spelling for doing phonetic transcription. In IPA, unlike in spelling, each symbol corresponds to only one sound and always the same sound.

The lesson is: When you are transcribing words, you need to forget about spelling.

PRACTICE 2.1: Segments and phonetic symbols

To get ready for transcription, try the following exercises.

1. Determine the number of speech sounds in each of the following words. Count diphthongs as single sounds.

    a. thing _____   d. phosphate _____

    b. comb _____   e. scene _____

    c. psychic _____   f. fright _____

2. a. When we say a word like *then*, do the letters *th* represent two separate sounds or one

    sound? _____

    b. Does the *th* spelling represent the same sound in all these words? *Thomas*, *think*, *though*?

    If not, how many different sounds does *th* represent? _____

    c. How many sounds are represented by the letters *ng* in the word *sung*? _____

    What about the *ng* in the word *hunger*? _____

    d. Does the letter *i* have the same sound in all of these words? _____

    kitten   kite   technique   university

    How many sounds are represented by *i* in these words? _____

    e. Sort the following list of words into two groups. In one group should be words with the sound made by *k* in the word *kite*. In the other group should be the words with the sound made by *ch* in the word *choke*:

ache	cello	each
arch	chain	kin
architect	choir	piccolo
batch	common	queen

    What is the correspondence between spelling and sound?

The Sound-Producing System (Section 2)

The **vocal tract** is the sound-producing system. It includes the lungs, trachea, larynx, pharynx, velum, oral cavity, and nasal cavity. Speech sounds are made as air passes through the vocal tract.

- **Larynx.** The larynx contains the vocal cords (or vocal folds), which provide the source of sound. The space between the vocal folds is the **glottis**. The **glottal states** that you should know are:

    Voiced: The vocal folds are vibrating.
    Voiceless: The vocal folds are open.
    Whisper: The front parts of the vocal folds are closed.
    Murmur: The vocal folds are relaxed to let some air through.

- **Pharynx:** The pharynx is the tube of the throat between the larynx and the oral cavity.

- **Oral cavity:** This is the mouth.

- **Nasal cavity:** The **velum** controls airflow through the nasal passages. Raising the velum cuts off airflow through the nasal passages. Lowering the velum allows air to flow through the nasal passages.

The pharynx, oral cavity, and nasal cavity act as filters that modify the sound in various ways. Together they comprise the vocal tract.

PRACTICE 2.2: Parts of the vocal tract

On this diagram, label the lungs, larynx, pharynx, oral cavity, nasal cavity, and velum.

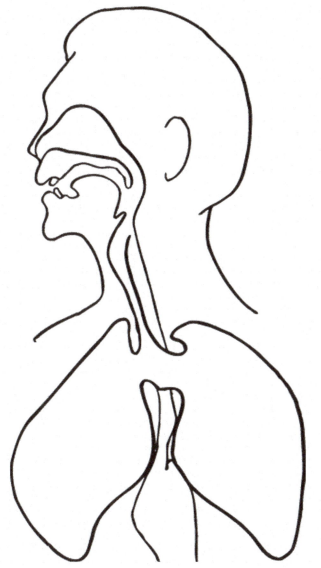

Sound Classes (Section 3)

Sounds produced with the vocal tract can be divided into three major classes: **consonants**, **vowels**, and **glides**. The defining characteristics of each class are given below.

- **Consonants.** Consonantal sounds are made with a narrow or complete obstruction in the vocal tract. Some of them come in **voiced/voiceless** pairs.

- **Vowels.** Vowel sounds are made with little obstruction in the vocal tract, and they are typically voiced. Vowels tend to be more **sonorous** than consonants. As a result, we perceive vowels as louder and longer lasting. Vowels are also classified as **syllabic** sounds, meaning that they can function as the **nucleus** of a syllable.

- **Glides.** Glides are sounds that have characteristics of both consonants and vowels. They are sometimes called semivowels or semiconsonants. Glides are like vowels in their articulation, but they are like consonants in that they do not function as the nucleus of a syllable.

PRACTICE 2.3: Identifying consonants, vowels, and glides

Each of the following words has one or more letters underlined. The underlined letters correspond to one sound. Identify this sound as a consonant, vowel, or glide. The first is done for you.

1. ro<u>tt</u>weiler   <u>consonant</u>

2. thr<u>ough</u>   _____

3. <u>l</u>ovely   _____

4. <u>y</u>ear   _____

5. my<u>th</u>   _____

6. <u>wh</u>istle   _____

7. s<u>u</u>ffer   _____

8. ju<u>dge</u>   _____

REMINDER

Some types of consonants can also be syllabic (i.e., function as the nucleus of a syllable). For this reason, you should think of sounds not just as being consonants, vowels, or glides, but as being syllabic or nonsyllabic elements. This will be useful in doing phonetic transcription and also when doing phonology (Chapter 3).

Consonant Articulation (Section 4)

All sounds, regardless of whether they are consonants, vowels, or glides, are described in terms of how they are articulated. This information is contained in the sound's articulatory description. Consonants and glides are described differently from vowels.

Consonants are sounds that are made with obstruction in the vocal tract. Consonants do not normally form the nucleus of a syllable and can be voiced or voiceless. There are three parameters necessary to describe consonant and glide articulation:

- **Glottal state** (Section 2.3)

- **Place of articulation** (Section 4.2)

- **Manner of articulation** (Section 5)

PRACTICE 2.4: Articulatory terms

Each place of articulation has an articulatory term to describe sounds made at that particular place in the vocal tract. In each blank, write the articulatory term for the type of sound made at that place of articulation. The first one is done for you.

1. lips   labial sounds _____

2. lips and teeth   _____

3. alveolar ridge   _____

4. alveopalatal region   _____

5. hard palate   _____

6. velum (soft palate)   _____

7. uvula   _____

8. pharynx   _____

9. larynx   _____

10. glottis   _____

Places of Articulation (Section 4.2)

Different places in the vocal tract can be modified to produce different sounds. Most of these places are found within the oral cavity, but there are two places of articulation outside the oral cavity.

PRACTICE 2.5: Locating places of articulation (See Figure 2.4)

On the following diagram, identify all the places of articulation and the kinds of sounds that are made at those places.

Manners of Articulation (Section 5)

Manner of articulation refers to the ways in which the airflow is modified as sounds are produced:

- **Stops** (Tables 2.3 and 2.4) stop the flow of air completely.

- **Fricatives** (Tables 2.5 and 2.6) allow a small stream of air to pass through, creating friction.

- **Affricates** (Table 2.7) begin as stops, but end as fricatives.

- **Nasals** (Tables 2.3 and 2.4) are produced when the velum is lowered and the air flows through the nasal cavity.

- **Liquids** (Table 2.10) allow a relatively free flow of air; the liquids are *l*'s and *r*'s.

- **Glides** allow the freest flow of air among the nonsyllabic sounds.

Although the consonant chart looks daunting, you will find that completing it will help you remember each phonetic symbol according to its place and manner of articulation.

PRACTICE 2.6: Consonants (Table 2.12)

Fill in the chart with the symbols corresponding to the consonant and glide sounds of American English.

		GLOTTAL STATE	PLACE OF ARTICULATION							
			Bilabial	Labiodental	Interdental	Alveolar	Alveopalatal	Palatal	Velar	Glottal
M A N N E R O F A R T I C U L A T I O N	Stop	voiceless								
		voiced								
	Fricative	voiceless								
		voiced								
	Affricate	voiceless								
		voiced								
	Nasal	voiced								
	Liquid									
	a. lateral	voiced								
	b. retroflex	voiced								
	Glide	voiced								

PRACTICE 2.7: Consonant sounds

1. Give the phonetic symbol for the first consonant sound in each of the following words.

    a. through _____   d. whistle _____

    b. shave _____   e. phone _____

    c. knee _____   f. quality _____

2. Give the phonetic symbol for the last consonant sound in each of the following words.

   a. laugh   _____   d. Ruth   _____

   b. sang   _____   e. lamb   _____

   c. choice   _____   f. box   _____

QUICK REMINDER!

Every sound has one and only one articulatory description. And every articulatory description corresponds to one and only one symbol in the International Phonetic Alphabet (IPA).

Voice Lag and Aspiration (Section 5.5)

Sometimes when voiceless **stops** [p, t, k] are pronounced, they are produced with a small puff of air. This puff of air is called **aspiration** and is represented as [ʰ].

Pronounce the words in the boxes on the next page, paying close attention to the first sound, and see if you can tell when aspiration does and does not occur. You can feel this extra release of air by putting your hand close to your mouth as you produce the words. (It is easier to feel the puff of air with **bilabial** and **alveolar** stops than with the **velar** stop.)

Voiceless stops in English can be both aspirated and unaspirated. Aspiration occurs only when there is a delay in the voicing of the vowel after the voiceless stop. This delay occurs in words such as *pit, take,* and *kill* because there is not enough time after the release of the voiceless stop to vibrate the **vocal folds** for the vowel articulation. The vowel therefore is not immediately voiced, and it is this initial voicelessness that is perceived as a puff of air. In words such as *spit, stake,* and *skill,* there is no delay in voicing, and therefore no aspiration. The delay does not occur because the presence of an extra sound provides the time necessary to get the vocal folds into position to immediately start voicing the vowel when the stop is released.

ASPIRATED VOICELESS STOPS	
[pʰ]	pit punk
[tʰ]	take tab
[kʰ]	kill car

UNASPIRATED VOICELESS STOPS	
[p]	spit spunk
[t]	stake stab
[k]	skill scar

PRACTICE 2.8: Aspiration

Pronounce the following words, and put a check mark beside those words containing aspirated voiceless stops.

1. scratch _____   4. pending _____

2. talk _____   5. stripe _____

3. segments _____   6. careful _____

Unreleased Stops. Sometimes when the voiceless stops [p, t, k] are pronounced they are not released. That is, the articulation ends with either the lips closed or the tongue on the place of articulation. The symbol for this articulation is a raised [˺].

Say the words in the boxes below. For the words in the first column, pay close attention to the first sound, and see if you can feel your lips opening or your tongue moving away from the place of articulation. For the words in the second column, pay close attention to the final sound and see if your lips remain closed or if your tongue remains at the place of articulation.

VOICELESS ASPIRATED STOPS	
[pʰ]	pit punk
[tʰ]	take tab
[kʰ]	kill car

VOICELESS UNRELEASED STOPS	
[p˺]	cap leap
[t˺]	pot most
[k˺]	back sack

Fricative and Affricate Articulations (Sections 5.3–5.4)

Strident/Sibilant. Some fricatives and affricates are noisier than are others. Say the words in the box below. See if you can hear which fricatives and affricates are noisier. The noisier fricatives and affricates are considered to be strident (sibilant). The quieter fricatives and affricates are considered nonstrident. This is an acoustic criterion used in describing fricatives and affricates.

NONSTRIDENT FRICATIVES	
[f] and [v]	fit vat
[θ] and [ð]	thick though

STRIDENT FRICATIVES AND AFFRICATES	
[s] and [z]	sip zen
[ʃ] and [ʒ]	ship pleasure
[tʃ] and [dʒ]	cherub gem

Now go back to the consonant chart in Practice 2.6, and put a box around the strident sounds.

Liquid and Nasal Articulation (Sections 5.6–5.7)

Voiced and voiceless liquids. Since [l] is normally voiced, *lateral* usually means voiced lateral. However, [l] can also be voiceless, in which case it is represented using [l̥]. Say the words in the table below and see if you can hear the difference between the voiced and voiceless laterals.

Voiced Lateral		Voiceless Lateral	
[l]	lip love lullaby lamp	[l̥]	please play clean clever

Like [l], [ɹ] is normally voiced. *Retroflex* therefore usually means voiced retroflex. Also like [l], [ɹ] can be voiceless, in which case it is represented using [̥]. English also has a flap sound, which is another type of sound commonly identified with *r*. A flap is made when the tip of the tongue strikes the alveolar ridge as it passes by. [ɾ] represents a flap. Say the words in the following table and see if you can hear the difference between the voiced and voiceless [ɹ], and the flap.

Voiced Retroflex		Voiceless Retroflex		Flap	
[ɹ]	ride right car	[ɹ̥]	pray train crayon	[ɾ]	kettle city

Clear and dark *l*. Most speakers of English pronounce the lateral ([l]) with two possible articulations. A **clear *l*** is produced with an alveolar articulation—i.e., with the tongue tip touching the alveolar ridge and the tongue body at a neutral position. The **dark *l*** is sometimes called a "velarized *l*" because it is produced with a secondary articulation in which the tongue body is raised toward the velum. There is dialectal difference, however, in the environments in which a speaker produces clear *l* or dark *l*.

Say the following words and pay close attention to the position of your tongue. Which words do you pronounce with the clear *l* and which do you pronounce with the dark *l*?

lip	peel	swallow
lop	pull	silly
love	gill	Sally
leave	gull	sully

Syllabic liquids and nasals. Liquid and nasal articulations can be either nonsyllabic or syllabic. Liquids (*l* and *r*) are syllabic when they can form the nucleus of a syllable.

Syllabic liquids occur in unstressed syllables at the ends of words whenever the liquid follows a consonant. An *r*-colored schwa [ɚ] occurs in one-syllable words such as *shirt* and *word*.

Syllabic nasals occur in unstressed syllables at the ends of words when the nasal follows a stop, fricative, or affricate. Say the words below and see if you can hear when the liquid or nasal is syllabic or nonsyllabic. See Table 2.11 of the text for further examples.

	SOME SYLLABIC SOUNDS	SOME NONSYLLABIC SOUNDS
Liquids	twink<u>le</u> fathe<u>r</u>	<u>l</u>awn <u>r</u>ain
Nasals	glutto<u>n</u> winso<u>me</u>	ha<u>n</u>dicraft <u>m</u>aster

PRACTICE 2.9: Liquids and nasals

1. Say the following words. Put a check mark beside those words containing a velarized (dark) *l*.

   a. malign _____

   b. silly _____

   c. allow _____

   d. pull _____

   e. lamb _____

   f. meal _____

2. Say the following words. Put a check mark beside those words containing a syllabic liquid or nasal.

   a. laugh _____

   b. bottom _____

   c. mad _____

   d. suffer _____

   e. kitten _____

   f. bushel _____

   g. rugby _____

   h. note _____

Facial Diagrams for Consonants (Figure 2.5)

There are four important parts to completing or deciphering facial diagrams for consonants.

Voicing/Voicelessness. Voiceless sounds are represented by two lines shaped like an ellipse. Voiced sounds are shown by two wavy lines where the larynx would be.

Nasal Passage. For oral sounds, the nasal passage is closed (the velum is raised); for nasal sounds, the nasal passage is open (the velum is lowered).

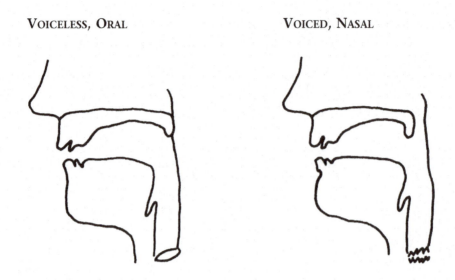

VOICELESS, ORAL   VOICED, NASAL

Place of Articulation. The narrowest point in the airstream passage is the **place of artic-ulation**.

Manner of Articulation. If no air escapes past a given articulator (i.e., a stop), then the articulator must touch the place of articulation. If the air does escape (i.e., a **fricative**), then there is a space between the articulator and the place of articulation. If the sound is an **affri-cate**, then the diagram is shown with the articulator touching the place of articulation and an arrow indicating the direction in which the articulator moves.

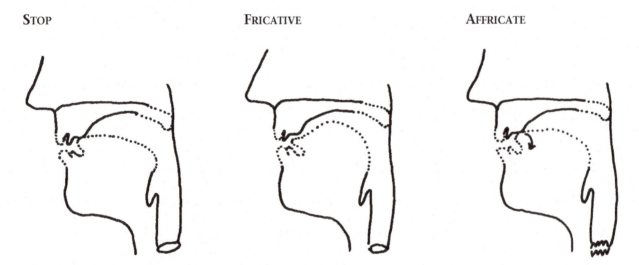

STOP   FRICATIVE   AFFRICATE

PRACTICE 2.10: Drawing facial diagrams

Complete the following diagrams so that each of the sounds listed below is depicted.

1. [s]   4. [n]
2. [b]   5. [g]
3. [dʒ]   6. [ð]

To complete the diagrams, you must:

- Draw in the lips: either closed or open.
- Draw the tongue to the place of articulation and to the manner of articulation.
- Draw in the velum: either closed or open.
- Draw in the glottal state: either voiced or voiceless.

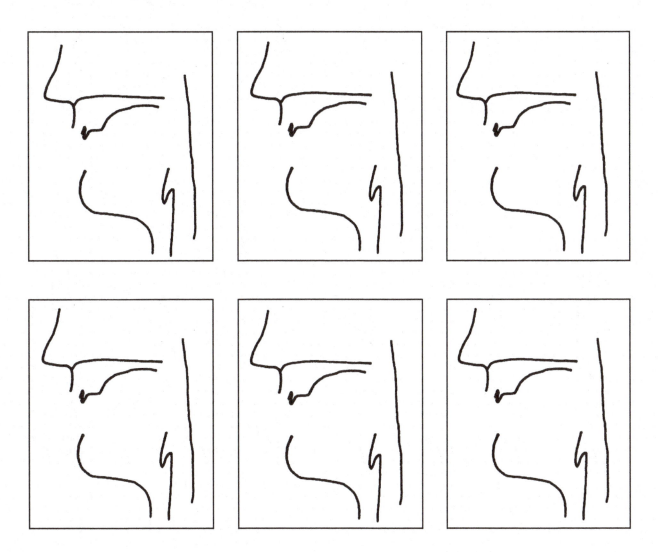

PRACTICE 2.11: Reading facial diagrams

For each of the following drawings, there is only one sound that could be produced by the vocal tract position. Figure out which consonant sound is represented, and write the phonetic symbol for that sound between the brackets below the drawing.

Make sure that you pay attention to voicing, to place and manner of articulation, and to the position of the velum.

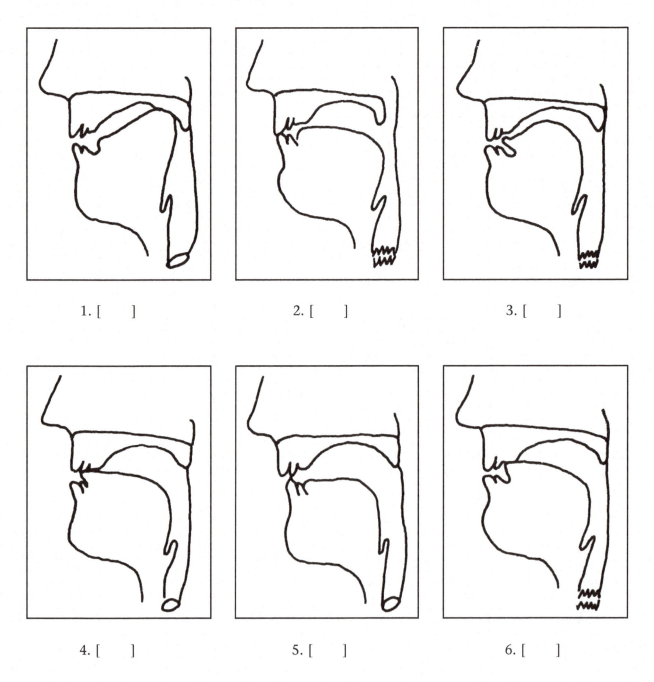

1. [   ]   2. [   ]   3. [   ]

4. [   ]   5. [   ]   6. [   ]

Vowel Articulation (Section 6)

Vowels are sounds that are sonorant, that are articulated with little obstruction in the vocal tract, and that are syllabic (can form the nucleus of a syllable). Vowels are also usually voiced.

Vowels are classified according to:

- tongue height:
    high vs. mid vs. low

- tongue backness:
    front vs. (central vs.) back

- lip rounding:
    rounded vs. unrounded

- tenseness:
    tense vs. lax

Simple Vowels and Diphthongs (Section 6.1)

Simple vowels are vowels whose quality does not change during their articulation, while diphthongs are vowels that exhibit a change in quality within a single syllable. This change in quality is the result of the tongue moving away from a vowel articulation to a glide articulation. Say the words in the table below and see if you can hear the change in quality during a diphthong articulation.

SOME SIMPLE VOWELS	SOME DIPHTHONGS
sit	buy
lost	now
cup	cry
met	pray
bat	sew

Diphthongs can be classified as either major or minor. The major diphthongs are those whose quality change is easy to hear. The quality change in the minor diphthongs is harder to hear. Say the words containing diphthongs in the above table again, and see if you can tell which are the major diphthongs and which the minor diphthongs. See Table 2.13 of the text for examples of simple vowels and major and minor dipthongs in American English.

PRACTICE 2.12: Vowels (Figure 2.11)

Fill in the following chart with the phonetic symbols corresponding to the vowel sounds of American English. In the blanks, indicate tongue position and height. Label the group of rounded vowels. Circle tense vowels.

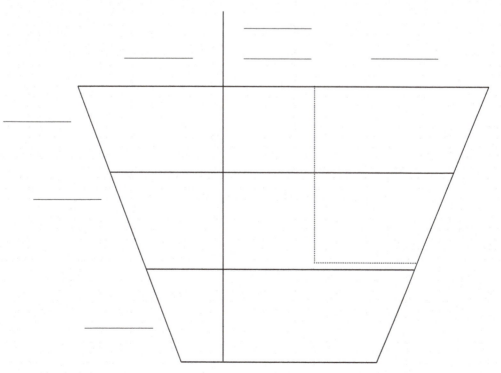

PRACTICE 2.13: Vowels

Give the phonetic symbol for the vowel sound in each of the following English words.

1. stool _____
2. sight _____
3. meet _____
4. pot _____
5. sit _____
6. put _____

Facial Diagrams for Vowels (Figure 2.9)

The following characteristics will help you read facial diagrams for vowels:

Tongue placement. The height (high, mid, or low) and backness of the tongue (front, central, or back) determine the particular vowel being depicted:

Front vowels: The tongue body is raised more toward the hard palate, as in [i], [ɪ], and [æ].

Back vowels: The tongue body is raised more toward the velum, as in [u], [ʊ], and [ɑ].

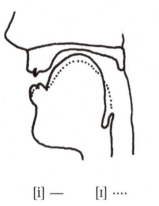

[i] — [ɪ] ····

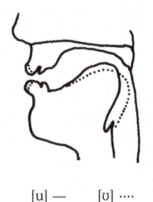

[u] — [ʊ] ····

High vowels: The tongue body is raised fairly high, as for [i], [ɪ], [u], and [ʊ].

REMINDER

For every articulatory description, you need to be able to provide the corresponding phonetic symbol, for example:

voiceless bilabial stop → [p]

For every phonetic symbol, you need to be able to provide the corresponding articulatory description, for example:

[ej] → mid front tense unrounded vowel

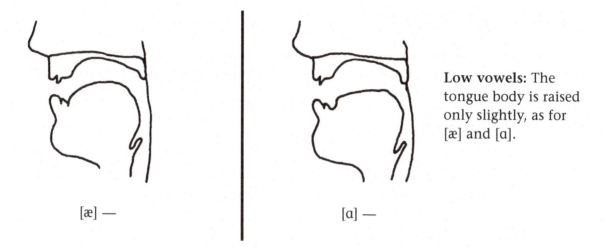

[æ] —   [ɑ] —   **Low vowels:** The tongue body is raised only slightly, as for [æ] and [ɑ].

Nasal passage. For oral vowels, the nasal passage is closed by the raised velum, as shown for all the English vowels here. For nasal vowels, the velum is lowered to allow air to flow through the nasal cavity.

Lip position. For rounded vowels, the lips protrude slightly. Compare the rounded vowels [u] and [ʊ] with the unrounded vowels [i] and [ɪ]. Also, the lips are closer together for high vowels and farther apart for low vowels.

These diagrams do not show the larnyx, but remember that all vowels in English are voiced.

PRACTICE 2.14: Facial diagrams for vowels

For each facial diagram, choose which vowel is being represented. Remember to look at the tongue height and position, the nasal passage, and the lip position.

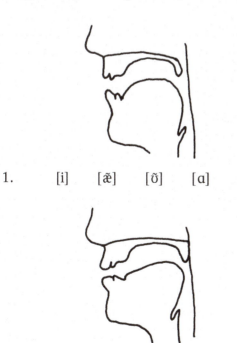

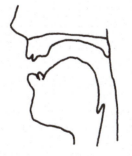

1.   [i]   [ǽ]   [ŭ]   [ɑ]   2.   [ĩ]   [ɛ]   [u]   [ɑ̃]

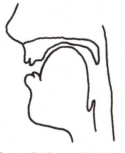

3.   [ĩ]   [ǽ]   [u]   [ɔ]   4.   [ĩ]   [ej]   [õw]   [ə]

[tɹænskɹɪpʃn̩ tajm] (Section 7)

Each box below contains examples of sounds that often cause difficulty when students are beginning to do transcription. For more examples of transcribed words, turn to the inside back cover of this book.

Syllabic Consonants

r	[ɹ]	for the *r* sound at the beginning of a syllable; e.g., *real, right;* for the *r* sound at the end of a syllable; e.g., *more, car*
	[ɾ]	for the *d*-like sound in *butter, writer, atom, duty*
	[ɹ̩]	for the syllabic *r* in an unstressed syllable at the end of a word after a consonant; e.g., *ladder, tailor, longer, laser*
	[ɚ]	for the *r*-colored schwa in *burr, earth, perceive*
l	[l]	for the *l* sound in *light, pill, please*
	[l̩]	for the syllabic *l* in an unstressed syllable at the end of a word after a consonant; e.g., *babble, poodle, little, couple, Russell, panel*
m	[m̩]	for the syllabic *m* in an unstressed syllable at the end of a word after a stop, affricate, or fricative; e.g., *chasm, Beecham, communism*
	[m]	for all other *m* sounds
n	[n̩]	for the syllabic *n* in an unstressed syllable at the end of a word after a stop, affricate, or fricative; e.g., *button, seven, brazen*
	[n]	for all other *n* sounds

Vowels

Diphthongs are transcribed as vowel-glide sequences. Remember that diphthongs are a single speech sound. Remember as well that diphthongs are described in terms of the vowel, not the glide.

• Use [a], not [ɑ], for the major diphthongs (i.e., [aj] and [aw], *not* [ɑj] and [ɑw]). The symbols [a] and [ɑ] represent different sounds.

• The mid tense vowels [e] and [o] are pronounced as minor diphthongs in most dialects of American English and are transcribed as [ej] and [ow].

• In some dialects of American English, the high tense vowels [i] and [u] are also pronounced as minor diphthongs. In these dialects, they would be transcribed as [ij] and [uw].

Vowels before [ɹ]: There is a good deal of dialectal variation in the pronunciation of vowels before *r.* Some alternatives are given here.

[biɹ] or [bɪɹ]	beer	[buɹ]	boor
[bejɹ] or [bɛɹ]	bear	[boɹ] or [boɹ]	bore
[bæɹi] or [bɛɹi]	Barry	[baɹ]	bar

Schwa and Wedge

Schwa [ə]	Wedge [ʌ]

• used for unstressed vowels
    [əbawt] about
• used for the words *the* and *a*
	• used when there is some degree of stress
	  on the vowel
	    [ˈsʌpɹ̩] supper
	• is not found before [ɹ] in the same syllable

Aspiration

p, t, k	Use [pʰ, tʰ, kʰ] for any *p, t, k* sound that occurs at the beginning of a syllable followed by a vowel that receives some degree of stress.
	    [pʰæt] pat, [tʰɔt] taught, [kʰejk] cake
	    [əˈpʰiɹ] appear, [əˈtʰæk] attack

	Use [p, t, k] for any other *p, t, k* sound. [spɛk] speck, [stɑp] stop, [skut] scoot

PRACTICE 2.15: [tɹænskɹɪpʃn̩ ɛksɚsajzəz]

Transcribe the following words as you would say them in normal everyday speech. Remember to include brackets, and remember to forget spelling. Watch out for syllabic consonants.

1. craft _____
2. sigh _____
3. health _____
4. beige _____
5. frog _____
6. paddle _____
7. angel _____

8. rich _____
9. tape _____
10. vague _____
11. rooster _____
12. instead _____
13. bottom _____
14. church _____

15. thought _____
16. had _____
17. exit _____
18. sugar _____
19. unit _____
20. question _____

REMINDER

There are many dialectical differences in the pronunciation of vowels and syllabic consonants. For more details, see the appendix to Chapter 2 in the textbook.

PRACTICE 2.16: Transcribing vowels

Remember that the tense mid vowels have an off-glide in phonetic transcription.

1. key	_____	5. cheese	_____	9. bone	_____
2. due	_____	6. ate	_____	10. east	_____
3. loaf	_____	7. wheeze	_____	11. baby	_____
4. made	_____	8. through	_____	12. throw	_____

PRACTICE 2.17: Transcribing vowels before [ɹ]

This time watch out for vowels before [ɹ] sounds.

1. cheer	_____	7. there	_____	13. chair	_____
2. car	_____	8. star	_____	14. score	_____
3. sir	_____	9. her	_____	15. floor	_____
4. oar	_____	10. horse	_____	16. course	_____
5. heart	_____	11. hard	_____	17. harm	_____
6. sharp	_____	12. shirt	_____	18. thwart	_____

PRACTICE 2.18: Diphthongs

Transcribe the following words as you would in normal everyday speech. Watch out for those diphthongs.

1. voice	_____	7. train	_____	13. bicycle	_____
2. hour	_____	8. oily	_____	14. goat	_____
3. eyes	_____	9. prize	_____	15. embroider	_____
4. shaking	_____	10. crow	_____	16. lazy	_____
5. prowl	_____	11. counter	_____	17. throne	_____
6. knifed	_____	12. down	_____	18. joint	_____

Remember: Transcription takes a lot of practice.

PRACTICE 2.19: Schwa, wedge, and syllabic consonants

For this group, pay close attention to the schwa, wedge, and syllabic consonant sounds. You might want to determine which vowel gets primary stress to help you out. Remember to use syllabic consonants where necessary.

1. sludge _____
2. quality _____
3. luck _____
4. notice _____

5. thunder _____
6. behave _____
7. emphasis _____
8. announce _____

9. hung _____
10. oven _____
11. stuff _____
12. understand _____

PRACTICE 2.20: Reading transcription

Give the correctly spelled English word for each of the following transcriptions.

1. [liʒɻ] _____
2. [æks] _____
3. [wɚði] _____
4. [wʌns] _____
5. [ʃejd] _____

6. [ʃaj] _____
7. [swit] _____
8. [tʰub] _____
9. [tʃɔjs] _____
10. [mʌtn̩] _____

11. [pʰajp] _____
12. [sɔfn̩] _____
13. [fowni] _____
14. [stætʃu] _____
15. [skwɛɹ] _____

Shared Phonetic Properties

Sounds are distinguished by their phonetic properties, but they can also share phonetic properties. Phonetic properties include such things as voice, place of articulation, manner of articulation, tongue height, and lip position.

PRACTICE 2.21: Shared phonetic properties

1. Each of the following groups of sounds contains at least one shared phonetic property. For each group of sounds, state the phonetic properties that the sounds have in common. Include as many as possible. The first is done for you.

   a. [b, d, g] _____ voiced (oral) stops _____

   b. [v, d, m] _____

   c. [s, tʃ, ʒ] _____

    d. [j, ɹ, n]   _____

    e. [ɑ, o, ʊ]   _____

    f. [æ, ɪ, ɛ]   _____

2. For each of the following groups of sounds, circle the sound that does not belong and state a phonetic property that the remaining sounds share. There may be more than one possible answer.

    a. [f ð v m]   _____

    b. [d t n g]   _____

    c. [ɑ o ɪ u]   _____

Suprasegmentals (Section 8)

Suprasegmentals are inherent properties that are part of all sounds regardless of their place or manner of articulation. The three main suprasegmentals are **pitch**, **length**, and **stress**. Pitch is further divided into tone and intonation.

- **Pitch: Tone languages** are languages in which pitch movement is used to signal differences in meaning. Mandarin Chinese is a good example. Tone languages may use register and/or contour tones. A **register tone** is a level pitch, while a **contour tone** is a moving pitch. Figure 2.14 of the text shows tones in Mandarin. Figures 2.12, 2.13, and 2.15 give examples from some other tone languages.

  Intonation is pitch movement that is not related to differences in word meaning. For example, rising pitch is often used to signal a question or an incomplete utterance, and falling intonation a statement or a complete utterance. Figures 2.16–2.19 in the text illustrate some intonation patterns.

- **Length: Long vowels** and long consonants (**geminates**) are sounds whose articulation simply takes longer relative to other vowels and consonants. Length is indicated with a [ː]. Yapese is an example of a language having long and short vowels. Italian is an example of a language having long and short consonants. Tables 2.19–2.20 in the text show examples of long and short vowels and consonants.

- **Stress:** Stress is associated with vowels. Stressed vowels are vowels that are perceived as more prominent than other vowels. The most prominent vowel receives **primary stress**. Primary stress is usually indicated with a ['] at the beginning of a stressed syllable. Section 8.3 in Chapter 2 discusses stress in more detail. See Table 2.21 for examples of stress placement in English.

PRACTICE 2.22: Stress

Transcribe the following words as you would say them in normal everyday speech. Mark primary stress.

1. scorned _____   6. duplicate _____

2. discover _____   7. dictate _____

3. explosion _____   8. occupied _____

4. genius _____   9. informative _____

5. macaroni _____   10. idolatry _____

Articulatory Processes (Sections 9.2–9.3)

Articulatory processes describe articulatory adjustments that occur during speech. Processes typically function to make words easier to articulate. Processes also occur to make speech easier to perceive. The main types of processes are:

- Assimilation
- Dissimilation
- Deletion
- Epenthesis
- Metathesis
- Vowel reduction

The following boxes define and illustrate the different processes found in language.

Assimilation

Assimilation involves sounds changing to become more like nearby sounds. While there are many different kinds of assimilation, in general, assimilation can be divided into three main types:

1. Voicing Assimilation:
   A sound takes on the same voice as a nearby sound.
   Includes: **voicing**, **devoicing**.

2. Place Assimilation:
   A sound takes on the same place of articulation as a nearby sound.
   Includes: palatalization, homorganic nasal assimilation, and more.

3. Manner Assimilation:
   A sound takes on the same manner of articulation as a nearby sound.
   Includes: **nasalization**, **flapping** (tapping), and more.

Note: In some types of assimilation, such as nasalization, a segment takes on some characteristic of the following segment (regressive assimilation). That is, a sound is influenced by what comes after it. Alternatively, a segment may take on some characteristic of the preceding segment (progressive assimilation). That is, a sound is influenced by what comes before it.

Dissimilation

A sound changes to become less like a nearby sound so that the resulting sequence of sounds is easier to pronounce; e.g., *fifths* [fɪfθs] → [fɪfts].

Deletion

The process of deletion simply removes a sound from a phonetic context. Deletion frequently occurs in rapid speech; e.g., *fifths* [fɪfθs] → [fɪfs]. Deletion of the schwa is especially common; e.g., *suppose* [sapowz] → [spowz].

Epenthesis

The process of epenthesis adds a segment to a phonetic context. Epenthesis is common in casual speech; e.g., *warmth* [wɔɹmθ] → [wɔɹmpθ].

Metathesis

Metathesis is a process that changes the order of segments; e.g., *ask* [æsk] → [æks]. Metathesis is common in the speech of young children.

Vowel Reduction

In vowel reduction, vowels move to a more central position when they are in unstressed syllables. That is, a vowel is pronounced as a full vowel when in a stressed syllable, and as a **schwa** when in an unstressed syllable; e.g., *blas'pheme* vs. *'blasphemy*.

Identifying processes: To identify processes, you need to look for differences between the starting and the ending pronunciation.

- If a sound is missing, **deletion** has occurred.
- If a sound has been added, **epenthesis** has occurred.
- If the order of sounds has changed, **metathesis** has occurred.
- If a sound has changed, you need to determine if either **assimilation** or **dissimilation** has occurred. To do this, follow these four steps:

1. Determine the phonetic property that has changed (voice, place of articulation, or manner of articulation).
2. Compare this phonetic property with the phonetic properties of the nearby sounds.
3. If the changed phonetic property matches a phonetic property of a nearby sound, then **assimilation** has occurred. The phonetic property that matches will tell you the specific type of assimilation that has occurred.
4. If the phonetic properties do not match, then **dissimilation** has occurred.

Remember: For assimilation, you also need to look at whether the influencing sound comes before or after the sound that is undergoing the change.

Consider the following example.

prince: [pɹɪns]   →   [pɹɪ̃nts]

In the above example, [t] occurs in the final pronunciation but not the starting pronunciation; therefore, epenthesis has occurred. As well, [ɪ] has changed to [ɪ̃]. Remember that [˜] indicates a nasalized sound. The vowel has therefore changed from an oral to a nasal sound, and since the following sound is a nasal, assimilation—in particular, nasalization—has occurred. The influencing sound is the following nasal, meaning the nasalization is regressive. So, the change in the pronunciation of the word *prince* from [pɹɪns] to [pɹɪ̃nts] involves two processes: epenthesis and nasalization.

PRACTICE 2.23: Identifying processes

Identify the process(es) at work in each of the following:

1. asterisk: [æstəɹɪsk]   →   [æstəɹɪks] _____

2. Peter: [pʰitɹ]   →   [pʰiɾɹ] _____

3. collards: [kɑlɚdz]   →   [kɑljɚdz] _____

4. frontal: [fɹʌntl̩]   →   [fɹʌ̃nl̩] _____

5. sixths: [sɪksθs]   →   [sɪksts] _____

6. walrus: [walɹəs]   →   [waləɹəs] _____

Review Exercises

1. For each part of the vocal tract, give its corresponding role in speech production.

   a. lungs _____

   b. larynx _____

   c. velum _____

2. Give the phonetic symbol for each of the following articulatory descriptions.

    a. [   ]   voiceless glottal stop

    b. [   ]   high front unrounded tense vowel

    c. [   ]   voiced bilabial nasal

    d. [   ]   voiceless labiodental fricative

3. Give the articulatory description that corresponds to each of the following phonetic symbols.

    a. [æ] _____

    b. [k] _____

    c. [j] _____

    d. [ʌ] _____

4. All the words in this exercise are transcriptions of words related to the study of phonetics. Write each term in conventional English spelling. Do you know the meaning of each term? If you do not, then you should review this chapter in the *Study Guide* and Chapter 2 in the textbook.

    a. [vowkl̩ tɹækt]   _____

    b. [sawnd klæsəz]   _____

    c. [aɹtʰɪkjələtɔɹi dɪskɹɪpʃn̩z]   _____

    d. [plejsəz əv aɹtʰɪkjəlejʃn̩]   _____

    e. [əmɛɹəkn̩ ɪŋglɪʃ kʰɑnsənənts]   _____

    f. [æspəɹejʃn̩]   _____

    g. [fejʃl̩ dajəgɹæmz]   _____

    h. [əmɛɹəkn̩ ɪŋglɪʃ vawəlz]   _____

    i. [sɛgmənts]   _____

    j. [trænskɹɪpʃn̩]   _____

    k. [ʃɛɹd fənɛɹɪk pɹɑpɹ̩tiz]   _____

    l. [supɹəsɛgmentl̩z]   _____

    m. [aɹtʰɪkjələtɔɹi pɹɑsɛsəz]   _____

5. Transcribe the following words as you would say them in normal everyday speech. Pay special attention to vowels. Watch out; they get harder.

1. days	_____	11. agitate	_____	21. gnome	_____
2. Xerox	_____	12. roast	_____	22. pinstripes	_____
3. guess	_____	13. theatrical	_____	23. masculine	_____
4. yellow	_____	14. bargain	_____	24. precious	_____
5. metal	_____	15. machine	_____	25. formula	_____
6. unicycle	_____	16. surrounded	_____	26. comedy	_____
7. extinguish	_____	17. costume	_____	27. graduate	_____
8. popular	_____	18. ponder	_____	28. irrigate	_____
9. isolate	_____	19. timetable	_____	29. unforgivable	_____
10. frighten	_____	20. euphemism	_____	30. called	_____

6. Identify all the processes at work in each of the following:

a. wash: [wɔʃ] → [wɔɹʃ]   _____

b. winter: [wɪntɹ̩] → [wɪ̃nɹ̩]   _____

c. clear: [kl̥iɹ] → [kəliɹ]   _____

d. especially: [ɪspɛʃəli] → [ɪkspɛʃli]   _____

e. kitchen: [kɪtʃn̩] → [tʃɪkn̩]   _____

☑ **RECAP**

Make sure you know the following material. (See also the Key Terms at the end of Chapter 2 of the main text.)

- the different parts of the vocal tract and sound-producing system
- the difference between voiced and voiceless sounds
- the difference between nasal and oral sounds
- the characteristics of consonants, glides, and vowels
- the places and manners of articulation for consonant sounds
- the different tongue placements required to describe vowels
- the difference between tense and lax, and rounded and unrounded vowels
- the symbols and articulatory descriptions for English consonants
- the strident fricatives and affricates
- the symbols and articulatory descriptions for English vowels
- when and why aspiration occurs
- how to complete and decipher facial diagrams
- how to identify articulatory processes
- the suprasegmentals of tone, intonation, length, and stress
- transcription

Questions? Problems?

three

Phonology: Contrasts and Patterns

Phonology is the study of how sounds vary and pattern in language. Following are some of the important topics and concepts covered in this chapter. Make sure you are familiar with them.

Phonemes and allophones	Phonetic and phonemic representations
Minimal pairs and near-minimal pairs	Syllables
Complementary distribution	Features
Cross-linguistic variation	Rules and generalizations
Phonology problems	Derivations and rule ordering

Since we will be dealing with many languages besides English, you will come across some phonetic symbols that have not yet been discussed. Articulatory descriptions will be provided for these unfamiliar sounds.

Phonemes and Allophones (Section 1.1)

Phonemes and allophones are two units of representation used in phonology. These are used to capture native-speaker knowledge about how sounds behave in that language.

Phoneme refers to:

- the way in which a sound is stored in the mind

- a contrastive sound in a language

- the underlying representation

Phonemes are:

- phonetically different sounds (i.e., they have different articulations)

- phonologically different sounds (i.e., they are found in unpredictable environments and make meaning differences)

Allophone refers to:

- the way a sound is pronounced

- a variant of a contrastive sound in a language

- the surface representation

Allophones may:

- refer to phonetically different sounds of the *same* phoneme (i.e., they have different articulations but are not perceived to be different sounds by native speakers)

- be in complementary distribution (i.e., they are found in mutually exclusive environments)

REMINDER

Don't forget that phonemes are indicated with / / slashes and allophones with [ ] brackets.

Minimal Pairs (Section 1.2)

Segments are said to contrast when their presence alone is responsible for forms having different meanings. Both consonant and vowel segments may contrast with each other. Determining which segments contrast is a first step in phonological analysis.

Minimal Pairs. A minimal pair is defined as two phonetic forms that differ by one segment that is in the same environment in both forms, and which have different meanings. Environment refers to the phonetic context in which the segment (sound) is found. A minimal pair means that sounds contrast.

e.g., English [pæt] 'pat' and [bæt] 'bat'

Near-Minimal Pairs. A near-minimal pair is defined as two phonetic forms that have segments in nearly identical environments. Like a minimal pair, these forms have different meanings, and like a minimal pair, a near-minimal pair means that sounds contrast.

e.g., Hungarian [vis] 'carry' and [viːz] 'water'

Phonemes. Sounds that contrast are said to belong to separate phonemes. Part of native speakers' phonological knowledge includes knowledge of which sounds are contrastive (distinctive) in their language. Phonemes are used to capture this knowledge. Sounds belonging to separate phonemes can be represented as follows.

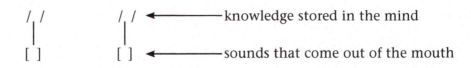

Which sounds contrast in the English and Hungarian examples above? Put together a phonemic representation of the contrastive sounds in each example.

PRACTICE 3.1: Recognizing minimal and near-minimal pairs

The following data are from Cofan, an indigenous language of Ecuador. For each pair, state whether the pair of words constitutes a minimal pair, a near-minimal pair, or neither. Make sure you pay attention to the meanings given in single quotation marks.

1.   [ʔoʔfa]   'vine'   [ʔoʔva]   'net bag'   _____

2.   [toja]   'still'   [dojaʔ]   'shall split'   _____

3.   [jokʰo]   'stimulant'   [ʒokʰo]   'stimulant'   _____

4.   [sisipa]   'sand'   [ʃipare]   'sting ray'   _____

5.   [daje]   'to change'   [doje]   'to split'   _____

6.   [batʰi]   'break through'   [vaʔtʰi]   'here'   _____

7.   [ʔoʔfɛ]   'star'   [ʔuʔfɛ]   'star'   _____

PRACTICE 3.2: Minimal pairs in English

For each of the following pairs of English consonant phonemes, find two minimal pairs. Wherever possible, one pair should show one contrast in initial position and the other pair in final position. The first pair is done for you. Don't be fooled by spelling.

1.   / p : b /   _____paste : baste_____   _____rope : robe_____

2.   / t : d /   _____   _____

3.   / k : g /   _____   _____

4.   / f : v /   _____   _____

5.   / s : z /   _____   _____

6.   / m : n /   _____   _____

7.   / ɹ : l /   _____   _____

8.   / t : θ /   _____   _____

9.   / tʃ : dʒ /   _____   _____

10.   / p : f /   _____   _____

Complementary Distribution (Section 1.3)

Not all segments found in a language contrast with each other. Some segments are in **complementary distribution**. Two phonetically similar segments are in complementary distribution when they never occur in the same phonetic **environment**. The term environment refers to the phonetic context in which the segments occur.

To understand what this means, look at this table for aspirated and unaspirated stops in English (a diagonal line through the box means the segment is not found in that environment):

ENVIRONMENT	ASPIRATED STOP	UNASPIRATED STOP
Beginning of a stressed syllable	YES	
Not at the beginning of a stressed syllable		YES

Aspirated and unaspirated stops are an example of predictable variation because they are found in predictable environments. They are in complementary distribution because aspirated stops and unaspirated stops are not found in the same environment.

Allophones are phonetic variants of a phoneme. So in our example in the previous paragraph, an aspirated stop and an unaspirated stop are allophones of the same phoneme in English. Native speakers of English have the phoneme /p/ in their minds, but sometimes they pronounce it as [p], and sometimes they pronounce it as [pʰ]. We can represent the relationship of a phoneme to its allophones like this:

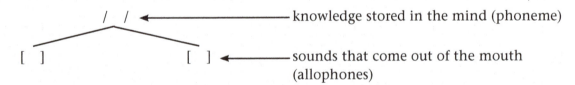

/ / ←———— knowledge stored in the mind (phoneme)

[ ]   [ ] ←———— sounds that come out of the mouth (allophones)

One allophone is chosen as the **underlying representation** (i.e., the phoneme). This is typically the allophone that occurs in the greatest number of phonetic environments. In the example of [p] and [pʰ], the aspirated stop [pʰ] occurs in only one environment (at the beginning of a stressed syllable), while the unaspirated stop [p] occurs everywhere else (i.e., at the beginning of an unstressed syllable, after [s], and at the end of a syllable). Therefore, we say that [p] occurs elsewhere and is the underlying representation.

REMINDER

The patterning of allophones can vary from language to language.

PRACTICE 3.3: Complementary distribution in English

1. In English, [p] has (at least) three allophones: [p]   – unaspirated
                                                          [pʰ] – aspirated
                                                          [p˺] – unreleased

The following list gives examples of words containing each allophone.

[p]	[pʰ]	[p˺]
spook	pig	collapse
spirit	police	apt
operate	appear	flipped
happening	repair	ape
		cop
		clap

a. Using the data in the above chart, determine which allophone occurs in each of the following environments:

 – at the beginning of a word (word initially)   _____

 – at the beginning of a stressed syllable   _____

 – before a consonant   _____

 – at the end of a word (word finally)   _____

 – after [s]   _____

b. Can [p], [pʰ], and [p˺] all occur in each of the following environments? Think about whether the words that result from using each of these sounds in the same environment have different meanings. Then, determine which sound can occur in each of the following environments. Make sure you pay attention to which vowel is stressed.

[hɪ _____ i]   [_____ ɑt]   [kɛ _____ t]

2. English [l] has (at least) three allophones: [l]   – alveolar (clear) l
                                                       [ɫ]   – velarized (dark) l
                                                       [l̩]   – syllabic l

The following list gives examples of words containing each allophone in one dialect.

[l]	[ɫ]	[l̩]
lip	swallow	paddle
love	silly	obstacle
allow	salt	twinkle
malign	ilk	bushel
slip	pull	hurdle

a. Using the data in the above chart, determine which allophone occurs in each of the following environments:

– at the end of a word after a consonant _____

– at the end of a word after a vowel _____

– right after a stressed vowel _____

– in the onset of a stressed syllable _____

– at the beginning of a word (word initially) _____

b. Can [l], [ɫ], and [l̩] all occur in each of the following environments? Think about whether the words that result from using each of these sounds in the same environment have different meanings. Then, determine which sound can occur in each of the following environments. Again, be sure to pay attention to which vowel is stressed.

[s_____ajd]   [mi_____]   [hæs_____]

REMINDER

The environments in Practice 3.3 are not a complete list of environments that can be used in phonological analysis. Many of these environments (e.g., word-initial and word-final positions) are environments in which predictable variation is often found across languages. Other environments used in the exercises have been simplified (e.g., before a consonant and between a consonant and a vowel).

PRACTICE 3.4: Complementary distribution in other languages

1. **Oneida:** Examine the following data from Oneida. Using the following chart, determine if the sounds [s] and [z] are or are not in complementary distribution. Note that [sh] represents [s] and [h], not [ʃ].

	[s]		[z]	
[lashet]	'let him count'	[kawenezuzeʔ]	'long words'
[laʔsluni]	'white men'	[khaiize]	'I'm taking it along'
[loteswatu]	'he's been playing'	[lazel]	'let him drag it'
[skahnehtat]	'one pine tree'	[tahazehteʔ]	'he dropped it'
[thiskate]	'a different one'	[tuzahatiteni]	'they changed it'
[sninuhe]	'you buy'	[wezake]	'she saw you'
[wahsnestakeʔ]	'you ate corn'		

	#_____ (word-initial)	_____C (before a consonant)	C_____ (after a consonant)	V_____V (between vowels)
[s]				
[z]				

2. **Oneida:** Now determine if the sounds [s] and [ʃ] are or are not in complementary distribution. Again, [sh] represents [s] and [h], not [ʃ]. Hint: Look at specific vowels or consonants in the environment.

	[s]		**[ʃ]**
[lashet]	'let him count'	[ʃjatuheʔ]	'you write'
[laʔsluni]	'white men'	[tehʃjaʔk]	'let you break'
[loteswatu]	'he's been playing'	[jaʔteʃjatekhahʃjahteʔ]	'they would suddenly
[skahnehtat]	'one pine tree'		separate again'
[thiskate]	'a different one'		
[sninuhe]	'you buy'		
[wahsnestakeʔ]	'you ate corn'		

3. **Japanese:** Examine the following data from Japanese, and determine if the sounds [t], [ts], and [tʃ] are or are not in complementary distribution. Set up a chart to help you. Hint: You may want to look at specific vowels in the linguistic environment.

The symbol [ts] is a single segment representing a voiceless alveolar affricate.

1.	[taijoː]	'the sun'	10.	[tʃigai]	'difference'
2.	[tatami]	'mat'	11.	[tʃiɽi]	'dust'
3.	[tambo]	'rice paddy'	12.	[itʃigo]	'strawberry'
4.	[buta]	'pig'	13.	[degutʃi]	'exit'
5.	[gaitoː]	'cloak, overcoat'	14.	[iɽigutʃi]	'entrance'
6.	[koto]	'fact'	15.	[tsunami]	'tidal wave'
7.	[tegami]	'letter'	16.	[tsukue]	'desk'
8.	[totemo]	'very'	17.	[doːbutsu]	'animal'
9.	[tʃiɲɲi]	'truly'	18.	[zatsudʒi]	'chores'

Language-Specific Phonemes and Allophones (Section 1.4)

Segments are said to **contrast** when their presence alone is responsible for forms having different meanings. Both consonant and vowel segments may contrast with each other, as shown by these minimal pairs in different languages.

	LANGUAGE	**SEGMENTS**	**FORMS**
Consonants	English	[kʰ] [g]	[kʰæp] 'cap' vs. [gæp] 'gap'
	Khmer	[kʰ] [k]	[kʰaːn] 'shaft' vs. [kaːn] 'act'
Vowels	English	[i] [æ]	[bit] 'beet' vs. [bæt] 'bat'
		[ow] [u]	[kʰowd] 'code' vs. [kʰud] 'cooed'
	Japanese	[i] [iː]	[toɽi] 'bird' vs. [toɽiː] 'shrine gate'
		[o] [oː]	[kibo] 'scale' vs. [kiboː] 'hope'

Whether particular segments contrast with each other is determined on a language-by-language basis. Sounds that are contrastive in one language may not be contrastive in another. Consider the following examples:

SEGMENTS	LANGUAGE	PHONETIC FORMS
[ɛ] [æ]	English	[bɛt] bet and [bæt] bat
	Turkish	[bɛn] 'I' and [bæn] 'I'
[i] [iː]	English	[si] see and [siː] see
	Thai	[krit] 'dagger' and [kriːt] 'to cut'

Do [ɛ] and [æ] contrast in English? In Turkish? How can you tell?

Do [i] and [iː] contrast in English? In Thai? How can you tell?

Solving Phonology Problems (Appendix)

The basic goal in solving a phonology problem is to determine if the sounds being examined belong to one phoneme or to separate phonemes.

When allophones belong to separate phonemes, they are:

1. Contrastive/distinctive
2. In unpredictable distribution
3. Easily perceived as different by native speakers
4. Not necessarily phonetically similar

When allophones belong to the same phoneme, they are:

1. Noncontrastive/rule-governed
2. Usually in predictable distribution
3. Not easily perceived as different by native speakers
4. Always phonetically similar

Problem-Solving Flowchart

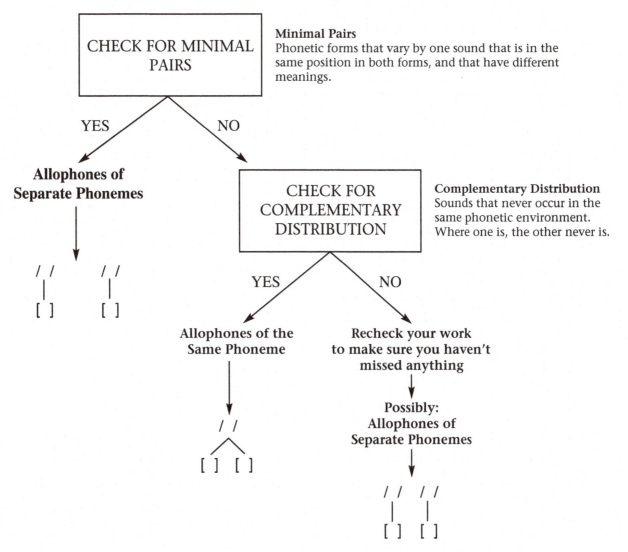

Repeat the above for each pair of sounds you are investigating.

PRACTICE 3.5: Distinguishing phonemes and allophones

1. **Sawai:** [e] and [ɛ]

Sawai belongs to the Eastern Malayo-Polynesian branch of the Austronesian language family. It is spoken in the Northern Maluku Province of Indonesia.

1.	[moke]	'father'	9.	[tɛptɛp]	'drop of blood'
2.	[tɛptep]	'edge of a river'	10.	[le]	'only, just'
3.	[ndʒɛ]	'that'	11.	[lawe]	'thread'
4.	[potʃɛ]	'there'	12.	[lɛ]	'no good' 3 SG
5.	[ndʒe]	'this'	13.	[delɛk]	'bay'
6.	[lokɛ]	'banana'	14.	[lɛmlɛm]	'lightning'
7.	[mokɛ]	'sea cucumber'	15.	[pote]	'here'
8.	[lɛmlɛm]	'dew'			

2. **Biblical Hebrew:** [d] and [ð]
   [ɣ] represents a voiced velar fricative.
   [q] represents a voiceless uvular stop.
   [ʕ] represents a voiced pharyngeal fricative.
   [x] represents a voiceless velar fricative.

1.	[gaðol]	'great'	8.	[zaðon]	'arrogance'
2.	[damim]	'blood'	9.	[duðim]	'cooking pots'
3.	[mɪgdal]	'tower'	10.	[mɪqdaʃ]	'sanctuary'
4.	[ʔaðam]	'man'	11.	[jəhuða]	'Judah'
5.	[davar]	'word'	12.	[hɪbdil]	'he distinguished'
6.	[dɛlɛt]	'door'	13.	[ʕeðɛn]	'Eden'
7.	[daɣeʃ]	'piercing'	14.	[dɛrɛx]	'way'

3. **German:** [ç] and [χ]
   [ç] represents a voiceless palatal fricative.
   [χ] represents a voiceless uvular fricative.
   [ʁ] represents a voiced uvular fricative.

1.	[naχ]	'to, after'	6.	[dɔχ]	'yet'
2.	[çemi]	'chemistry'	7.	[kɪʁçə]	'church'
3.	[dɪç]	'you'	8.	[aχaːt]	'agate'
4.	[maχt]	'power'	9.	[ʁeçnən]	'to count'
5.	[ʁɛçt]	'right'	10.	[nɔχ]	'still, yet'

4. **Zinacantec Tzotzil:** [p] and [p'], [k] and [k']
   Zinacantec Tzotzil is a Mayan language of Mexico.
   [p'] represents a glottalized sound, made with simultaneous closure of the glottis and
       constriction of the throat.
   [k'] represents a glottalized sound, made with simultaneous closure of the glottis and
       constriction of the throat.

1.	[pim]	'thick'	7.	[p'in]	'pot'
2.	[bikil]	'intestines'	8.	[bik'it]	'small'
3.	[ka]	'particle'	9.	[kok]	'my leg'
4.	[nopol]	'nearby'	10.	[p'ol]	'to multiply'
5.	[p'us]	'hunchback'	11.	[k'ok']	'fire'
6.	[k'a]	'horse'	12.	[pus]	'jail'

PRACTICE 3.6: More practice with phonemes and allophones

The following pages contain data sets from a number of different languages (some of the data may have been regularized). Each data set contains sufficient data to make valid conclusions about the sounds under consideration. For each data set:

- state your conclusion (i.e., allophones of the same phoneme or of separate phonemes)

- provide evidence to support your conclusion

- provide a representation of the phoneme(s)

1. **English: Long and short vowels**
   [V:] When a colon-like symbol follows a vowel, it means that the vowel is long. This means that we take a longer time saying the vowel; do not confuse this use of the term *long vowel* with what you may have learned in elementary school (where the term referred to a vowel that sounds like the name of the letter).

1.	[gɪft]	'gift'	7.	[hʌːg]	'hug'
2.	[ɹɑːbd]	'robbed'	8.	[nowt]	'note'
3.	[lʌk]	'luck'	9.	[gɪːv]	'give'
4.	[moːwd]	'mowed'	10.	[sliːz]	'sleaze'
5.	[slæpt]	'slapped'	11.	[pɑt]	'pot'
6.	[mejs]	'mace'	12.	[kɹæːb]	'crab'

   You could treat each vowel individually. However, it will be more efficient if you treat long vowels as a class. Assume that English has either short and corresponding long vowels as separate phonemes, or short and corresponding long vowels as allophones of the same phonemes.

2. **Siona: [t'] and [ɾ]**
   Siona is an indigenous language of South America, spoken by about 500 people on the border between Ecuador and Colombia.
   [t'] represents a glottalized [t], with a complete closure of the glottis at the same time as the alveolar closure.
   [ɾ] represents the flap.
   [ɨ] represents a high central unrounded vowel.
   [ɲ] represents a palatal nasal.
   [ã] a tilde over a vowel represents a nasalized vowel.

1.	[t'iohi]	'he is causing to submerge'	10.	[saʔəɾo]	'entrance'
2.	[t'aijɨ]	'I am coming'	11.	[tuɾupɨ]	'kind of shoulder bag'
3.	[t'ɛhi]	'it is hanging'	12.	[tʃuɾu]	'kind of snail'
4.	[t'ahi]	'he is bringing'	13.	[taɾi]	'kind of turtle'
5.	[t'ɨihi]	'he is submerging'	14.	[hoɾo]	'flower'
6.	[t'o]	'just that and nothing more'	15.	[p'ɛoɾu]	'all'
7.	[t'uʔt'u]	'first'	16.	[kɨʔəɾo]	'home site'
8.	[t'aɲã]	'hairs'	17.	[p'ɨʔp'ɨɾi]	'kind of buzzard'
9.	[t'oʔt'ojɨ]	'I am boring'	18.	[kuɾa]	'chicken'

3. **Inuktitut:** [k] and [q]

   [q] represents a voiceless uvular stop.

   (Note: Assume a relatively broad transcription as far as vowels are concerned.)

1.	[qisik]	'sealskin'	7.	[imaq]	'water'
2.	[kamik]	'sealskin boots'	8.	[tuvaq]	'sea ice'
3.	[gimmik]	'dog, Huskie'	9.	[savik]	'snow knife'
4.	[iqaluk]	'fish'	10.	[qukiut]	'gun, rifle'
5.	[amaruq]	'Arctic wolf'	11.	[nukaq]	'younger sibling'
6.	[tasiq]	'lake'	12.	[saku]	'harpoon head'

4. **English:** [g], [gʲ], and [gʷ]

   [gʲ] represents a fronted [g], made with the back of the tongue at or near the hard palate.

   [gʷ] represents a rounded [g], made with simultaneous lip rounding.

1.	[gɔn]	'gone'	7.	[gʲik]	'geek'
2.	[gʷufi]	'goofy'	8.	[igɹ]	'eager'
3.	[gli]	'glee'	9.	[gejm]	'game'
4.	[slʌg]	'slug'	10.	[gowfɹ]	'gopher'
5.	[gɹin]	'green'	11.	[gædʒət]	'gadget'
6.	[ɹægʷu]	'Ragu'	12.	[gʲis]	'geese'

5. **Yakut:** [i], [ɨ], [y], and [u]

   Yakut is a Turkic language of northeastern Siberia.

   [ɨ] represents a high central unrounded vowel.

   [y] represents a high front rounded vowel.

   For these sounds to be allophones of separate phonemes, you must find a minimal pair for:

   - [i] and [ɨ]
   - [ɨ] and [y]
   - [i] and [y]
   - [ɨ] and [u]
   - [i] and [u]
   - [y] and [u]

   You may use the same data item in more than one pair.

1.	[bit]	'mark'	8.	[ɨt]	'shoot'
2.	[il]	'peace'	9.	[tys]	'descend'
3.	[sil]	'saliva'	10.	[byt]	'end'
4.	[kir]	'nibble'	11.	[sur]	'gray'
5.	[tɨs]	'paw'	12.	[kur]	'belt'
6.	[ik]	'wring'	13.	[uk]	'insert'
7.	[sɨl]	'year'	14.	[tus]	'directly'

6. **Italian:** [ʤ] and [g]

   Note: When a consonant is doubled in the phonetic transcription, it is geminate, meaning it is pronounced for a longer period of time.

1.	[ʤiro]	'circle'	9.	[ʤelato]	'ice cream'
2.	[gusto]	'taste, flavor'	10.	[albɛrgo]	'hotel'
3.	[ʤɛtto]	'throwing'	11.	[ʤirɔvago]	'wandering, strolling'
4.	[goffadʤine]	'clumsiness'	12.	[ingurʤitare]	'to gulp down'
5.	[auʤe]	'height, peak'	13.	[gregarjo]	'gregarious'
6.	[rɛdʤere]	'to hold up'	14.	[fulʤido]	'bright, shining'
7.	[ingrɛsso]	'entrance'	15.	[borgata]	'hamlet'
8.	[negliʤɛnte]	'negligent'	16.	[singolo]	'single'

REMINDER

When you find allophones of the same phoneme, there is a quick way to determine if your solution is in all likelihood correct. If your rule and statement describe an articulatory process such as assimilation, which is the result of neighboring sounds interacting with each other, then your solution is probably correct. If your rule and statement do not describe such a process, then you might want to rethink your analysis.

Phonetic and Phonemic Representation (Section 1.7)

There are two types of representation: phonetic and phonemic.

- **Phonetic representation** is a representation of normal, everyday speech. That is, it is a representation of pronunciation. Phonetic representation includes all phonetic information, both the predictable and the unpredictable. Phonetic representation is always indicated with [ ] brackets.

- **Phonemic representation** is representation that contains only the phonemes of the language. Phonemic representation only includes unpredictable phonetic information: all predictable phonetic information is excluded. Phonemic representation is always indicated with / / slashes.

To understand the difference between phonetic and phonemic representation, let's reconsider the English problem concerning allophones of /g/ on p. 50. Remember that in English, [g], [gʷ], and [gʲ] are allophones of the same phoneme, with [gʲ] occurring before front vowels, [gʷ] occurring before back vowels, and [g] occurring elsewhere. Given this information, we can convert English phonetic representation into English phonemic representation:

Phonetic	Phonemic	
[gʷufi]	/gufi/	'goofy'
[gʲik]	/gik/	'geek'
[slʌg]	/slʌg/	'slug'

Notice that in the phonemic representation, only the phoneme /g/ has been used, while in the phonetic representation, the allophones [gʲ] and [gʷ] have both been used, along with [g]. Also notice that in the phonetic representation, [gʲ] occurs only before front vowels, and [gʷ] occurs only before back vowels, while in phonemic representation, /g/ occurs in all environments. See Table 3.10 in the textbook for other examples of phonetic and phonemic representation.

Remember: The main difference between phonetic and phonemic representation is that

- phonetic representation includes both predictable and unpredictable phonetic information, while

- phonemic representation includes only the unpredictable information. Anything that is predictable is excluded.

PRACTICE 3.7: Phonemic representation

To practice phonemic representation, return to the phonology problems in Practice 3.6, and wherever allophones of the same phoneme were found, convert the first few words in the data set from the phonetic representation provided into phonemic representation. Identify the predictable phonetic property that is missing from the phonemic representation.

Classes and Generalizations (Section 1.7)

Phonetic variation in language does not typically affect individual segments but groups of sounds that share a common phonetic property—i.e., **classes** of sounds. One of the goals of phonological analysis is to uncover and make **generalizations** about the broad patterning of sounds in language.

For example, the phonemes /p, t, k/ in English have aspirated allophones when they occur at the beginning of a stressed syllable.

- These three sounds comprise the natural class of voiceless stops.

- We can make the generalization that any of these voiceless stops in English will behave in the same predictable way.

PRACTICE 3.8: Generalizations

1. **Mon diphthongs**
   Mon belongs to the Mon-Khmer language family and is spoken in southern Myanmar (Burma). Some sounds of Mon are pronounced with breathy voice; this is not included in the transcription here.

   Some vowels in Mon become diphthongs by adding the off-glide [j] or [w].

1.	/wi/	→	[wij]	'to treat'
2.	/dun/	→	[duwn]	'to cook'
3.	/ke/	→	[kej]	'clear'
4.	/kɛ/	→	[kɛj]	'to say'
5.	/proa/	→	[prowa]	'rain'
6.	/mɔŋ/	→	[mɔwŋ]	'to exist, to live'

   a. Which vowels take [j] as the off-glide? _____

What property do these vowels share? _____

    b. Which vowels take [w] as the off-glide? _____

What property do these vowels share? _____

2. **Mon schwa insertion**
A schwa is inserted before some vowels in Mon.

    1. /bi/ → [bəi] 'ocean'
    2. /hui/ → [həui] 'to mix, to associate'
    3. /pɛ/ → [pəɛ] 'to look at'
    4. /klɛŋ/ → [kləɛŋ] 'canoe'
    5. /so/ → [səo] 'hair'
    6. /tɔ/ → [təɔw] 'to be'

    a. Which vowels have a schwa inserted before them? _____

What property do all these vowels share? _____

    b. The word for 'to be' also shows another allophonic change. What is it?

_____

3. **Hausa palatalization**
Palatalization refers to moving the place of articulation closer to the palate.
Hausa is a language spoken in northern Nigeria.
[ɗ] represents a voiced alveolar implosive, in which the larynx moves downward,
    sucking air in.

Nonpalatalized consonants		**Palatalized consonants**	
1. [maːtaː]	'women'	[matʃɛ]	'woman'
2. [saːtaː]	'theft'	[jaː saːtʃi kuɗi]	'he stole money'
3. [gʊduː]	'running'	[gʊdʤe]	'to run away'
4. [gaːdo]	'inheritance'	[naː gaːdʤe ta]	'I inherited from her.'
5. [maːsu]	'spears'	[maːʃi]	'spear'
6. [dasaː]	'to transplant'	[daʃe]	'transplanting'
7. [kaːzaː]	'chicken'	[kaːdʒi]	'chickens'
8. [bazo]	'to scatter (here)'	[badʤe]	'to scatter around'

    a. The vowels [i, ɪ, e, ɛ] trigger palatalization. What properties do these vowels share?

_____

    b. What are the consonants that are palatalized before those vowels?

_____

What is the palatalized allophone of each consonant? _____

What properties do the nonpalatalized consonants share?

_____

Syllables (Section 2)

A **syllable** is another phonological unit of representation. Sounds can be grouped together to form a syllable, which consists of a syllabic element (usually a vowel) plus any preceding or following sounds.

Syllable Structure

Syllables have internal structure, which is represented above the individual sounds making up the syllable. A syllable (σ) consists of an onset (O) and a rhyme (R). The rhyme consists of a nucleus (N) and a coda (Co). The elements that can make up these constituents are defined below:

- The **nucleus** of a syllable contains a vowel (including diphthongs) or a syllabic consonant (either a syllabic liquid or a syllabic nasal).

- The **onset** contains consonants occurring before the nucleus.

- The **coda** contains consonants occurring after the nucleus.

- The nucleus plus the coda make up the **rhyme**.

In any syllable, the nucleus—and therefore, the rhyme—must be included. This is true for all languages. Onsets and codas may not be present in every syllable, although this will depend on individual languages. See Figure 3.6 in Section 2.2 of the text for an example of the constituents making up a basic syllable.

Basic Syllables

Basic syllables contain the structure outlined above. In addition, there are two restrictions on the structure of basic syllables in languages that allow more than one consonant in either the onset or the coda.

1. **Sonority Requirement.** Not all sounds have the same degree of sonority. Vowels are the most sonorant, while obstruents (stops, fricatives, and affricates) are the least sonorant. Of the sonorant consonants, glides are the most sonorant, followed by liquids, and finally nasals. This can be diagrammed as follows:

increasing sonority

$\longrightarrow$

0	1	2	3	4
Obstruents	Nasals	Liquids	Glides	Vowels

Sonority provides the basis for the following two restrictions on syllable structure:

- Consonants must rise in sonority before the nucleus (i.e., in the onset).

- Consonants must fall in sonority after the nucleus (i.e., in the coda).

See Figure 3.11 in Section 2.3 for an example of a syllable in English that meets this requirement. See Table 3.15 for examples of some English onsets that meet the Sonority Requirement.

2. **Binarity Requirement.** Each constituent can, at the most, be binary (branching). This means that an onset can have a *maximum* of two consonants. That is, an onset can consist of zero, one, or two consonants. The same is true for codas.

PRACTICE 3.9: Syllables in English

Examine the words below. For each word, determine how many syllables are in the word. For each syllable in the word, determine whether it is or is not a basic syllable. Remember to put the words into their phonemic representation first.

1. garden
2. parks
3. trained
4. beauty
5. twinkle
6. lovely
7. understand
8. triangle
9. tent
10. angry
11. cleanser
12. splashdown

Syllable Representations

There are three steps to putting together a representation of a basic syllable. These are illustrated for the word *blackboard* /blækbɔɹd/.

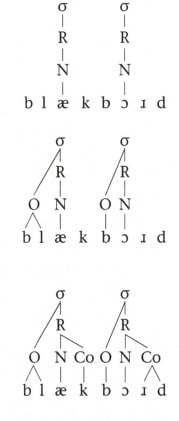

1. Assign the nucleus, the rhyme, and the syllable node. Vowels (including diphthongs) and syllabic consonants may occupy the nucleus position. Remember every syllable (σ) must have a nucleus (N) and a rhyme (R).

2. Assign the onset. These are consonants to the left of the nucleus. Assign the longest possible string of sounds that can begin a syllable to the onset. Do this for every syllable in the word. Remember that a syllable does not have to have an onset (O).

3. Assign the coda. These are consonants to the right of the nucleus. Do this for every syllable in the word. Remember that a syllable does not have to have a coda (Co).

See Figures 3.7 to 3.9 in Section 2.2 of the text for another example of the procedure for setting up syllable representations.

Complex Syllables

Complex syllables are those that fail to meet either the Sonority Requirement or the Binarity Requirement. For example, in the word *stop*, the onset *st* does not rise in sonority, since both consonants are obstruents. In *scratch*, the onset (*scr*) contains three sounds, not two. Similarly, in *kept*, the coda does not fall in sonority (again, both consonants are obstruents), while in *tanks*, the coda (*nks*) contains three sounds.

Sounds that do not meet the Sonority Requirement or the Binarity Requirement are not part of either the onset or the coda. Rather, they are sometimes called **appendices**. Appendices are typically found at either the beginning or end of a word.

When representing a complex syllable, a fourth step in the procedure outlined on the previous page is necessary:

4. Assign any sounds that violate either sonority or binarity to the syllable node.

Why is /s/ assigned to the syllable node in the above example? What requirement does it violate and why?

See Figure 3.13 in Section 2.4 of the text for an example of the representation of a complex syllable.

Some Definitions

*   An **open syllable** is a syllable that does not include a coda—that is, the rhyme only consists of the nucleus.

*   A **closed syllable** is a syllable that includes a coda—the rhyme consists of the nucleus plus the coda.

*   A **heavy syllable** is a syllable whose rhyme contains a vowel plus either a glide or a consonant.

*   A **light syllable** is a syllable whose rhyme contains only a vowel or a syllabic consonant.

Variations in Syllable Structure: All languages have syllables, but not all languages have the same syllable structure. All languages allow onsets, but not all languages allow codas (e.g., Hawaiian). Some languages allow only a single sound to occupy the onset position (e.g., Korean), some allow two sounds (e.g., French), and some three (e.g., English). There are also languages that require every syllable to have an onset. But no language requires that every syllable have a coda. Finally, onsets usually allow a greater range and type of consonants than do codas.

PRACTICE 3.10: Drawing syllable structure

The exercises in this set are designed to help you discover how to draw syllable structure using language-specific constraints.

> **REMINDER**
>
> - Assign onsets before codas. This reflects a universal preference in language for onsets over codas.
>
> - A syllable does not have to have either an onset or a coda. A syllable, however, must have a nucleus and therefore also a rhyme.

1. **English**
   Write the English word under each transcription below. Then draw the syllable structure for each word.

   a. / p ʌ b l ɪ ʃ /   b. / t ɹ ɑ m b o n /   c. / s p ɹ a j t l i /

2. **Japanese**
   In Japanese, onsets are not required. The only allowable coda is a nasal or the first member of a geminate consonant. Draw the syllable structure for each of the following words. They are already in phonemic transcription.

   a. / i g a k u /   b. / h a m p a /   c. / n a n i /
   'medicine'   'haphazard'   'what'

3. **Fante**

   Fante is a language spoken in Ghana. A syllable nucleus can be either a vowel or syllabic liquid or nasal. Onsets are not required; if there is an onset, only one consonant is allowed in the onset. Syllable codas are not allowed. Fante is a tone language, but tones are not shown here. Draw the syllable structure for each of the following words. They are already in phonemic transcription.

   a. /ɔ f ɛ r/   b. /n s u/   c. /o b i s a/
      'he is shy'   'water'   'he asks'

4. **Bemba**

   Bemba is a Bantu language spoken in Zambia and some neighboring countries. In Bemba, all syllables must be open. Onsets are not required; if there is an onset, it may be a single consonant, or it may be a cluster of one of the following types: nasal + C; nasal + C + glide. Draw the syllable structure of each of the following words. They are already in phonemic transcription.

   a. /i s a/   b. /s o m a/   c. /j a m b a/   d. /i m p w a/
      'come'   'read'   'begin'   'eggplants'

5. **Persian (Farsi)**

   In Persian, onsets are required, except word-initially. However, complex onsets are not allowed (i.e., only one C in an onset). Codas are allowed and may have a maximum of two consonants. Draw the syllable structure of each of the following words. They are already in phonemic transcription.

   [ɣ] represents a voiced velar fricative.

   [ɒ] represents a low back rounded vowel.

a. /t æ ʔ s i r/   b. /e ɣ r ɒ r/   c. /m i k æ r d æ n d/
   'impression'   'confession'   'they did'

Syllable-Based Phonology (Section 2.6)

Syllables are often relevant to stating generalizations about the distribution of allophones. For example, in English:

- Voiceless aspirated stops are found at the beginning of a syllable that is word initial or stressed, and unaspirated stops are found elsewhere. See Tables 3.19 and 3.20 in Section 2.6 of the text for some examples of English aspiration, as well as the distribution of aspirated stops in English.

- Vowels are long when followed by a voiced obstruent in the coda position of the same syllable. See Tables 3.21 and 3.22 for some examples of long and short vowels in English, including their distribution.

PRACTICE 3.11: Syllables and phonology

1. **Korean:** In Korean, stress is generally on the second syllable of a multisyllabic word. However, this is not always the case. Using the following data, determine the two conditions that will cause the first syllable of the word to be stressed.

   [ɟ]   represents a voiced palatal stop.
   [ː]   indicates a long vowel.
   [cʰ] represents an aspirated voiceless palatal stop.
   [ɯ]   represents a high back unrounded vowel.

1.	[gaˈɟaŋ]	'most'	8.	[ˈbeːda]	'to cut'
2.	[ˈgaːɟan]	'disguise'	9.	[ˈhɛnnimi]	'sun'
3.	[ˈzanzu]	'landscape'	10.	[ˈzuːbag]	'watermelon'
4.	[zʌˈli]	'frost'	11.	[ˈcʰulgu]	'exit'
5.	[ˈzʌːli]	'acting head'	12.	[ˈbʌdginɯn]	'take off'
6.	[ˈibgo]	'wearing'	13.	[taˈtɯtʰan]	'warm'
7.	[beˈgɛ]	'pillow'	14.	[ˈweːtʰulɯl]	'coat'

2. **Larike:** Larike belongs to the Malayo-Polynesian branch of the Austronesian language family. It is spoken on Ambon Island in Indonesia.

Larike has four allowable syllables: V, CV, VC, CVC. It can also have CCVC in borrowed words.

First, draw the syllable structure for the word for 'government' and the word for 'to ask' in the space above each word.

Then, consider [i] and [ɪ]: [ɪ] is an allophone of /i/. Describe the conditions under which /i/ is realized as [ɪ].

1.	[parɪnta]	'government'		9.	[diəmata]	'sun'
2.	[sɛnɪn]	'Monday'		10.	[ʔntudo]	'it sleeps'
3.	[tahalɪl]	'funeral service'		11.	[ʔimɪrduma]	'your PL house'
4.	[ʔimɪrʔure]	'your banana'		12.	[matɪrhaho]	'their pig'
5.	[ʔise]	'tree sap'		13.	[margrɪb]	'evening prayer'
6.	[hɛtike]	'to snap'		14.	[hiru]	'to toss'
7.	[pakiniəku]	'to ask'		15.	[ʔilaŋa]	'to lose'
8.	[titu]	'peak, summit'		16.	[miso]	'earthquake'

p a r ɪ n t a   p a k i n i ə k u

Features (Section 3)

Features represent individual properties of a sound. Features are usually divided into four groups as follows:

Major Class Features	Manner Features
<ul><li>[+/−consonantal]</li><li>[+/−syllabic]</li><li>[+/−sonorant]</li></ul>	<ul><li>[+/−continuant]</li><li>[+/−nasal]</li><li>[+/−lateral]</li><li>[+/−delayed release]</li></ul>
Laryngeal Features	**Place Features**
<ul><li>[+/−voice]</li><li>[+/−spread glottis (SG)]</li><li>[+/−constricted glottis (CG)]</li></ul>	<ul><li>[LABIAL] [+/−round]</li><li>[CORONAL] [+/−anterior], [+/−strident]</li><li>[DORSAL] [+/−high], [+/−low], [+/−back], [+/−tense], [+/−reduced]</li></ul>

- Since features represent articulation, they are always enclosed in square (i.e., [ ]) brackets.

- Except for [LABIAL], [CORONAL], and [DORSAL], all features are binary and are specified as either plus or minus. [LABIAL], [CORONAL], and [DORSAL] are used to represent the articulator that is active in executing the articulation:

  - [LABIAL] for the lips;

  - [CORONAL] for the tongue tip or blade; and

  - [DORSAL] for the body of the tongue.

- All other place features have plus and minus specifications. These features are used to represent place of articulation features specific to the active articulator. That is, labial sounds are [+/–round]; coronal sounds are [+/–anterior] and [+/–strident]; and dorsal sounds are [+/–high], [+/–low], [+/–back], [+/–tense], and [+/–reduced].

Features are used:

- **To capture natural classes.** **Natural classes** are groups of sounds that share a feature or features, or that pattern together in a sound system. For example, voiceless stops can be considered a natural class, as can rounded vowels.

- **To define contrast.** When sounds contrast they are responsible for meaning differences. However, it is not the sound that contrasts, but one property of the sound that contrasts: that is, a feature. This is called the distinctive feature: the only feature that distinguishes between the sounds. For example [nasal] is a distinctive feature for the /b/ and /m/ contrast in English.

- **To understand the nature of allophonic variation.** Allophonic variation is a change in the specification of a feature of an allophone. For example, voiceless sounds often change and become voiced when near other voiced sounds. This can be captured with a single feature [voice].

Features and Rules

Allophones are the predictable variants of phonemes and their distribution can be described using a rule. Remember that rules have three parts: an individual phoneme or class of contrastive sounds, the allophone or change, and the environment in which the change occurs. Include features for each component of the rule. Rules can be written using phonological notation, or more formally using feature notation.

For example, the rule (given here as a statement) "voiceless unaspirated stops[1] become[2] aspirated[3] syllable initially[4]" can be formulated using feature notation as shown below.

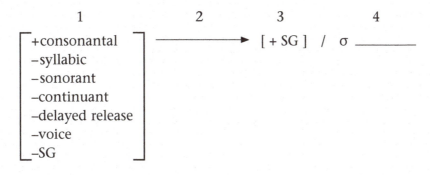

PRACTICE 3.12: Features

1. State the feature that distinguishes each of the following pairs of sounds. (There may be more than one correct answer.) The first one is done for you.

   a. [θ] / [ð] _____ [+/–voice] _____

   b. [p] / [f] _____

   c. [s] / [θ] _____

   d. [b] / [m] _____

   e. [tʃ] / [ʃ] _____

2. Each of the following sets contains three sounds that belong to the same natural class. Add one other segment to each set, making sure that the natural class is preserved. Indicate the feature (including its value) that distinguishes the natural class. The first one is done for you.

	Segment Added	Distinctive Feature
a. [l̩ ə n̩]	[o]	[+ syllabic]
b. [θ s f]	[ ]	_____
c. [i e u]	[ ]	_____
d. [t g n]	[ ]	_____
e. [j ɹ n]	[ ]	_____
f. [i æ ɛ]	[ ]	_____

3. Name the natural class that each of the following phonetic matrices describes.

   a. $\begin{bmatrix} -\text{consonantal} \\ -\text{syllabic} \end{bmatrix}$

   b. $\begin{bmatrix} +\text{consonantal} \\ -\text{syllabic} \\ -\text{sonorant} \\ +\text{continuant} \\ +\text{voice} \end{bmatrix}$

4. In each of the following sets, all the sounds except one belong to the same natural class. Draw a circle around the sound that does not belong, and state the feature that the remaining sounds share.

    a. [t ɡ v dʒ]   _____

    b. [b m ɹ w]   _____

    c. [n ɡ t j]   _____

    d. [i ɛ u æ]   _____

5. In each of the following systems, some segments are boxed. Determine if the boxed segments belong to the same natural class. If they do, state the feature that distinguishes that natural class.

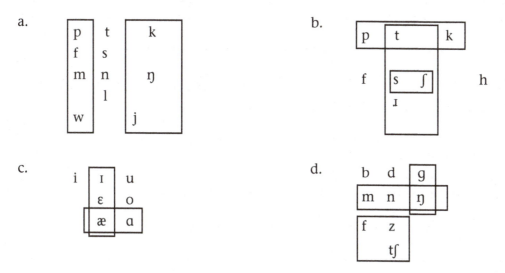

6. For each of the following groups of sounds, provide a feature matrix for features shared by the group. Then tell which feature or features distinguish individual sounds in the group from each other.

    a. [ð θ f v]   c. [u o]

    b. [ɡ dʒ]   d. [i ɪ e ɛ æ]

Rules and Generalizations (Section 4)

When a phonological analysis uncovers allophones belonging to the same phoneme, a rule can be put together to capture the distribution. You need to remember that:

*   Allophones belonging to the same phoneme represent a predictable sound change. Such sound changes occur because segments are often affected by the phonetic characteristics of neighboring sounds. These changes are described using processes such as assimilation. Rules, therefore, are descriptions of articulatory processes.

- The sound changes represented in allophonic distributions usually affect classes of sounds rather than individual sounds. For this reason, rules are formulated as generally as possible.

The format and function of rules:

- Rules are given in phonological notation:

  e.g., $/l/ \rightarrow [\r{l}] \ / \left\{ \begin{array}{l} p \\ t \\ k \end{array} \right\}$ ————

- Rules link the phonemic and phonetic levels together.
  1. the phoneme (e.g., /l/)
  2. The change that takes place as captured by the non-elsewhere allophone (e.g., [l̥])
  3. The environment in which the change from the phoneme to the non-elsewhere allophone takes place (e.g., $\left\{ \begin{array}{l} p \\ t \\ k \end{array} \right\}$ ————)

- The rule is read: "A voiced lateral liquid becomes voiceless after voiceless stops."

What type of assimilation does the above rule describe? Think about the phonetic property of the phoneme that changed to arrive at the allophone.

PRACTICE 3.13: Rules and statements

1. Convert these statements into rules. Watch out for natural classes.

   a. Voiced oral stops become voiceless at the beginning of words.

   _____

   _____

   b. Alveopalatal affricates become fricatives between vowels.

   _____

   c. Vowels become nasalized before nasals.

   _____

   d. Schwa is deleted word-finally.

   _____

   e. A schwa is inserted between a voiceless bilabial stop and a voiced lateral liquid.

   _____

2. Convert the following rules into statements.

a. t $\longrightarrow$ t$^\text{?}$ / ? _____

_____

b. $\begin{Bmatrix} f \\ \theta \\ s \\ \int \end{Bmatrix} \longrightarrow \begin{Bmatrix} v \\ ð \\ z \\ ʒ \end{Bmatrix}$ / V_____V

_____

c. $\begin{Bmatrix} i \\ e \end{Bmatrix} \longrightarrow \begin{Bmatrix} ɪ \\ ɛ \end{Bmatrix}$ / _____#

_____

d. $\begin{Bmatrix} t \\ d \end{Bmatrix} \longrightarrow ɾ$ / V_____V

_____

PRACTICE 3.14: Discovering rules

For each of the following problems, decide what phonological process is in operation. Write a rule that captures the process.

1. **Polish: Voiced and voiceless stops**
   Voiced and voiceless stops are separate phonemes in Polish.

1.	[klubi]	'clubs'		7.	[klup]	'club'
2.	[trupi]	'corpses'		8.	[trup]	'corpse'
3.	[trudi]	'labors'		9.	[trut]	'labor'
4.	[koti]	'cats'		10.	[kot]	'cat'
5.	[wugi]	'lyes'		11.	[wuk]	'lye'
6.	[soki]	'juices'		12.	[sok]	'juice'

2. **South Midland and Southern American English:** [ɪ] and [ɛ]

   In some areas of the United States the phonemes [ɪ] and [ɛ] have merged in certain words. Write a rule to explain it.

1.	[bɪn]	'Ben'	7.	[sɪt]	'sit'	
2.	[pʰɪn]	'pin'	8.	[sɪnt]	'cent'	
3.	[bɛt]	'bet'	9.	[ɹɛk]	'wreck'	
4.	[bɪt]	'bit'	10.	[hɪm]	'hem'	
5.	[pʰɪn]	'pen'	11.	[hɛlow]	'hello'	
6.	[sɛt]	'set'	12.	[hɪm]	'hymn'	

3. **Fante:** [t] and [tʃ]; [d] and [dʒ]

   In Fante, a language spoken in Ghana, [t] and [tʃ] are allophones of one phoneme, and [d] and [dʒ] are allophones of one phoneme. Examine the following data, and write a rule that will account for both. Fante is a tone language, but tones are not shown here.

   [tʃ]   represents a voiceless alveolar affricate.

   [dʒ]   represents a voiced alveolar affricate.

1.	[tutu]	'dig up'	10.	[itʃir]	'head'	
2.	[abodʒin]	'title'	11.	[medʒe]	'I took'	
3.	[tɔŋ]	'sell'	12.	[otʃei]	'he listens'	
4.	[adaka]	'box'	13.	[dom]	'bless'	
5.	[tʃie]	'listen'	14.	[dʒin]	'name'	
6.	[atar]	'dress'	15.	[tʃew]	'pluck'	
7.	[dʒi]	'eat'	16.	[dɔm]	'to team up'	
8.	[ntoma]	'cloth'	17.	[adʒe]	'thing'	
9.	[edur]	'medicine'				

Derivations (Section 4.1)

Derivations are a representation of how phonemes and allophones are related. Phonetic forms are derived from phonemic forms by applying rules. There are three parts to a derivation. These parts are very similar to the components of a **phonological rule**.

- **Underlying representation (UR).** The underlying representation is a representation of native speaker knowledge and therefore is always in phonemic representation.

- **Rules.** Remember that phonemes and allophones are linked by a rule. The rule applies to change the phoneme into the allophone. This, of course, only occurs when the structural description (environment) specified in the rule is found in the underlying representation.

- **Phonetic representation (PR).** The phonetic representation is also called the **surface representation**. Since the surface representation always represents pronunciation, it is in phonetic representation.

Recall that in English, liquids and glides become voiceless after a voiceless stop at the beginning of a syllable. This is an example of devoicing.

The following derivation illustrates how the phonetic form is derived from the underlying representation using this rule.

UR	# pliz #	'please'	# læf #	'laugh'
Liquid glide devoicing	# pl̥iz #		———	
PR	[pl̥iz]		[læf]	

- In the word *please,* liquid/glide devoicing applies because [l] occurs after a voiceless consonant (i.e., [p]). The structural description of the rule has been met. Notice that after the rule has applied, [l] has become voiceless (i.e., [l̥]).

- The rule does not apply to the word *laugh,* as indicated by the line, since the structural description necessary for the rule to apply was not met: [l] occurs at the beginning of the word and not after a voiceless consonant. The phonetic form, therefore, remains the same as the underlying form.

See Figure 3.15 in the textbook for an example of a derivation involving aspiration and vowel lengthening in English.

PRACTICE 3.15: Rules and derivations

1. **Tamil:** [p] and [b], [k] and [g], [t] and [ḍ], [t̪] and [d̪]
   [t], [ḍ] are retroflex.
   [̪] means that a sound is dental.
   [ɨ] represents a high central unrounded vowel.

   Remember: When looking for complementary distribution, you must record the immediate surrounding phonetic environment around each occurrence of a sound.

1. [pal]	'tooth'	11. [id̪ɨ]	'this'
2. [abayam]	'refuge'	12. [aḍɨ]	'that'
3. [kappal]	'ship'	13. [katti]	'knife'
4. [saabam]	'curse'	14. [kuḍi]	'jump'
5. [kaakkaaj]	'crow'	15. [pat̪t̪i]	'ten'
6. [mugil]	'cloud'	16. [paaḍam]	'foot'
7. [t̪ugil]	'veil'	17. [idam]	'place'
8. [t̪at̪t̪ɨ]	'plate'	18. [kaat̪paaḍi]	'name of a town'
9. [padɨ]	'lie down'	19. [pattɨ]	'silk'
10. [t̪uukkɨ]	'carry'		

- Are the pairs of sounds separate phonemes or allophones of the same phoneme? What is the evidence for your answer?

- If these are allophones of the same phoneme, identify the articulatory process at work. Provide a statement and write a rule using feature notation. Make your rule as general as possible. Watch out for natural classes.

- Provide a derivation for 3, 6, and 14.

2. **Standard Spanish and Andalusian Spanish**

	Spelling	Standard	Andalusian	Gloss
1.	doy	[doj]	[doj]	'I give'
2.	lado	[laðo]	[laːo]	'side'
3.	robledo	[roβleðo]	[roβleːo]	'oak grove'
4.	lindo	[lindo]	[lindo]	'pretty'
5.	verdad	[berðað]	[beːðaː]	'truth'
6.	arder	[arðer]	[aːðeː]	'to burn (intransitive)'
7.	verde	[berðe]	[beːðe]	'green'
8.	pecado	[pekaðo]	[pekaːo]	'sin'
9.	anda	[anda]	[anda]	'he/she walks'
10.	virtud	[birtuð]	[biːtuː]	'virtue'
11.	donde	[donde]	[donde]	'where'
12.	florido	[floriðo]	[floriːo]	'florid, robust'
13.	conde	[konde]	[konde]	'count (aristocratic title)'
14.	mercado	[merkaðo]	[meːkaːo]	'market'

a. When does [d] become [ð] in Standard Spanish? Write a rule using features.

b. When does [d] become [ð] in Andalusian Spanish? Write a rule using features.

c. When is Standard Spanish [r] deleted in Andalusian Spanish?

d. When is Standard Spanish [ð] deleted in Andalusian Spanish?

e. Some of the rules that derive the Andalusian Spanish phonetic form must be ordered. Write derivations for *verdad* and *mercado*.

REMINDER

To solve a phonology problem, you must have a firm grasp on minimal pairs, near-minimal pairs, complementary distribution, and phonemes and allophones. If you don't, then you need to get some help.

Review Exercise

Determine whether the sounds under consideration are allophones of the same phoneme or are separate phonemes. Provide evidence to support your conclusion. If the sounds are allophones of the same phoneme in complementary distribution, provide a phonological rule.

1. **French:** Voiced and voiceless nasals and liquids
   Note: The diacritic [̥] under a symbol means that it is voiceless, e.g., [m̥] represents a voiceless [m]; [l̥] represents a voiceless [l].
   A tilde over or after a vowel represents a nasalized vowel, e.g., [ã, ɛ̃] are nasal [a] and [ɛ].
   [ʁ] represents a voiced uvular fricative.
   [y] represents a high front tense rounded vowel.
   [ø] represents a mid front tense rounded vowel.

1. [pl̥i] 'fold'
2. [blø] 'blue'
3. [komynism̩] 'communism'
4. [aluʁdiʁ] 'to weigh down'
5. [ãpl̥] 'wide'
6. [sɛ̃pl̥] 'simple'
7. [ʁale] 'to moan, groan'
8. [tãpl̥] 'temple'
9. [dʁol] 'funny'
10. [sm̥ɔkiŋ] 'tuxedo'
11. [ʁezyme] 'to sum up'
12. [mufl̥] 'mittens'
13. [kl̥aksɔne] 'to honk the horn'
14. [sn̥ɔb] 'snob'

2. **Kpelle:** Nasalized and oral vowels

Kpelle is a tone language spoken in Liberia and Sierra Leone. Tones have been omitted in the data here. A tilde [˜] over a vowel indicates that it is nasalized.

1. [sĩi] 'spider'
2. [nsũa] 'my nose'
3. [nũui] 'the person'
4. [mela] 'split it'
5. [ntĩa] 'my taboo'
6. [kpɛla] 'water chevrotain'*
7. [põja] 'a design, mark'
8. [mɛ̃la] 'its horn'
9. [ntɛɛ] 'send me'
10. [nsoŋ] 'catch me'

* A water chevrotain is a hornless ruminant, also called a mouse deer.

3. **Hausa:** [r] and [ɽ]

Hausa is a language spoken in northern Nigeria. Tones are not shown here.

[r] represents a trill.

[ɽ] represents a retroflex flap.

[ɓ] represents a voiced bilabial implosive, in which the larynx moves downward, sucking air in.

1. [ʃaːɽaː] 'sweeping'
2. [ʃahararreː] 'famous'
3. [ɓaɽgoː] 'marrow'
4. [ɽuɓeːwaː] 'rotting'
5. [baraː] 'begging'
6. [rubuːtuː] 'writing'
7. [bargoː] 'blanket'
8. [ʃaːɽaɽɽeː] 'swept'
9. [kʷoːɽaː] 'ringworm'
10. [gʷoːro] 'kola nut'

4. **Bemba:** [s] and [ʃ]

Bemba is a Bantu language spoken in Zambia and elsewhere in East Africa. Tones are not shown here.

1. [ukuʃika] 'to be deep'
2. [amakalaʃi] 'glasses'
3. [umuʃikaːle] 'soldier'
4. [ameːnʃi] 'water'
5. [umwaːnakaʃi] 'woman'
6. [insoːkoʃi] 'socks'
7. [nʃi] 'what'
8. [insa] 'clock, hour'
9. [isabi] 'fish'
10. [fuseːke] 'go away!'
11. [ukusela] 'to move'
12. [akasuba] 'sun'
13. [soma] 'read!'
14. [pasoːpo] 'beware!'

5. **Syrian Arabic:** [s] and [sˤ], [z] and [zˤ]
[sˤ] and [zˤ] are pharyngealized; they are formed with a secondary articulation involving a constriction in the pharynx.
[ħ] represents a voiceless pharyngeal fricative.

1.	[nəsˤsˤ]	'half'	9.	[sˤeːf]	'summer'
2.	[buːzˤa]	'ice cream'	10.	[nəsər]	'eagle'
3.	[sˤadˤme]	'shock'	11.	[naːs]	'people'
4.	[seːf]	'sword'	12.	[wəsˤex]	'dirty'
5.	[nizˤaːm]	'discipline'	13.	[sahəl]	'easy'
6.	[zahər]	'flower'	14.	[buːz]	'muzzle'
7.	[sˤəhər]	'sister's husband'	15.	[ħəzer]	'careful'
8.	[fazˤzˤ]	'crude'	16.	[zˤaːher]	'apparent'

6. **Mandarin Chinese:** [tɕ] and [k]; [tɕʰ] and [kʰ]; [ɕ] and [x]
In Mandarin Chinese, there are three pairs of voiceless palatal and velar obstruents:

Palatals		Velars	
IPA	Description	IPA	Description
[tɕ]	voiceless unaspirated affricate	[k]	voiceless unaspirated stop
[tɕʰ]	voiceless aspirated affricate	[kʰ]	voiceless aspirated stop
[ɕ]	voiceless unaspirated fricative	[x]	voiceless unaspirated fricative

Examine the data set below, and decide whether each pair of palatal and velar obstruents listed above—namely, [tɕ] and [k], [tɕʰ] and [kʰ], and [ɕ] and [x]—represents two separate phonemes or two allophones of one phoneme. Describe the environments in which palatal obstruents occur and the environment in which velar obstruents occur, and make a generalization.

Chinese is a tone language:
[ˉ] represents a level tone.
[ˇ] represents a contour tone that is falling, then rising.
[ˊ] represents a rising tone.
[ˋ] represents a falling tone.

1.	[tɕiɛ̄]	'street'	10.	[kǎi]	'correct'
2.	[tɕʰuə̄]	'lack'	11.	[tɕī]	'hit'
3.	[kə̄]	'song'	12.	[xǎo]	'good'
4.	[kʰə̄]	'piece'	13.	[tɕʰī]	'seven'
5.	[ɕī]	'west'	14.	[tɕʰí]	'hardworking'
6.	[xə̄]	'drink'	15.	[kʰāi]	'open'
7.	[kʰŏŋ]	'afraid'	16.	[kāŋ]	'steel'
8.	[tɕiàn]	'see'	17.	[ɕùn]	'instruct'
9.	[ɕuə̀]	'blood'	18.	[xóŋ]	'red'

7. **Brazilian Portuguese**
   In most dialects of Brazilian Portuguese, [l] becomes [w] in a particular environment.

1.	aquilo	[akilu]	'that'		6.	melado	[meladu]	'molasses'
2.	gols	[gows]	'goals'		7.	sol	[sɔw]	'sun'
3.	bolo	[bolu]	'cake'		8.	futebol	[futʃibɔw]	'football'
4.	sulco	[suwku]	'groove'		9.	voltar	[vowtah]	'to come back'
5.	mel	[mɛw]	'honey'		10.	Raul	[hauw]	(man's name)

   a. Draw the syllable structure for the words below. Treat [w] as a consonant. The syllable structure constraints for Brazilian Portuguese are:

   - Consonant clusters are allowed in onsets, but only for an obstruent + liquid sequence.

   - Codas may include a cluster of glide + obstruent.

   - A syllable with an onset is preferred over a syllable without an onset.

   a   k   i   l   u   g   o   w   s   s   u   w   k   u

   b. Describe the environment in which [l] does *not* change to [w].

   _____

   c. In what environment does [l] → [w]? (Try to supply the most economical explanation.)

   _____

☑ **RECAP**

Make sure you know how to do the following. (See also the Key Terms at the end of Chapter 3.)

- define phonemes and allophones
- spot minimal and near-minimal pairs
- determine complementary distribution
- use phonemic and phonetic representation
- construct syllable representations
- identify basic and complex syllables
- identify consonantal and vowel features
- spot classes of sounds
- put together feature matrices
- translate rules into statements and statements into rules
- put together rules using feature notation
- construct derivations
- solve phonology problems

Questions? Problems?

_____

_____

_____

_____

_____

_____

_____

_____

_____

_____

_____

_____

_____

_____

_____

four

Morphology: The Analysis of Word Structure

Morphology is the study of words and how they are formed and interpreted. Following are some of the important topics and concepts covered in this chapter. Make sure you are familiar with them.

Morphological terminology
Identifying morphemes
Identifying lexical categories
Analyzing word structure
Derivation

Compounding
Inflection
Morphological processes
Morphology problems
Morphophonemics

Morphological Terminology (Section 1)

The following terms are crucial to understanding morphology. You should know them. (Remember also to review the Key Terms at the end of Chapter 4 of the main text.)

TERM	DEFINITION
Word	Words are the smallest free forms found in language. **Free forms** are elements that can appear in isolation, or whose position is not fixed. Words can be **simple** or **complex**. See Table 4.1 in the text for some examples.
Morpheme	A morpheme is the smallest meaning or functional unit found in language. Morphemes can be **free** or **bound**.
Allomorphs	**Allomorphs** are the different forms of a morpheme.
Root	A **root** is the core of a word. It is the portion of the word that carries most of the word's meaning. The majority of English words are built from roots that are free morphemes, making English a word-based language. Some English words, though, are built from roots that are bound morphemes (e.g., unkempt). Think of some examples.

Affixes	**Affixes** are different types of bound morphemes. There are three types of affixes found in language: **prefixes**, **suffixes**, and **infixes**. See Tables 4.3 and 4.4 in the text for examples.
Base	A **base** is any form to which an affix is added. The base may be the same as the root, but it can also be larger than the root. See Figure 4.3 in the text for an illustration of the difference between roots and bases.
Stem	A **stem** is a base to which an inflectional affix is added.

Identifying Morphemes (Section 1.1)

Morphemes are the building blocks of words. A word may contain only one morpheme, making it a simple word, or a word may contain more than one morpheme, making it a complex word. Below are some hints for determining the number of morphemes that a word contains.

- A morpheme can carry information about meaning or function. For example, the word *haunt* cannot be divided into the morphemes *h* and *aunt,* since only *aunt* has meaning. However, the word *bats* has two morphemes, since both *bat* and *-s* have meaning. The *-s,* of course, means that there is more than one.

- The meanings of individual morphemes should contribute to the overall meaning of the word. For example, *pumpkin* cannot be divided into *pump* and *kin,* since the meaning of *pumpkin* has nothing to do with the meaning of either *pump* or *kin.*

- A morpheme is not the same as a syllable. Morphemes do not have to be a syllable, or morphemes can consist of one or more syllables. For example, the morpheme *treat* has one syllable, the morpheme *vampire* has two syllables, but the morpheme *-s* (meaning 'plural') is not a syllable.

- Often as words are built, changes in pronunciation and/or spelling occur. These do not affect a morpheme's status as a morpheme. For example, when *-y* is attached to the word *scare,* it becomes *scary,* and when *-er* is attached to *scary,* it becomes *scarier.* The root, however, is still *scare,* not *scar.*

PRACTICE 4.1: Identifying morphemes

Identify the number of morphemes in each of the following words.

1. desert   _____

2. memory _____

3. format   _____

4. flowchart   _____

5. bug   _____

6. debug   _____

7. supply	_____	10. faster	_____
8. supplies	_____	11. power	_____
9. supplier	_____	12. processor	_____

Free and Bound Morphemes (Section 1.1)

A free morpheme can stand on its own as a word (e.g., *scare*, *treat*, *vampire*). A bound morpheme must be attached to another element and cannot be a word by itself (e.g., scar*y*, treat*ed*, pumpkin*s*).

PRACTICE 4.2: Free and bound morphemes

For each of the following words, fill in the number of morphemes and write the free and bound morphemes in the appropriate blanks. The first one is done for you.

WORD	# OF MORPHEMES	FREE	BOUND
1. eraser	2	erase	-er
2. wicked	____	_____	_____
3. invalid (A)	____	_____	_____
4. invalid (N)	____	_____	_____
5. Jack's	____	_____	_____
6. optionality	____	_____	_____
7. refurnish	____	_____	_____
8. inabilities	____	_____	_____
9. denationalize	____	_____	_____
10. deride	____	_____	_____
11. activation	____	_____	_____

Identifying Lexical Categories (Section 1.2)

In morphology, we are concerned with four **lexical categories**: nouns, verbs, adjectives, and prepositions. Nouns typically refer to people and things; and prepositions typically indicate relations in space or time.

PRACTICE 4.3: Lexical categories

For each of the following words, fill in the number of morphemes, and identify the root, the lexical category of the root, and the lexical category of the entire word. Be careful: the root's lexical category and the word's lexical category may or may not be the same. The first one is done for you.

	WORD	# OF MORPHEMES	ROOT	ROOT CATEGORY	WORD CATEGORY
1.	healthiest	3	health	noun	adjective
2.	amazement				
3.	reusable				
4.	dishonest				
5.	Baltimore				
6.	lovelier				
7.	historic				
8.	uncontrolled				
9.	impersonal				
10.	trees				
11.	faster				
12.	rereads				
13.	beautiful				
14.	child				

Word Structure (Section 1.2)

A word **tree** is a representation of a word's internal structure. To put together a word tree, you need to be able to determine the number of morphemes in a word, identify roots and affixes, and assign lexical categories.

Remember: Prefixes are attached to the front of a base, while suffixes are attached to the end of a base. Infixes are a type of affix that occurs inside another morpheme. Infixes are generally not found in English.

Below are some examples of how to draw a word tree.

1. Words with a single affix.

    a. Root + suffix

    A
    |
    kindness

    1. Identify the root and determine its lexical category.

    2. Attach the suffix and determine the lexical category of the resulting word. This may or may not be the same as the lexical category of the root.

    b. Prefix + root

    A
    |
    unkind

    A
    /\
    Af A
    | |
    unkind

    1. Identify the root and determine its lexical category.

    2. Attach the prefix and determine the lexical category of the resulting word. This is typically the same as the lexical category of the root.

2. Words with multiple suffixes.

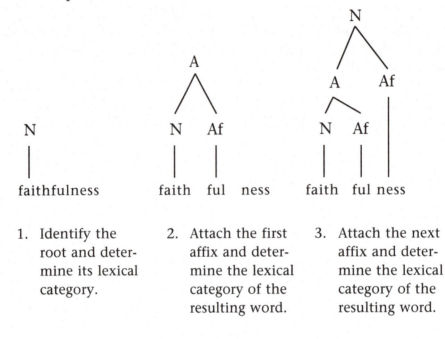

1. Identify the root and determine its lexical category.

2. Attach the first affix and determine the lexical category of the resulting word.

3. Attach the next affix and determine the lexical category of the resulting word.

3. Words with both a prefix and a suffix.

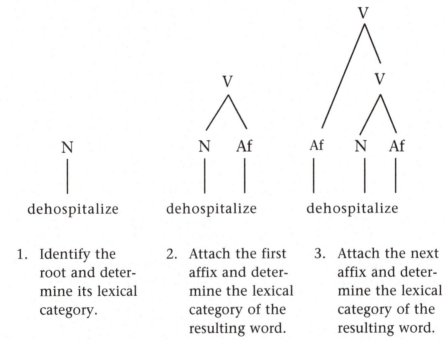

1. Identify the root and determine its lexical category.

2. Attach the first affix and determine the lexical category of the resulting word.

3. Attach the next affix and determine the lexical category of the resulting word.

Note: In this example, the suffix must be attached before the prefix. Why is that?

4. Words that are structurally ambiguous.

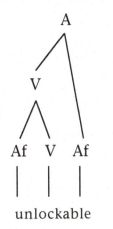
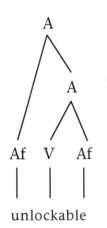

The prefix *un-* is first attached to create the verb *unlock.* The suffix *-able* is then attached to create the adjective *unlockable.*

The suffix *-able* is first attached to create the adjective *lockable.* The prefix *un-* is then attached to create the adjective *unlockable.*

PRACTICE 4.4: Drawing word trees

To practice, draw word trees for the following words:

1. trees
2. lovelier
3. dishonest
4. beautiful

5. amazement
6. reusable
7. impersonal
8. Baltimore

REMINDER

To be able to draw word trees correctly, you need to be able to identify nouns, verbs, adjectives, and prepositions. If you are having difficulty with these, refer to Section 1.2 of the text for help.

Derivation (Section 2)

Derivation is a process of affixation. Affixation is a morphological process that adds affixes to words. Derivational affixes are affixes that:

- build a word having a different (but usually related) meaning than that of its base,
- usually change the lexical category of a word,
- are restricted in the class of bases to which they can attach.

English has many derivational affixes. English derivational suffixes have all of the characteristics of derivation just described. For example:

- The suffix -*ity* combines with an adjective such as *stupid* to create the noun *stupidity*, meaning the state or quality of being stupid.
- The suffix -*en* combines with an adjective such as *hard* to create the verb *harden*, meaning to become hard.
- The suffix -*ous* combines with a noun such as *poison* to create the adjective *poisonous*, meaning producing or possessing poison.

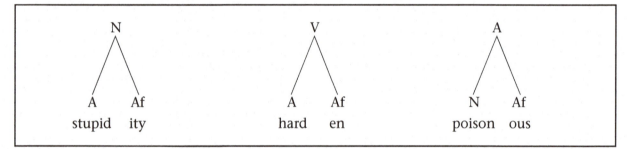

English also has many derivational prefixes. These cause a meaning change to the base, but usually do not change the lexical category of the base. It is the meaning change that makes them derivational. For example:

- The prefix *ex*- combines with a noun such as *friend* to create the noun *ex-friend*, meaning someone who is no longer a friend.
- The prefix *re*- combines with a verb such as *think* to create the verb *rethink*, meaning to think again.
- The prefix *in*- combines with an adjective such as *complete* to create the adjective *incomplete*, meaning not complete.

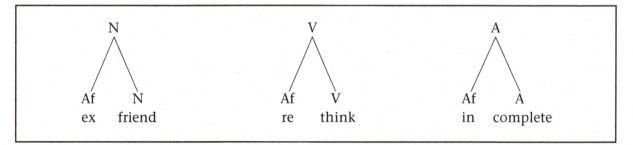

For more examples of English derivational prefixes and suffixes, see Table 4.6 of the textbook.

Derivational affixes are often subject to restrictions. For example:

- Derivational affixes combine with bases of particular lexical categories.
  e.g., In English, *-ize* must be attached to a noun or adjective; *-er* must be attached to a verb.

- Derivational affixes combine with bases having certain phonological properties.
  e.g., In English, *-en* must be attached to a base having one syllable and ending in an obstruent.

- Derivational affixes combine with bases of specific origin.
  e.g., In English, *-ant* must be attached to a base of Latin origin.

Some derivational affixes cause a phonological change in the base. For example:
- In English, *-ity* and *-(a)tion* change the stress of a word.

  e.g., 'modern → mo'dernity, 'modernize → moderni'zation

The affixes in English that cause phonological change in the base are **Class I affixes**. **Class II affixes** do not cause phonological change in the base. See Tables 4.9 and 4.10 of the text for examples of both types of affixes.

PRACTICE 4.5: Derivational affixes

1. Draw trees for the following words. Remember that a word can contain more than one derivational affix.

   a. disappear   d. unbreakable
   b. homeless   e. institutional
   c. electricity   f. lodger

   Now go back and identify which words have a Class I affix.

2. For each word below, write the affix and how the affix changes the lexical category of the word. Some words may have more than one affix. The first one is done for you.

WORD	AFFIX	CHANGE
1. affordable	-able	V → A
2. racial		
3. silliness		
4. disconnect		
5. organization		
6. combative		

7. humorous   _____   _____

8. morality   _____   _____

9. remarry   _____   _____

10. Brazilian   _____   _____

11. demonize   _____   _____

12. validate   _____   _____

13. lighten   _____   _____

14. unpleasant   _____   _____

15. unbend   _____   _____

Compounding (Section 3)

Compounding is another process for building words. Compounding involves the combination of two or more words into a new word. Most English compounds are nouns, verbs, and adjectives. There are four important concepts about English compounds:

- **Headedness.** The **head** of a compound is the morpheme that determines the category of the entire compound. Most English compounds are right-headed. That is, the category of the entire compound is the same as the category of the last member of the compound. For example, the compound *blackboard* is a noun, since the last member, *board,* is a noun. The head of *dry clean* is *clean*, and the head of *nationwide* is *wide*.

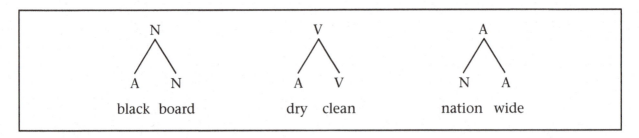

- **Stress patterns.** Even though compounds can be spelled as one word, as two words, or with a hyphen separating the morphemes, a generalization can be made about the stress patterns found on them. Stress tends to be more prominent on the first member of the compound rather than the second: for example, *'greenhouse* (a garden center) versus *green 'house* (a house that is green).

- **Tense/Plural.** Tense and plural markers are usually added to the compound as a whole and not to the first member of the compound. For example, the plural of *fire engine* is *fire engines* and not *fires engine*. Similarly, the past tense of *drop kick* is *drop kicked* and not *dropped kick*.

- **Meaning relationships.** In an **endocentric compound**, the entire compound denotes a subtype of the head. For example, a *teacup* is a type of *cup*, and a *lunchroom* is a type of *room*. In an **exocentric compound**, the meaning of the compound does not come from the head. For example, a *redneck* is not a type of *neck*, but a type of person.

Compounds can be formed from smaller compounds. As well, compounding can be used in conjunction with derivation to build words. For example, the compound *blackboard* can combine with the derived word *eraser* to create the larger compound *blackboard eraser*.

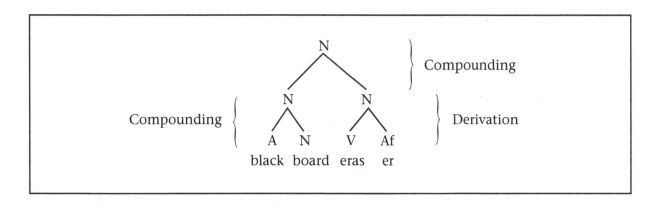

See Figures 4.10 and 4.11 in the text for other examples.

PRACTICE 4.6: Compounds

1. For each of the following compounds, identify the lexical categories making it up and give another example of that type of compound. Give a different example for each compound. The first one is done for you.

COMPOUND	LEXICAL CATEGORIES	EXAMPLE
a. bathroom	noun + noun	movie star
b. scarecrow		
c. skin-deep		
d. bittersweet		
e. upstairs		

Now go back and draw a word tree for each compound.

2. Compounding can be used in conjunction with derivation to build words. Draw trees for each of the following words.

   a. washer-dryer

   b. presidential election

   c. (an) undertaking

   d. overgrown

Inflection (Section 4.1)

Inflection is commonly a process of affixation. Inflectional affixes are affixes that:

- function to provide grammatical information (e.g., singular or plural, tense),
- do not change the lexical category of a word,
- occur at the outer edges of a word (e.g., last).

English has eight inflectional affixes. They are found on nouns, verbs, and adjectives.

NOUNS

1. PLURAL: *-s*
                                         dogs, cats, roses

2. POSSESSIVE: *-'s*
                                           Mary's book, Pat's book, the judge's book

VERBS

1. THIRD-PERSON SINGULAR: *-s*
                                           She likes jazz. He walks slowly. He hisses loudly.

2. PAST TENSE: *-ed*
                                         She filled the gas tank. He wanted a dog.

3. PROGRESSIVE: *-ing*
                                         I am sighing. You are singing. She is walking.
                                         We are talking. He was running. They were leaving.

4. PAST PARTICIPLE: *-en / -ed*
                                         I have spoken. He has filled the gas tank.

ADJECTIVES

1. COMPARATIVE: *-er*
                                         greener, louder, faster, softer

2. SUPERLATIVE: *-est*
                                           greenest, loudest, fastest, softest

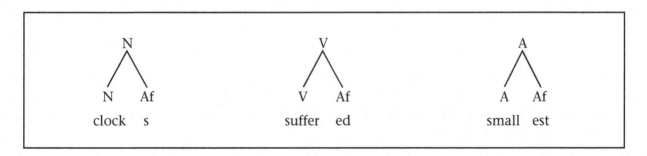

See Table 4.15 of the text for some other examples of these English inflectional affixes.

PRACTICE 4.7: Recognizing lexical categories and inflection

For each of the following words, identify the lexical category of the root and the type of inflectional information found (e.g., past tense, superlative, plural). The first one is done for you.

WORD	LEXICAL CATEGORY	INFLECTIONAL INFORMATION
1. watched	verb	past tense
2. runs		
3. sorriest		
4. lamps		
5. playing		
6. driven		
7. lovelier		

Inflection versus Derivation (Section 4.2)

It can sometimes be hard to determine whether an affix is an inflectional affix or a derivational affix. The boxes below provide some criteria for helping determine whether an affix is inflectional or derivational.

Inflectional affixes	Derivational affixes
• do not change the lexical category or meaning of the base.	• typically change both the lexical category and meaning of the base.
• are attached after derivational affixes have been attached.	• occur closer to the root than inflectional affixes.
• are productive, meaning there are relatively few exceptions on the class of bases to which they can attach.	• are less productive than inflectional affixes, meaning there are restrictions on the class of bases to which they can attach.
• are semantically transparent, meaning that it is easy to determine the contribution of the affix to the meaning of the resulting word.	• are less semantically transparent than inflectional affixes, meaning that it is not always easy to determine the contribution of the affix to the meaning of the resulting word.

PRACTICE 4.8: Identifying affixes

Each of the following English words contains at least one affix. For each word, identify all the affixes, and for each affix state whether it is inflectional (Infl) or derivational (Deriv). The first is done for you.

WORD	AFFIX(ES)	INFL / DERIV
1. trucks	-s	inflectional (plural)
2. instructional		
3. reuse		
4. girl's		
5. smaller		
6. delightful		
7. nationalize		
8. watched		
9. mistreat		
10. unhealthiest		

PRACTICE 4.9: Form versus function of affixes

Many affixes have the same form, but different functions. That is, affixes having the same form can be either inflectional or derivational, or they can be different inflectional affixes or derivational affixes.

In each of the following groups of words, two words have the same type of affix, one word has a different affix, and one word has no affix at all. Underline the affix in each word. Then, next to each word, write S (same), D (different), or N (none), based on the items in the set. You may want to use a dictionary. The first one is done for you.

1.	ovens	S	3.	leaven	
	lens	N		harden	
	hens	S		spoken	
	listens	D		thicken	
2.	greedy		4.	rider	
	ivory			colder	
	jealousy			silver	
	dirty			actor	

5. greener   _____   7. intelligent   _____

   farmer   _____   inhale   _____

   colder   _____   incongruous   _____

   water   _____   inhuman   _____

6. friendly   _____   8. candied   _____

   slowly   _____   shopped   _____

   intelligently   _____   cleaned   _____

   early   _____   candid   _____

Word Trees to Show Inflection, Derivation, and Compounding

Remember that more than one process can be used to build a single word. A word like *black-boards*, for example, is a compound noun (*black + board*) with an inflectional suffix *-s* for the plural. If you are in doubt about the lexical category of an entire word, you can look at the affixes; sentence context can also help you determine the lexical category.

For example, the word *creamiest* might be diagrammed as follows.

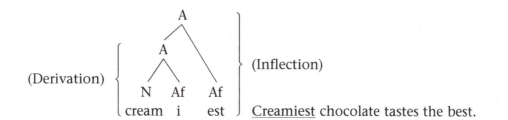

Creamiest chocolate tastes the best.

PRACTICE 4.10: Drawing word trees

Draw a tree diagram for each of the following words, and identify whether inflection, derivation, and/or compounding was used to build the word.

WORD	CONTEXT SENTENCE
1. taken	The baby has <u>taken</u> his first steps.
2. spoonfeeding	Mother is <u>spoonfeeding</u> the baby.
3. retry	She should <u>retry</u> the recipe.
4. silkiest	Sandra used the <u>silkiest</u> material.
5. introductions	Mary performed the <u>introductions</u>.
6. steps	John <u>steps</u> up the ladder.

7. steps   I hate those steep <u>steps</u>.

8. thickener   Flour is a type of <u>thickener</u>.

9. skiers   The <u>skiers</u> were rich.

10. insightful   Your answer is rather <u>insightful</u>.

11. stone-cold   Your French fries are <u>stone-cold</u>.

12. making   Jill is <u>making</u> candy.

13. boxing   We watched the <u>boxing</u> on TV.

14. unbreakable   Joan always buys <u>unbreakable</u> dishes.

15. attractive   That room is very <u>attractive</u>.

16. moonrocks   The astronauts collected many <u>moonrocks</u>.

17. blessing   Give me your <u>blessing</u>.

18. blessing   She is <u>blessing</u> the bread.

19. school teacher   My mother was a <u>school teacher</u>.

20. clumsiness   I detest <u>clumsiness</u>.

21. ex-Iowan   Herb is an <u>ex-Iowan</u>.

22. hammered   John <u>hammered</u> on the door.

23. overthink   Don't <u>overthink</u> the problem.

24. unlocked   We <u>unlocked</u> the door.

25. impure   <u>Impure</u> water is dangerous.

26. criticize   You <u>criticize</u> too much.

27. treatment center   He needs to go to a good <u>treatment center</u>.

28. defrosting   The steaks are <u>defrosting</u>.

29. stringier   Her hair is <u>stringier</u> than yours.

30. selfishness   <u>Selfishness</u> is not very attractive.

QUICK REMINDER!

Remember that *all* English prefixes are derivational even though they do not cause a lexical category change.

Processes Related to Inflection (Section 5.1)

In addition to affixation, inflection can be marked by using **internal change**, **suppletion**, **reduplication**, and **tone placement**. See Tables 4.17–4.21 in the text for more examples.

PROCESS	DEFINITION
Internal Change	This process provides grammatical information by changing a portion of the morpheme. That is, the tense or number of a word is marked by changing a sound within the morpheme. e.g., *run → ran*
Suppletion	This process provides grammatical information by changing the entire morpheme. That is, the tense, number, etc., of a word is marked by replacing one morpheme with an entirely different morpheme. e.g., *go → went* Partial suppletion is sometimes used to describe the change in words such as *think → thought* in which more than a segment has been changed, but not the entire morpheme.
Reduplication	A process that copies all (full) or a portion (partial) of the base to mark a semantic or grammatical contrast. This process has only limited use in English. e.g., Vietnamese: *mau* 'rapidly' *mau-mau* 'very rapidly' Tagalog: *tawag* 'call' *tatawag* 'will call'
Tone Placement	This process is found in tone languages in which differences in tone can mark grammatical information such as change in tense or number. e.g., Mashi (Shi), spoken in the Democratic Republic of Congo (An acute accent marks a high tone; no accent means a low tone) *nagánja* 'I counted' *nágánja* 'I will count'

PRACTICE 4.11: More inflection

Each of the following words has been inflected. For each, identify the type of inflectional process that has been used to mark the grammatical contrast. The first has been done for you.

WORD	TYPE OF INFLECTION
1. drove	internal change
2. was	

3. (is) jumping   _____

4. *kitsji* 'small'
   kitsji kitsji 'very small'
   (from Fa d'Ambu)   _____

5. better   _____

6. lovelier   _____

7. George's   _____

8. *gavu* 'good'
   gagavu 'very good'
   (from Fa d'Ambu)   _____

9. mice   _____

REMINDER

Many more inflectional phenomena, including case and agreement, are widely used in language.

Other Morphological Processes (Section 5.2)

In addition to derivation and compounding, other common word-building processes include:

PROCESS	DEFINITION
Cliticization	Clitics are morphemes that behave like words in terms of meaning and function. Clitics differ, though, in that they cannot stand alone as a word. Cliticization attaches these elements to either the beginning of a following word or the end of a preceding word. e.g., *re* from *are* is attached to *they* as in *they're*
Conversion	A process that assigns an existing word to a different lexical category. e.g., *butter* (N) → *(to) butter* (V)
Clipping	A process that shortens a word by removing one or more syllables. e.g., *condominium* → *condo*
Blending	A process that creates a new word by combining portions of two existing words. e.g., *spiced* + *ham* → *spam*

Backformation	A process that creates a word by removing a supposed affix from an existing word. e.g., *donation → donate*
Acronym	A new word created by using the initial letters of the words in a phrase or title. e.g., *radar, UNICEF* Acronyms are different from initialisms, in which each letter making up the word is pronounced. e.g., *IBM, NBA*
Onomatopoeia	Words that have been created to sound like the thing they name. e.g., *buzz, hiss, sizzle*
Coinage	A process that creates a totally new word. e.g., *Teflon*
Eponyms	New words can also be created from names. e.g., *boycott*
Borrowing	New words can be borrowed from other languages. e.g., *feng-shui*

See Tables 4.22–4.26 in the text for more examples.

PRACTICE 4.12: Word-formation processes

1. Identify the process responsible for the formation of each of the following English words. Choose from any of the morphological and word-formation processes in the preceding two tables as well as inflection, derivation, and compounding. The first one is done for you.

   1. Ebonics   blending (**eb**ony + ph**onics**)

   2. (to) ship   _____

   3. swam   _____

   4. layoff   _____

   5. splat   _____

   6. jumped   _____

   7. healthy   _____

   8. demo   _____

   9. export   _____

  10. he's   _____

  11. Facebook   _____

12. beep _____

13. NASA _____

14. Delmarva (Peninsula) _____

15. yoga _____

2. There are many examples of different word-formation processes in the following passage. Find all the examples of acronym, backformation, blending, clipping, coinage, compounding, conversion, and onomatopoeia.

> When Dave woke up, he should have been ready for brunch since he'd slept late. Despite the cheerful chirping of the birds outside and the annoying buzz of the infomercial coming from the TV at the foot of the bed, the external world held no charm. Dave had a headache hammering behind his right eyeball, his stomach hurt, and his nose was running. As he reached for a Kleenex, he reflected bitterly on his luck. Today was supposed to be his first scuba lesson, but instead he'd come down with the flu. As he fingered the blanket, he recalled that the last time he'd gone to the clinic had not inspired confidence. The med student who saw him enthused about his condition in a most off-putting way; he sent Dave for a CAT scan and a blood test, and even suggested hopefully that laser surgery might be in order. In Dave's present condition, this all seemed like too much effort. Maybe, Dave thought as he reached for the remote, he should just laze around for the day, drink Coke, and eat sandwiches while channel-surfing.

3. Word formation in French (1–6) and German (7–12): Write the word formation process that created the word in column 2 from the word in column 1. Words are in French and German orthography, not phonetic transcription.

COLUMN 1 →	COLUMN 2	WORD FORMATION PROCESS
French:		
1. *justice + escargot* 'snail'	*justice escargot* 'slow-moving justice'	_____
2. *esclave* 'slave'	*esclavage* 'slavery'	_____
3. *moquer* 'to make fun of' (V)	*moquerie* 'mockery' (N)	_____
4. *laboratoire* 'laboratory'	*labo* 'laboratory'	_____
5. *français* 'French' (A)	*français* 'French person' (N)	_____
6. *automobile + omnibus*	*autobus* 'city bus'	_____

German:

7. *Nacht* 'night' +
    wandeln 'to walk'   *nachtwandeln* 'to sleepwalk'   _____

8. *ernst* 'serious' (A)   *Ernst* 'seriousness' (N)   _____

9. *ja* 'yes' + *n<u>ein</u>* 'no'   *jein* 'yes and no'   _____

10. *Pinke* 'money'   *Pinkepinke* 'dough'   _____

11. *criminal* 'criminal' +   *Kriminalroman*   _____
    Roman 'novel'   'crime novel'

12. *Kriminalroman*   *Krimi* 'crime novel'   _____
    'crime novel'

Introduction to Morphology Problems (Appendix)

The goal in tackling morphology problems is to isolate and identify all the morphemes in the data given. To do this, you must identify recurring strings of sounds and match them with recurring meanings. It sounds harder than it really is. Here are a few easy ones to try.

PRACTICE 4.13: Easy morphology problems

All data are given in phonetic representation.

1. **Kisar** (Indonesia)
    Examine the data, and fill in the morphemes below. Data are in phonetic transcription.
    [t] here represents a voiceless alveopalatal stop.

    1. [lereni]   'this day'   5. [moʔoniţa]   'one boy'
    2. [mawekonne]   'that girl'   6. [muʔueni]   'this banana'
    3. [papeni]   'this father'   7. [pipionne]   'that goat'
    4. [ornohiţa]   'one mouse'

    Write the morphemes for:

    day   _____   banana   _____

    girl   _____   goat   _____

    father _____   this   _____

    mouse   _____   that   _____

    boy   _____   one   _____

2. **Kiswahili** (East Africa)

1.	kisu	'knife'	visu	'knives'
2.	kitanda	'bed'	vitanda	'beds'
3.	kijiti	'stick'	vijiti	'sticks'
4.	kifungo	'button'	vifungo	'buttons'
5.	kitana	'comb'	vitana	'combs'

a. What is the morpheme meaning SINGULAR? _____

b. What is the morpheme meaning PLURAL? _____

c. If *viti* means 'chairs', how would you say 'chair'? _____

d. If *kikombe* means 'cup', how would you say 'cups'? _____

3. **Toba Batak**
Toba Batak is a Malayo-Polynesian language of Sumatra. Although tones are marked, you may disregard them for this exercise.

1.	[deŋgán]	'good'	[duméŋgan]	'better'
2.	[tíbbo]	'tall'	[tumíbbo]	'taller'
3.	[rɔá]	'ugly'	[rumɔa]	'uglier'
4.	[gokan]	'full'	[gumokán]	'fuller'
5.	[rahis]	'steep'	[rumáhis]	'steeper'
6.	[holom]	'dark'	[humolom]	'darker'

a. What morpheme indicates the comparative? _____

b. What kind of affix is this morpheme? _____

c. If [datu] means 'wise', what is the form for 'wiser'? _____

d. If [sɔmal] means 'usual', what is the form for 'more usual'? _____

e. If [ʤumɛppɛk] means 'shorter', what is the form for 'short'?_____

f. If [lumógo] means 'drier', what is the form for 'dry'? _____

4. **Danish**
Examine the data from Danish, fill in the morphemes, and answer the questions below. The data are in Danish orthography (Danish spelling).

1.	en rød bil	'a red car'
2.	en stor mand	'a big man'
3.	en stor bil	'a big car'
4.	en rød bog	'a red book'
5.	en bil er rød	'a car is red'
6.	en mand er stor	'a man is big'
7.	en bils dør	'a car's door'
8.	bilens dør	'the car's door'

9. mandens   'the man's'
10. bilen er rød   'the car is red'
11. bilen er stor   'the car is big'
12. manden er stor   'the man is big'
13. bilens farve er rød   'the car's color is red'
14. mandens hat er sort   'the man's hat is black'

a. Fill in the morphemes for each of the following:

red   _____   man   _____

book   _____   hat   _____

color   _____   big   _____

black   _____   car   _____

door   _____

is   _____   POSSESSIVE   _____

b. What is the morpheme for 'a'? _____

    Is this morpheme bound or free? _____

c. What is the morpheme for 'the'? _____

    Is this morpheme bound or free? _____

PRACTICE 4.14: More morphology problems

The following pages contain somewhat more difficult problems based on data sets from different languages. These data sets are intended to give you practice in doing morphological analysis. Each contains sufficient data to make valid conclusions; however, the data may have been regularized somewhat. Data are in phonetic representation unless otherwise noted.

1. **Bahasa Indonesian**

1.	baik	'kind'	9.	olahragawan	'sportsman/woman'
2.	bebas	'free'	10.	berolahraga	'to play sports'
3.	bersih	'clean'	11.	kebebasan	'freedom'
4.	olahraga	'sport'	12.	kebersihan	'cleanliness'
5.	ilmu	'science'	13.	ilmuwan	'scientist'
6.	kebaikan	'kindness'	14.	berbaik	'to be kind'
7.	membersihkan	'to clean up, purify'	15.	membebaskan	'to set free'
8.	berilmu	'to be learned or scholarly'			

a. What affix means 'to be [Adjective]/do [Noun]'? _____

b. What affix means 'person who does/engages in [Noun]'? _____

c. Fill in the boxes with the morphemes meaning:

'to cause to be [Adjective]'

	BASE	

abstract noun

	BASE	

2. **Turkish**

[y] represents a high front rounded vowel.
[œ] represents a mid front rounded vowel.

1. [ʃehiɾ] 'city'
2. [ʃehiɾden] 'from the city'
3. [el] 'hand'
4. [elim] 'my hand'
5. [elimde] 'in my hand'
6. [kœpɾy] 'bridge'
7. [kœpɾyleɾ] 'bridges'
8. [kœpɾyleɾe] 'to the bridges'
9. [kœpɾyde] 'on the bridge'
10. [zilim] 'my bell'
11. [zilleɾ] 'bells'
12. [eve] 'to the house'
13. [evde] 'in the house'
14. [evden] 'from the house'
15. [kœpɾyden] 'from the bridge'
16. [elleɾinize] 'to your hands'
17. [sesleɾiniz] 'your voices'
18. [otobysleɾ] 'buses'

a. What morphemes mean:

1. city _____
2. hand _____
3. bridge _____
4. bell _____
5. house _____
6. voice _____
7. bus _____

8. from _____
9. to _____
10. on, in _____
11. my _____
12. your _____
13. PLURAL _____

b. What is the order of morphemes?

Fill in the boxes with: PLURAL, POSSESSIVE, POSTPOSITION, ROOT

c. What do the following mean in English?

1. [ʃehiɾde] _____
2. [elleɾiniz] _____

d. How would you say 'to the buses' in Turkish? _____

3. **Classical Nahuatl**

Nahuatl is an Aztecan language of Mexico.

1.	[tikʷiːka]	'you (SG) sing'	8.	[kikʷa]	'he eats it'
2.	[kʷiːka]	's/he sings'	9.	[kikʷaʔ]	'they eat it'
3.	[tikʷiːkaʔ]	'we sing'	10.	[aːltia]	'he bathes'
4.	[ankʷiːkaʔ]	'you (PL) sing'	11.	[aːltiaʔ]	'they bathe'
5.	[kʷiːkaʔ]	'they sing'	12.	[kikʷaːni]	'he customarily eats it'
6.	[kʷa]	'he eats'	13.	[aːltiaːni]	'he customarily bathes'
7.	[kʷaʔ]	'they eat'	14.	[tiaːltiaːni]	'you (SG) customarily bathe'

a. What are the morphemes for:

1. sing _____   6. it (object) _____

2. eat _____   7. we (subject) _____

3. bathe _____   8. you (PL) (subject) _____

4. you (SG) (subject) _____   9. they (subject) _____

5. s/he (subject) _____

b. What is the suffix that marks a plural subject in the present? _____

c. How is the customary present marked? _____

REMINDERS

1. An affix is an infix only when it is inserted into a root.
2. Don't forget to use morphological boundary markers (i.e., hyphens) for all bound affixes (prefixes, suffixes, and affixes). Root words do not need morphological boundaries.

Morphophonemics (Section 6)

Morphemes do not always have the same form. Allomorphs are the different forms of a morpheme. Consider the following English example.

- **The Allomorphs:** The English plural morpheme *-s* has three different phonetic forms:

   [-s] in words like *cats*
   [-z] in words like *dogs*
   [-əz] in words like *dishes*

- **The Conditioning Environment:** Which phonetic form is realized depends on the phonological characteristics of the final segment in the preceding word:

   [-s] occurs after a base ending in a voiceless consonant that is not strident.
   [-z] occurs after a base ending in a voiced segment that is not strident.
   [-əz] occurs after a base ending in a strident consonant.

The specific environment in which the different allomorphs occur is often referred to as the distribution of the allomorphs. This interaction between morphology and phonology is called **morphophonemics**.

PRACTICE 4.15: Morphophonemics

Spot the allomorphs in the following exercises, and answer the questions that follow.

1. **English**

1.	[ɪnɛdɪbl̩]	'inedible'	5.	[ɪnsəpɔɹtəbl̩]	'insupportable'
2.	[ɪmpɑsɪbl̩]	'impossible'	6.	[ɪnəbɪləti]	'inability'
3.	[ɪŋkejpəbl̩]	'incapable'	7.	[ɪmɔɹl̩]	'immoral'
4.	[ɪntɑləɹənt]	'intolerant'	8.	[ɪŋkəmplit]	'incomplete'

   a. What are the three different allomorphs of the morpheme meaning 'not'?

   _____

   b. State the environment (in words) in which the allomorphs occur.

   1. _____

   2. _____

   3. _____

2. **Turkish**
   Vowel harmony is a process that results in all vowels of a word sharing a certain feature or features. Morphophonemic rules of vowel harmony are found in many languages. Look at the data from Turkish, and answer the following questions.
   [y] represents a high front rounded vowel.
   [œ] represents a mid front rounded vowel.

1.	[gœz]	'eye'	[gœzleɾ]	'eyes'
2.	[mum]	'candle'	[mumlaɾ]	'candles'
3.	[top]	'gun'	[toplaɾ]	'guns'
4.	[at]	'horse'	[atlaɾ]	'horses'
5.	[ip]	'thread'	[ipleɾ]	'threads'
6.	[gyl]	'rose'	[gylleɾ]	'roses'
7.	[mektup]	'letter'	[mektuplaɾ]	'letters'
8.	[anne]	'mother'	[anneleɾ]	'mothers'
9.	[liman]	'harbor'	[limanlaɾ]	'harbors'
10.	[ʃule]	'flame'	[ʃuleleɾ]	'flames'

   a. What are the allomorphs of the plural morpheme? _____ _____

   b. What phonological feature distinguishes the vowels of the allomorphs?

   _____

c. What feature of the last vowel in the root determines the choice of the plural allomorph?

_____

3. **Dutch**

In Dutch, there are "strong verbs" and "weak verbs" depending on the form of the past tense and past participle (the past participle is the verb form used with *have* in English, e.g., *has* <u>done</u>). Examine the data from Dutch, which is in Dutch orthography, and answer the following questions.

WEAK VERBS

Root	Infinitive	Past Participle	
werk	werken	gewerkt	'work'
luister	luisteren	geluisterd	'listen'
poets	poetsen	gepoetst	'brush'
winkel	winkelen	gewinkeld	'go shopping'
regen	regenen	geregend	'rain'
zag	zagen	gezagd	'saw, harp on something'

STRONG VERBS

Infinitive	Past Participle	
bijten	gebeten	'bite'
laten	gelaten	'let, leave off'
sterven	gestorven	'die from'
nemen	genomen	'take'

a. How is the infinitive formed for weak verbs in Dutch? _____

b. How is the past participle formed for weak verbs in Dutch? _____

What are the two forms of the past participle of the weak verb?

_____   _____

Under what conditions is each form used?

_____   _____

c. It is interesting that the two forms of the past participle of the weak verb in Dutch are pronounced the same. What do you think is the pronunciation, and what phonological process has occurred? _____

d. Strong verbs undergo internal change, which need not concern us here. What affix is added to form the past participle of strong verbs in Dutch? _____

e. *Iemand* <u>*heeft mijn auto gestolen*</u> means 'Someone <u>has stolen my car</u>.' Is *gestolen* a weak verb or a strong verb? How do you know? _____

Review Exercises

The following exercises will provide review in solving morphology problems.

1. **Ancient Egyptian**
   Ancient Egyptian was written in hieroglyphs (see Chapter 14 in the main text). We do not know how the vowels were pronounced, so it is transliterated without vowels. The following data have been transcribed with IPA symbols instead of the traditional orthography for ancient Egyptian.
   [tʲ] represents a palatalized [t].

1. sn	'brother'	snwj	'2 brothers'	snw	'brothers'
2. snt	'sister'	sntj	'2 sisters'	snwt	'sisters'
3. ntʲr	'god'	ntʲrwj	'2 gods'	ntʲrw	'gods'
4. ntʲrt	'goddess'	ntʲrtj	'2 goddesses'	ntʲrwt	'goddesses'

   a. What morphemes mean:

      1. sibling   _____

      2. deity   _____

      3. FEMININE   _____

      4. MASCULINE   _____

      5. DUAL   _____

      6. PLURAL   _____

   b. What is the order of morphemes?
      Fill in the boxes with terms from this list: DUAL, FEMININE, PLURAL, ROOT

      1. M SG   [   ]

      2. F SG   [   ][   ]

      3. M PL   [   ][   ]

      4. F PL   [   ][   ][   ]

      5. M DU   [   ][   ][   ]

      6. F DU   [   ][   ][   ]

2. **Luganda**
   Luganda is a Bantu language of eastern Africa.

1. [muntu]	'person'	4. [bitabo]	'books'
2. [kati]	'stick'	5. [magulu]	'legs'
3. [kitabo]	'book'	6. [miti]	'trees'

7.	[muti]	'tree'	14.	[katiko]	'mushroom'
8.	[kutu]	'ear'	15.	[matu]	'ears'
9.	[butiko]	'mushrooms'	16.	[buti]	'sticks'
10.	[kintu]	'thing'	17.	[bintu]	'things'
11.	[musege]	'wolf'	18.	[muwala]	'girl'
12.	[bawala]	'girls'	19.	[misege]	'wolves'
13.	[kugulu]	'leg'	20.	[bantu]	'people'

Five noun classes are represented here according to the forms for singular and plural. Fill in the following chart. In the boxes labeled "CLASS," give an arbitrary number to the class. For each class, in the box labeled "SG," write the morpheme for the singular. In the box labeled "PL," write the morpheme for the plural. In the box labeled "STEMS," write the stems (the morphemes without the singular or plural), and in the corresponding space in the box labeled "GLOSS," write the meaning of the stem between single quotes. Some of the data have been filled in for you.

CLASS	SG	PL	STEMS	GLOSS
1	mu-	ba-		

3. **Fore** (Papua New Guinea)

1.	[natuwi]	'I ate yesterday.'	8.	[natuni]	'We ate yesterday.'
2.	[nagasuwi]	'I ate today.'	9.	[nagasuni]	'We ate today.'
3.	[nakuwi]	'I will eat.'	10.	[nagasusi]	'We (DUAL) ate today.'
4.	[nataːni]	'You ate yesterday.'	11.	[nakuni]	'We will eat.'
5.	[nataːnaw]	'You ate yesterday?'	12.	[nakusi]	'We (DUAL) will eat.'
6.	[nakiyi]	'He will eat.'	13.	[nataːwi]	'They ate yesterday.'
7.	[nakiyaw]	'He will eat?'	14.	[nataːsi]	'They (DUAL) ate yesterday.'

- Don't forget that what are inflectional affixes in many languages can be translated into separate words in English.

- 'Yesterday,' 'today,' and 'tomorrow' are translations of the English past, present, and future tenses (respectively).

a. Identify the Fore morphemes that correspond to the following English words:

1. I _____ 3. we _____

2. he _____ 4. they _____

5. we (DUAL) _____   8. yesterday _____

6. they (DUAL) _____   9. today _____

7. eat _____   10. will _____

b. What morphemes mark a: QUESTION? _____

STATEMENT? _____

c. Describe the order of the morphemes in terms of personal pronouns, question/statement markers, verbs, and adverbs.

d. Give the Fore words for the following:

1. He ate yesterday? _____

2. They (DUAL) will eat? _____

3. They ate today. _____

4. **Twi** (Ghana)

(Data are in Twi orthography, not phonetic transcription, although you will recognize some phonetic symbols that are used in the orthography.)

1. Woyε Amerikani.   'You (SG) are an American.'
2. Wɔyε Amerikafoɔ.   'They are Americans.'
3. Yεyε Ghanafoɔ.   'We are Ghanaians.'
4. M'agya yε Ghanani.   'My father is a Ghanaian.'
5. M'agya nyε Ghanani.   'My father is not a Ghanaian.'
6. Wɔnyε Amerikafoɔ.   'They are not Americans.'
7. Wonyε Amerikani.   'You (SG) are not an American.'

a. Write the morphemes for:

America _____

Ghana _____

is/are _____

we _____

you (SG) _____

they _____

'citizen of' _____

'citizens of' _____

b. What is the morpheme for 'not'? _____

What is the rule for the placement of this morpheme?

_____

c. How would you say 'We are not Ghanaians'?

_____

Now examine the following additional data:

8. Mepɛ Ghana.   'I like Ghana.'
9. Mefiri Ghana.   'I come from Ghana.'
10. Mempɛ Ghana.   'I do not like Ghana.'
11. Memfiri Ghana.   'I do not come from Ghana.'

d. Write the morphemes for:

I   _____

like   _____

come from   _____

e. What is the morpheme for 'not'? _____

Why is this morpheme different from the one you isolated in question b above?

_____

5. **English**
The data here are all names for breeds of dogs. For each item, write the word-formation process (or processes) that has produced this name.

1. Chihuahua   _____

2. greyhound   _____

3. labradoodle (cross of a
    Labrador and poodle)   _____

4. Peke (Pekinese)   _____

5. minpin (miniature pinscher)   _____

6. Jack Russell (terrier)   _____

7. bulldog   _____

8. Dalmatian   _____

9. dorgi (cross of a
    dachshund and corgi)   _____

10. Shar Pei   _____

6. **Iraqi Arabic (Past Tense)**
   Examine the data, and answer the questions below. The data are in phonetic representation.
   [tˤ] represents a [t] pronounced with a constriction in the pharynx.
   [x] represents a voiceless velar fricative.

1.	[tˤubaxit]	'I cooked'		13.	[kitab]	'he wrote'
2.	[kitabtu]	'you (PL) wrote'		14.	[tˤubaxti]	'you (F SG) cooked'
3.	[ʔakal]	'he ate'		15.	[ʔakalit]	'you (M SG) ate'
4.	[ʔakalna]	'we ate'		16.	[kitabna]	'we wrote'
5.	[tˤubxaw]	'they cooked'		17.	[tˤubxat]	'she cooked'
6.	[tˤubax]	'he cooked'		18.	[ʔaklaw]	'they ate'
7.	[kitabti]	'you (F SG) wrote'		19.	[kitabit]	'I wrote'
8.	[ʔakalit]	'I ate'		20.	[ʔakaltu]	'you (PL) ate'
9.	[tˤubaxna]	'we cooked'		21.	[kitbat]	'she wrote'
10.	[ʔaklat]	'she ate'		22.	[kitabit]	'you (M SG) wrote'
11.	[ʔakalti]	'you (F SG) ate'		23.	[tˤubaxtu]	'you (PL) cooked'
12.	[kitbaw]	'they wrote'				

   a. Write the affixes that are used for the following meanings:

   1 SG (I) _____

   1 PL (we) _____

   2 M SG (you) _____

   2 F SG (you) _____

   2 PL (you all) _____

   3 M SG (he) _____

   3 F SG (she) _____

   3 PL (they) _____

   b. What change occurs in the stem for the 3 F SG and the 3 PL?

   _____

   c. How would you say 'you M SG cooked'?

   _____

☑ **RECAP**

Make sure you know how to do the following. (See also the Key Terms at the end of Chapter 4 in the main text.)

- define morphological terms
- divide a word into its morphemes
- assign lexical categories
- build word trees
- identify inflection and derivation
- construct compound words
- recognize endocentric and exocentric compounds
- recognize morphological processes used to build words
- do morphological analysis
- identify morphemes and morphological processes in unfamiliar languages
- find allomorphs

Questions? Problems?

five

Syntax: The Analysis of Sentence Structure

Syntax is the study of the system of rules and categories that underlies sentence formation. Following are some of the important topics and concepts covered in this chapter. Make sure you are familiar with them.

Lexical and nonlexical categories
Phrases
Phrase structure and phrase structure tests
Sentences
Complement clauses
Complement options
Merge and Move
Yes-no and *Wh* questions
Deep and surface structure
Verb raising
Modifiers
Relative clauses
Passives
VP internal subjects

Lexical and Nonlexical Categories (Section 1.1)

There are two types of **syntactic categories**: **lexical** and **nonlexical**. Some of the major characteristics of each include:

Lexical:
- words that have meaning (semantic content)
- words that can be inflected
- includes **nouns** (N), **verbs** (V), **adjectives** (A), **adverbs** (Adv), and **prepositions** (P)

Nonlexical:
- words whose meaning is harder to define
- words that have a **grammatical** function
- includes **determiners** (Det), **auxiliary verbs** (Aux), **degree words** (Deg), and **conjunctions** (Con)

The lexical category to which a word belongs can be determined by examining (1) its meaning, (2) the type of inflectional affixes that it can take, and (3) the nonlexical category words with which it can co-occur.

Be careful: Some words can belong to more than one category.

PRACTICE 5.1: Syntactic categories

Each of the following sentences contains some underlined words. Identify the category of each underlined word. Note that the underlined word can be either lexical or nonlexical.

Words can often be assigned to more than one category, so pay close attention to how the word is being used in the sentence.

1. Pamela's heart <u>beat</u> <u>really</u> fast and her hands trembled a lot as she <u>listened</u> to the <u>intermittent</u> <u>knocking</u> on the front <u>door</u> of her shanty located <u>near</u> the railroad <u>tracks</u> <u>beside</u> a hobo jungle and she <u>thought</u>, "That's a <u>bum</u> rap, if I ever <u>heard</u> one."

2. "The <u>leg</u>, he is fractured," he <u>said</u> <u>in</u> broken English.

3. The Great Barrier Reef is 900 miles <u>long</u> <u>and</u> Wilmer Chanti, the <u>great</u> explorer, <u>says</u> it <u>could</u> <u>be</u> <u>circumnavigated</u> in forty days.

4. When <u>I</u> <u>turned</u> the <u>key</u> to open <u>my</u> lab door, I thought it <u>would</u> be a <u>very</u> <u>dull</u> day, until I noticed that my little cucaracha <u>had</u> <u>flopped</u> over on <u>his</u> back, and <u>was</u> waving his <u>little</u> legs <u>frantically</u>, and <u>I</u> <u>realized</u> that someone had <u>bugged</u> my bug.

5. It was <u>a</u> <u>rather</u> dark, <u>but</u> calm night, its <u>green</u> <u>clarity</u> diluted <u>by</u> my roommates who, as usual, <u>were</u> <u>making</u> cutting remarks as they drank <u>that</u> bottle <u>of</u> old scotch.

6. "I <u>hate</u> <u>pineapples</u>," said Tom <u>dolefully</u>.

7. Here's how to make a <u>fortune</u>. <u>Buy</u> fifty female <u>pigs</u> and fifty <u>male</u> deer. Then you <u>will</u> have a hundred sows and bucks.

REMINDER

There are two types of auxiliary verbs: modal and nonmodal. Modal auxiliary verbs include *will, would, can, could, may, must, should, might*. . . . Nonmodal auxiliary verbs include all the different forms of *be* (*am, are, is, was, were, been, being*) and *have* (*has, had*).

Go back over the above exercise, and for any word that you identified as an auxiliary verb, determine if it is a modal or nonmodal auxiliary verb.

Phrases (Section 1.2)

Words are grouped together to form **phrases**. Although a phrase can consist of a single word, a phrase usually consists of two or more words. There are three important components to a phrase.

- **Heads.** A phrase must have a head. The **head** of a phrase is the obligatory core around which the phrase is built. Four categories usually function as the head of a phrase, thereby allowing for four types of phrases.

1. NP (noun phrase)
2. AP (adjective phrase)
3. VP (verb phrase)
4. PP (prepositional phrase)

The head of a noun phrase is, of course, a noun; the head of an adjective phrase, an adjective; the head of a verb phrase, a verb; and the head of a prepositional phrase, a preposition.

- **Specifiers.** A phrase can optionally contain a specifier. **Specifiers** help to make the meaning of the head more precise. Specifiers mark phrasal boundaries. In English, specifiers occur before the head, thus marking the beginning of a phrase.

  1. Det (determiners) specify a noun
       e.g., *the, a, these, that*

  2. Adv (preverbal adverbs) specify a verb
       e.g., *always, often, never*

  3. Deg (degree words) specify an adjective or a preposition
       e.g., *very, quite, really*

- **Complements.** A phrase can also optionally contain a complement. **Complements** provide more information about entities that are implied by the head of the phrase. In English, complements come after the head, thus marking the end of a phrase. Complements are always phrases (even if they are only one word).

REMINDER

Specifiers can help determine the category to which a word belongs. This is because the type of specifier found in a phrase depends on the category of the head. So, if a word can occur with a determiner, it is a noun; if it occurs with an adverb, it is a verb; and if it occurs with a degree word, it is an adjective or preposition.

A phrase can consist of a single word or many words. If a phrase consists of a single word, that word must be the head of the phrase. If a phrase consists of a number of words, the phrase may consist of:

- a specifier and a head;
- a head and a complement; or
- a specifier, a head, and a complement.

Below are some possibilities for each type of phrase.

Following are some examples of the four different types of phrases.

1. Noun Phrase (NP)

   a. *presidents*   —contains only the head noun (*presidents*)

   b. *the presidents*   —contains a specifier (*the*) and the head noun (*presidents*)

c. *presidents*
   of the USA
   —contains the head noun (*presidents*) and a complement prepositional phrase (*of the USA*)

d. *the presidents*
   of the USA
   —contains a specifier (*the*), the head noun (*presidents*), and a complement prepositional phrase (*of the USA*)

The complement prepositional phrase *of the USA* consists of a head preposition (*of*) and a complement noun phrase (*the USA*). The noun phrase *the USA* then consists of a specifier (*the*) and a head noun (*USA*).

In addition to the noun phrases shown above, noun phrases can also contain pronouns (e.g., *I*, *you*, *them*) and proper nouns (i.e., names). When these are used to indicate possession, they are called possessive noun phrases. Possessive noun phrases function as specifiers for nouns. Some examples are shown below.

a. *Bob's*
   coat
   – contains a specifier (*Bob's*) and a head noun (*coat*)

b. *his*
   coat
   – contains a specifier (*his*) and a head noun (*coat*)

c. *the boy's*
   coat
   – contains a specifier (*the boy's*) and a head noun (*coat*)

In (a) and (b), the specifier is a noun phrase consisting only of the head noun [*Bob's* in (a) and *his* in (b)], while in (c) the specifier noun phrase *the boy's* consists of a specifier (*the*) and a head noun (*boy's*).

2. Adjective Phrase (AP)

a. *happy*   —contains only the head adjective (*happy*)

b. *very happy*   —contains a specifier (*very*) and the head adjective (*happy*)

c. *happy with*
   the results
   —contains the head adjective (*happy*) and a complement prepositional phrase (*with the results*)

d. *very happy*
   with the results
   —contains a specifier (*very*), the head adjective (*happy*), and a complement prepositional phrase (*with the results*)

The complement prepositional phrase *with the results* consists of a head preposition (*with*) and a complement noun phrase (*the results*). The noun phrase *the results* then consists of a specifier (*the*) and a head noun (*results*).

3. Verb Phrase (VP)

a. *sings*   —contains only the head verb (*sings*)

b. *often sings*   —contains a specifier (*often*) and the head verb (*sings*)

c. *sings a song*   —contains the head verb (*sings*) and a complement noun phrase (*a song*)

    d. *often sings*   —contains a specifier (*often*), the head verb (*sings*), and a
       a song   complement noun phrase (*a song*)

The complement noun phrase *a song* consists of a specifier (*a*) and a head noun (*song*).

4. Prepositional Phrase (PP)

    a. *in the car*   —contains the head preposition (*in*) and a complement
                   noun phrase (*the car*)

    b. *almost in*   —contains a specifier (*almost*), the head preposition (*in*),
       the car   and a complement noun phrase (*the car*)

The complement noun phrase the car contains a specifier (*the*) and a head noun (*car*).

REMINDER

Phrases have hierarchical structure.

Give an example of:

1. a noun phrase containing a specifier, a head noun, and a complement. Then make the specifier a possessive noun phrase.
2. an adjective phrase containing a specifier and a head adjective.
3. a verb phrase containing a head verb and a complement.
4. a prepositional phrase containing a head preposition and a complement.

REMINDER

Prepositional phrases are different from the other three types of phrases in that prepositional phrases must almost always contain a complement, and that complement is usually a noun phrase.

PRACTICE 5.2: Heads, specifiers, and complements

For each of the following phrases, determine the head of the phrase, any specifiers, and any complements. Remember that every phrase must have a head, but not every phrase has a specifier and complement. The first one is done for you.

	HEAD	SPECIFIER	COMPLEMENT	TYPE OF PHRASE
1. the rat	rat	the	none	
2. George				

3. in the barn   _____ _____ _____ _____

4. really mean   _____ _____ _____ _____

5. worked   _____ _____ _____ _____

6. worked at the station _____ _____ _____ _____

7. extremely boring   _____ _____ _____ _____

8. that destruction of the city _____ _____ _____ _____

9. never walks to the park _____ _____ _____ _____

10. very small   _____ _____ _____ _____

11. in the room   _____ _____ _____ _____

12. awfully cute   _____ _____ _____ _____

13. seldom smiles   _____ _____ _____ _____

14. swept the floor   _____ _____ _____ _____

15. the poem about love _____ _____ _____ _____

16. pancakes   _____ _____ _____ _____

Go back and determine the type of each phrase. Remember, the lexical category of the head determines the type of phrase.

Phrase Structure Tests (Section 1.4)

A number of tests can be done to determine whether a group of words is or is not a phrase. Three frequently used tests are the **substitution test**, the **movement test**, and the **coordination test**. Be careful, though; not every test works for every phrase.

Substitution Test

The substitution test states that a group of words is a phrase if you can substitute expressions such as *they*, *do so*, or *there*, and still be grammatical. The expression used as a substitute tells you the type of phrase you have.

NP: A noun phrase can be substituted with a pronoun.
        e.g., *The boys* played in the mud. *They* played in the mud.
        (*they = the boys*)

VP: A verb phrase can be substituted with *do so*.
        e.g., The girls will *play in the mud*, if the boys *do so*.
        (*do so = play in the mud*)

PP: A prepositional phrase can sometimes be substituted with *there* or *then*.
          e.g., The girls played *in the mud,* and the boys played *there* too.
          (*there = in the mud*)

Movement Test

The movement test states that a group of words is a phrase if it can be moved to another position in the sentence and still be grammatical.

      e.g., The children bought candy *at the store.* ⟶
         At the store, the children bought candy.

Coordination Test

According to this test, a group of words is a phrase if it can be joined to another group of words using a conjunction (*and, but, or*) and still be grammatical.

      e.g., The children *bought candy* and *left the store.*
         (two verb phrases joined with the conjunction *and*)

PRACTICE 5.3: Phrase structure tests

1. Apply the substitution test to determine which of the bracketed sequences in the following sentences are phrases.

    1. [Juanita and Juan] arrived [in San Juan] [on Epiphany].
    2. The cabbage [rolls were] salty.
    3. They moved [the desk with the wooden top].
    4. Little Andrew swallowed [all the pills].
    5. Mike is [writing a book about American soldiers in Afghanistan].

2. Apply the movement test to determine which of the bracketed sequences in the following sentences are phrases.

    1. The [army was surrounded] by the enemy.
    2. Leona likes [Viennese waltzes and Argentinean tangos].
    3. Shawn ate his lunch [in the revolving restaurant].
    4. Eat, drink, and [be merry for] today will become yesterday.
    5. The polar bears [were swimming among] the ice floes.

3. Use a conjunction (*and, but, or*) and join each of the following phrases with a phrase of the same type. Use the substitution test to determine the type of phrase.

    1. the new desk
    2. assembled the new desk
    3. new
    4. in a hole
    5. rather huge

6. worked on a movie
7. beside the fence
8. really lovely
9. talked to the girls
10. a dentist

Phrase Structure Trees (Section 1.2)

Specifiers, heads, and complements are arranged using the **X'** (X-bar) **schema** in which X stands for any head.

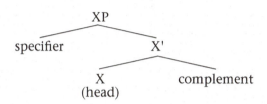

The representation of a phrase using the above schema is often referred to as a tree diagram.

Some things to remember about tree diagrams:

- All phrases have a head (X).
- If there is a specifier, it is attached at the XP level
- If there is a complement, it is attached at the X' level.
- The X' level is usually omitted from the tree diagram if there is no specifier and/or no complement.

See Figures 5.4–5.8 in the text for examples of tree diagrams of phrases containing specifiers, heads, and complements in various configurations.

Merge (Section 1.2)

Merge is responsible for building the phrase structure in a manner compatible with the X' schema. Essentially, Merge combines words together to make phrases, phrases to make sentences, and sentences to make larger sentences.

The following example illustrates how Merge operates.

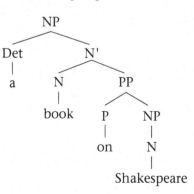

Merge created the above complex phrase by combining the noun phrase *Shakespeare* with the preposition *on* to create the prepositional phrase *on Shakespeare*. This phrase was then combined with the noun *book* and the specifier *a* to create the noun phrase *a book on Shakespeare*.

PRACTICE 5.4: Drawing phrase structure trees

Draw tree diagrams for each of the following phrases. Remember, specifiers come before the head, and complements come after the head. You will not always need to include the X' level.

1. the rat
2. George
3. really mean
4. ran
5. in the barn
6. ran into the shed
7. rather boring

8. those trucks
9. the publication of the book
10. very small
11. under the stove
12. seldom smiles
13. swept the floor
14. George's hand

15. the poem about love
16. silly
17. read your poem
18. really happy with him
19. usually eats lunch
20. looks good

REMINDER

Use the substitution test to help determine the type of phrase you are dealing with. The substitution test not only can tell you if a group of words is or is not a phrase, but also can tell you the type of phrase you have.

Sentences (Section 1.3)

A **sentence** is the largest unit of syntactic analysis. Sentences have the same structure as do phrases in that they consist of a specifier, head, and complement.

- **NP.** The noun phrase is typically referred to as the subject. The subject is the specifier of T. Every T in English will have a specifier.

- **T (Tense).** This is the obligatory head of the sentence and is used to refer to tense. There are two possibilities for T: +Pst (past) and –Pst (nonpast); +Pst is used for sentences in the past tense, and –Pst is used for sentences in either the present or future tense.

  Modal auxiliaries occur under T. This is because modals have an inherent tense (usually non-past), so T is a natural place for them to occur. T, then, has two possibilities:

  - tense (either +Pst or –Pst) *or*

  - a modal auxiliary (+/–Pst is not necessary, as tense is inherent in the modal auxiliary)

- **VP.** The verb phrase is the complement of T. In the sentences you will work with here, every T will have a verb phrase.

Sentences, like phrases, are built according to the X' schema. Since T is the head of a sentence, TP is used to represent the sentential phrase.

Below are two diagrammed sentences, the first without a modal auxiliary and the second with a modal auxiliary. For each sentence, there is a full diagram with the X' level and an abbreviated diagram without intermediate levels.

(1) *The children saw a deer.*

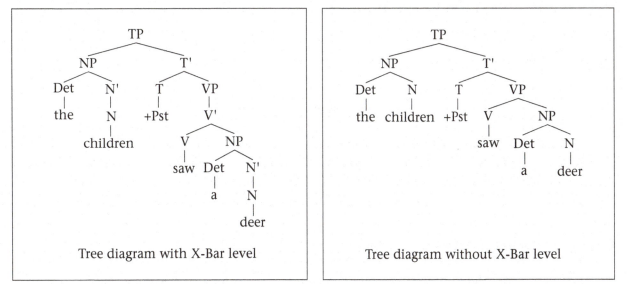

Tree diagram with X-Bar level   Tree diagram without X-Bar level

(2) *The children will see a deer.*

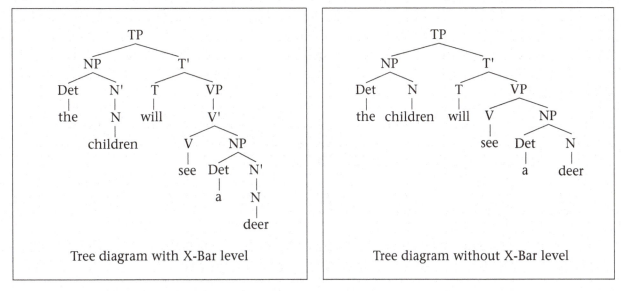

Tree diagram with X-Bar level   Tree diagram without X-Bar level

PRACTICE 5.5: Diagramming simple sentences

Draw a tree diagram for each of the following sentences.

1. Abner should conceal the document.

2. They usually watch the sunset.

3. A penguin walked into the room.

4. Carla might sell her car.

5. The air smells really fresh.

6. Grandparents often live in condominiums.

7. The chair of the department retired.

8. Those monsters never hide under Daniel's bed.

9. Gerard may seem tired of work.

10. Dogs will sometimes run in the park.

REMINDER

A noun phrase (NP), a prepositional phrase (PP), or an adjective phrase (AP) are all potential complements of a verb. The particular complement that occurs depends on the verb. Some verbs can take more than one complement. See Figure 5.13 in the text for an example.

Complement Options (Section 2)

To ensure that the Merge operation builds grammatical sentences, the individual words in a sentence must occur with complements of the right type. For example, many verbs (e.g., *throw*) require a complement noun phrase and must therefore appear in a structure containing a noun phrase in the complement position. If such a verb were entered into a structure without a noun phrase complement, the result would be an ungrammatical sentence. The complement(s) with which a word can occur are called its complement options. Merge, therefore, combines words into sentences in a manner consistent with both the X' schema and the complement options of the individual words.

Information on the complement options of words along with the meaning and pronunciation of words is found in a speaker's mental **lexicon**. Information about a word's complement options is often referred to as **subcategorization**.

PRACTICE 5.6: Complement options

1. Determine the complement options that the verbs listed below require. Do this by thinking of grammatical and ungrammatical sentences containing the verb.

1. panic	4. write
2. watch	5. wonder
3. imagine	6. play

2. Nouns, adjectives, and prepositions also have restrictions on the types of complements with which they can and cannot occur. Determine the complement options required by the following lexical items.

1. pleasure	4. intelligent
2. with	5. at
3. contribution	6. upset

Sentences with Complement Clauses (Section 2.3)

In addition to noun phrases, adjective phrases, and prepositional phrases, a sentence (TP) may also function as a complement. When a sentence functions as a complement, it can occur in the complement position of a verb phrase. The sentence contained within the verb phrase is called a complement clause (CP). The sentence within which the CP is found is called the matrix clause.

A CP is like any other type of phrase in that it consists of a specifier, a head, and a complement.

- **Specifier.** The specifier position of a CP functions as a landing site for phrases under-going the Move operation (see the section on Move).

- **Complementizer.** The head of a CP is a complementizer (C). Complementizers include words such as *that, if,* and *whether.*

- **TP.** The complement of a complementizer is a TP (i.e., a sentence).

Below is a tree diagram of the sentence *John thinks that Mary might sing*, which contains a CP inside the VP. See Figure 5.15 in the text for another example. See Table 5.9 in the text for examples of verbs that can have CP complements.

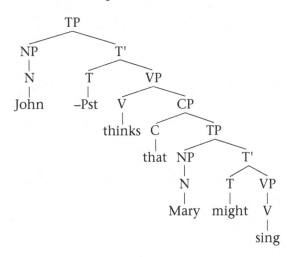

SOME HINTS FOR DRAWING PHRASE STRUCTURE TREES

1. Every sentence (TP) has the following structure.

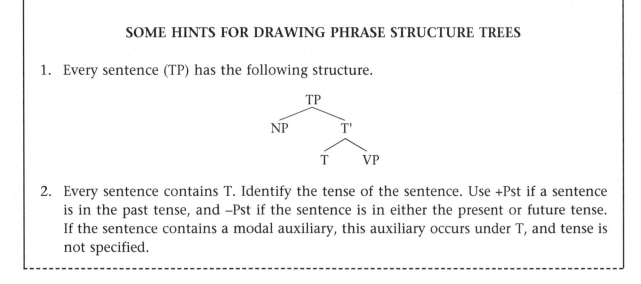

2. Every sentence contains T. Identify the tense of the sentence. Use +Pst if a sentence is in the past tense, and –Pst if the sentence is in either the present or future tense. If the sentence contains a modal auxiliary, this auxiliary occurs under T, and tense is not specified.

3. Every sentence has a verb. Identify the verb. Check if this verb has a specifier and/or a complement. Remember that the specifier of a verb is a preverbal adverb and marks the beginning of the phrase. If there is a complement, it can be either a phrase or a sentence.

    -   If the complement is a phrase, identify the type of phrase and then diagram the phrase using the X' schema. Remember you may be able to omit the intermediate (X-Bar) level.
    -   If the complement is a sentence, it will begin with the following structure.

    Identify the complementizer. Since a CP contains a TP, you will also need to identify and diagram the NP, T, and VP for this embedded TP.

4. Every sentence has a subject NP. Identify the noun. Check if this noun has a specifier and/or a complement. Remember that the specifier of a noun is a determiner and that this determiner marks the beginning of this noun phrase. If there is a complement, it will be a prepositional phrase. Diagram this phrase using the X' schema. You may be able to omit the intermediate (X-Bar) level.

    For more hints on drawing tree diagrams of phrases and sentences, see the Appendix to Chapter 5 in the text.

PRACTICE 5.7: Diagramming sentences with complement clauses

Draw a tree diagram for each of the following sentences.

1. Stan hopes that Kaley will become a pilot.

2. Kasey wonders whether aliens exist.

3. Sailors know that ships can sink.

4. He thought that the plane would never land.

PRACTICE 5.8: More practice with sentences

The following exercise contains many examples of simple sentences as well as sentences with complement clauses. Draw a tree diagram for each. Watch out: they get harder.

1. The repairman fixed the watch.

2. Neighbors can be unfriendly.

3. She never complains.

4. The train often leaves on time.

5. The children ran up the hill.

6. The assistant should send those e-mails.

7. Children are very curious.

8. Sally's friend lives in the capital of the country.

9. The student must rewrite that essay.

10. Your soup tastes really great.

11. The squirrels will often scurry across the road.

12. Sandra is almost at the restaurant.

13. The captain of the team fired that player.

14. The doctor's team was quite correct in their diagnosis.

15. The driver of that car sped down the highway.

16. George hoped that Fred would win a car.

17. The salesman wondered if those customers might buy that sofa.

18. Kayleigh usually thinks that classes in linguistics are fun.

19. The media reported that the candidate won the election.

20. The captain hoped that the tourists would perhaps see a whale.

Move (Section 3)

Move is a second syntactic operation. Move transports elements from one position in a sentence to another. This is all that a Move operation can do: Move cannot change the categories of words, nor can it eliminate any part of the structure.

There are three important points to remember about how Move operates.

CP. Move transports elements to positions with a CP. For this to occur, every TP must be found within a larger CP. This CP is a shell that contains a TP.

- Remember that C is the head of CP. C contains information on whether the sentence is a question or a statement: if C contains +Q, the structure is a question, and if C has –Q, it is a statement. It is the +Q that can trigger a Move operation. See Figure 5.16 in the text for an example of a TP within a CP shell.

- Remember that a CP can function as a complement clause, in which case it is embedded in a larger sentence. When a CP is embedded within a larger sentence, C can contain a complementizer such as *that, if,* or *whether.* Refer to Figure 5.12 in the text for an example of a sentence with an embedded CP.

Trace. Moved elements leave behind a **trace** (t). A trace records (1) that a movement occurred and (2) where in the structure the moved element originated. This is necessary as Move cannot change the structure that Merge builds.

Levels of Representation. Two levels of representation result: **deep** and **surface structure**.

- Merge occurs first to build the syntactic structure. The structure that Merge generates is called the deep structure (**D-structure**).

- Move may then apply. The surface structure (**S-structure**) is the result of applying Move.

If a Move operation has taken place, then the deep and surface structure are usually not the same. If no Move operation takes place, then the deep and surface structures are the same.

Questions (Sections 3.1, 3.2)

Merge is responsible for building the structure of a sentence using both subcategorization information (i.e., the complement options) and the X' schema. However, Merge cannot create all the structures of a language. Some structures require a second operation. Move transforms an existing structure (e.g., a statement) into another type of structure (e.g., a question) by transporting elements from one position in a sentence to another.

Move operates to create both *yes-no* and *wh* **questions**.

Yes-No Questions

Yes-no questions are so named because the response to such a question is usually "yes" or "no." *Yes-no* questions are formed by moving an auxiliary verb from its position in T to the complementizer position within a CP. This is informally called **Inversion**.

Inversion: Move T to C
e.g., Mary **will** sing → **Will** Mary **t** sing
(D-structure) (S-structure)

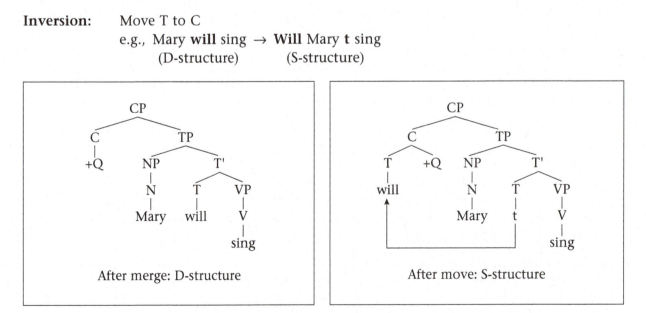

After merge: D-structure   After move: S-structure

Wh Questions

Wh questions are so named because they begin with a *wh* word. These are question words that typically begin with a *wh*. *Who, what, which, where, when, why,* and *how* are all examples of *wh* words. See Table 5.10 in the text for the syntactic categories of *wh*-words.

Wh questions are the result of *Wh* Movement. *Wh* Movement is normally preceded by Inversion.

Wh Movement: Move a *wh* phrase to the specifier position under CP.

    e.g.,   Mary **should** buy *what* → *What* **should** Mary *t* buy *t*
                 (D-structure)   (S-structure)

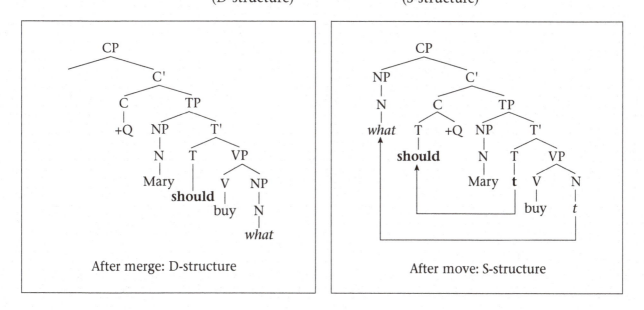

Wh Movement can:

- move a *wh* phrase occurring as the complement of the verb (as in the previous example)
- move a *wh* phrase occurring in the subject position (as in the following example)

         e.g.,   *Who* will sing → *Who t* will sing
                 (D-structure)   (S-structure)

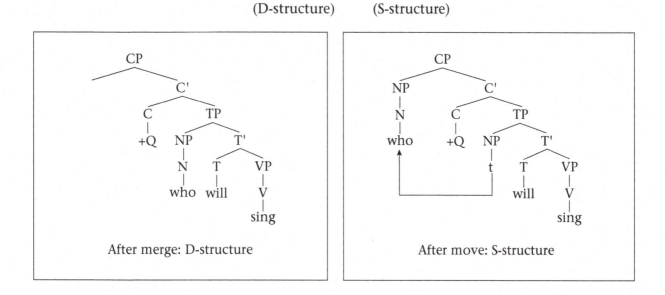

Compare the above deep and surface structures. Is the word order in the deep and surface structure the same? Is Inversion required when *Wh* Movement moves a subject NP?

See Figures 5.17 to 5.21 in the text for more examples of tree diagrams of the deep and surface structures of sentences in which Inversion and *Wh* Movement have taken place.

PRACTICE 5.9: Questions

For each of the following sentences, draw a tree diagram for both the deep and surface structures. On the surface structure, indicate with arrows the elements that have moved and where they have moved.

1. Will Paul enjoy the trip?
2. What could the spy uncover?
3. Who saw the lion?
4. Should Joan visit that museum?
5. Who might Leyna play with?

REMINDER

1. Each movement leaves a trace in its original position. When you draw the surface structure tree, do not forget to include a *t* in the original position of a moved element.

2. *Wh* Movement moves an entire phrase.

Verb Raising (Section 4.1)

Move can also transport a verb to a new position in the sentence. This is often called **Verb Raising**. Verb Raising is found in many different languages and can affect auxiliary verbs in English.

There are two types of auxiliaries: modal and nonmodal. Modal auxiliaries occur in T and are not specified for either +Pst or –Pst. Nonmodal auxiliaries (*have* and *be*) are a special type of verb. As such, they occur in V. They also take a verb phrase as a complement.

Below is a tree diagram of a sentence containing a nonmodal auxiliary verb.

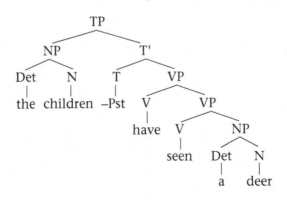

A sentence can have more than one auxiliary. For example, the sentence *The choir has been singing many songs* contains two nonmodal auxiliaries. How would you diagram the verb phrase of this sentence? What about the sentence *The choir will be singing more songs*, which contains both a modal and a nonmodal auxiliary? How would you diagram the verb phrase for this sentence? See Figure 5.25 in the text if you are unsure.

Remember: Nonmodal auxiliaries can also occur as the only verb in the sentence (e.g., *Mary is happy*, or *John has a cat*). They still occur in V, but they take a noun phrase, adjective phrase, or prepositional phrase rather than a verb phrase as a complement.

Both modal and nonmodal auxiliaries can be inverted when forming a *yes-no* question:

- Modal auxiliaries occur in T and are moved from T to C using Inversion.

- Nonmodal auxiliaries occur in V. Before moving from T to C, they must first be moved from V to T. The move from V to T is called Verb Raising.

Verb Raising: Move V to T.

e.g., Mary **is** leaving → Mary **is** *t* leaving → **is** Mary *t t* leaving

(D-structure)   (S-structure)

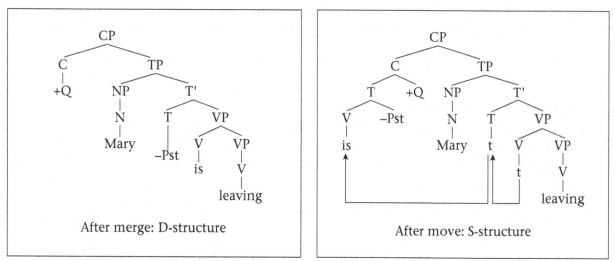

After merge: D-structure   After move: S-structure

Verb Raising can also occur during the formation of *wh* questions.

e.g.,   What was Sylvia thinking?

Sylvia **was** thinking *what* → Sylvia **was** *t* thinking *what* → **was** Sylvia *t t* thinking *what* → *what* **was** Sylvia *t t* thinking *t*

PRACTICE 5.10: Verb Raising

1. Draw a tree diagram of both the deep structure and the surface structure for *What was Sylvia thinking?* On the S-structure, draw arrows from the traces to the moved elements.

2. For each of the following sentences, draw a tree diagram of both the deep and surface structures.

   a. Had the elves swept the floor?   c. Are the neighbors moving?

   b. What was Sally painting?   d. Which restaurant is the city closing?

REMINDER

Verb Raising is a good example of the variation that occurs across languages. In English only auxiliary (nonmodal) verbs can move to T; regular (main) verbs cannot move. What this means is that only auxiliary verbs (both modal and nonmodal) can be inverted to create questions. This is not true of all languages. For example, in French, any type of verb can move into T. This means that both regular (main) verbs and auxiliary verbs can be inverted in French. The idea is that all languages use the Move operation, but how this operation is instantiated can vary from language to language.

See Figures 5.23 and 5.24 in the text for tree diagrams illustrating Verb Raising in French and Figure 5.26 for an example of Verb Raising in English.

Identifying Deep Structure and Movements (Section 3.3)

You need to be able to determine the deep structure for any sentence you are given, and to do so you need to be able to identify any of the movements that have occurred. Remember, Inversion, *Wh* Movement, and Verb Raising are all applications of the Move operation.

Here are some clues to help you identify which movements have occurred and put surface structure sentences back into deep structure:

YOU SEE:	YOU THINK:	YOU DO:
A modal auxiliary verb ahead of the subject.	Inversion has taken place.	Put the modal auxiliary back into its deep structure position in T.
A nonmodal auxiliary verb ahead of the subject.	Inversion has taken place. Verb Raising has taken place.	Put the nonmodal auxiliary back into its deep structure position under V.
A *wh* word or phrase.	*Wh* Movement has taken place.	Examine each verb in the sentence. Determine if a verb is missing either a subject or an object, and put the *wh* word or phrase into that position. Examine each preposition in the sentence. Determine if a preposition is missing its object. Put the *wh* word or phrase into that position.

See the Appendix to Chapter 5 in the text for more guidance on how to analyze sentences involving the Move operation.

PRACTICE 5.11: Practice with complements, questions, and movements

Draw a tree diagram of each sentence. If movement has occurred, draw both the deep and surface structure, and list all transformations that have occurred to derive the surface structure.

1. Can the clown amuse that boy?

2. Which coat should Hilary wear?

3. Who broke my lamp?

4. Margo dreamt that Frances flew to England.

5. Has the player left the team?

6. What was Joanne eating?

7. Could the vandals destroy the billboard?

8. Christopher hopes that he has discovered the treasure.

9. Who might these clothes fit?

10. Were the maids cleaning the house?

11. Will the winner be claiming the prize?

12. What might Mary's sister want?

13. The jury believed that the prisoner was guilty.

14. Who prepared the meal?

15. Colin was wondering whether George would order pizza.

REMINDER

1. You are trying to determine which elements have already moved; therefore, you must never move any additional words or phrases.

2. No movements may have occurred, only one movement may have occurred, or more than one movement may have occurred.

3. To find the deep structure, you need to find all instances of Move.

4. Include a trace (t) for every movement.

Other Structures (Section 5)

Some other syntactic structures include **modifiers**, **relative clauses**, **passives**, and **VP internal subjects**. Each of these structures builds on the basic syntactic system (i.e., Merge and Move) for forming sentences.

Modifiers (Section 5.1)

Modifiers are words and phrases that denote properties of heads. There are two main types of modifiers.

- Adjective phrases modify nouns, in that they indicate a property of the noun.

  e.g.,   A **very cold** wind is blowing.

- Adverb phrases modify verbs, in that they can provide information on the manner (for example) of the verb.

  e.g.,   The ballerina danced **gracefully**.

The modifier phrase is the sister of X' (not of the head). See Figure 5.27 in the text for some examples of diagrams of phrases containing modifiers.

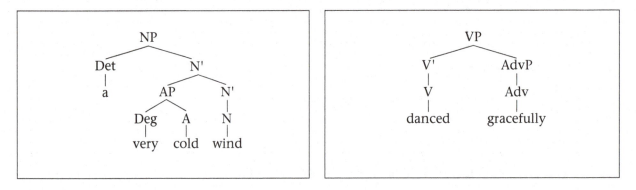

Relative Clauses

A relative clause is a special type of CP that modifies nouns; that is, it is a clause that provides more information about a noun. A relative clause occurs after the noun that it modifies. A relative clause is like a *wh* question in two ways:

- It begins with a *wh* word (e.g., *who* or *which*) called a relative pronoun.

  e.g., The house [**which** Jerry designed]$_{CP}$ won an award.

- The *wh* word occurs within the sentence and is moved to the specifier position of C, leaving a trace behind. This is *Wh* Movement.

  e.g., The house [**which** Jerry designed *t*]$_{CP}$ won an award.

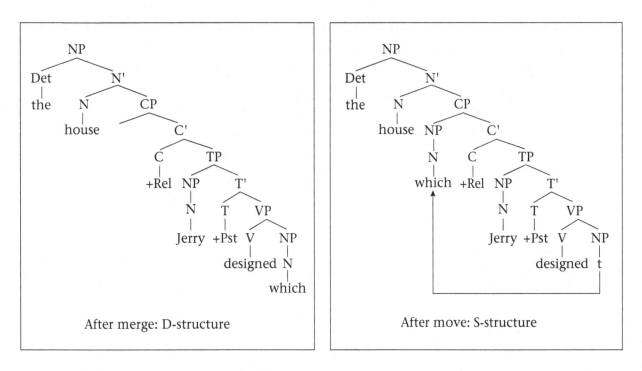

After merge: D-structure   After move: S-structure

- The *wh* word can start out as the complement of the verb (direct object), as in the above example, or it can start out as the subject of the sentence as in the example below.

  e.g., Architects [**who**   t designed the house]_{CP} won an award.

As with subject *wh* questions, in a subject relative clause, the *wh* word is assumed to move from the subject position to the specifier position under C. Draw a tree diagram of both the D- and S-structures of the above sentence.

See Figure 5.30 in the text for a diagram of the S-structure of a subject relative clause. See Figures 5.28 and 5.29 in the text for another example of a tree diagram of the deep and surface structures of an object relative clause.

The presence of +Q in C triggers *Wh* Movement during the formation of *wh* questions. What triggers *Wh* Movement during the formation of relative clauses?

Passives (Section 5.3)

A sentence may be either **active** or **passive**. Active and passive sentences differ in the following ways:

- In an active sentence, the agent (doer of the action) occurs in the subject position. In a passive sentence, this agent is often absent. If the agent is present, it is found within a prepositional phrase (usually headed by *by*) that occurs at or near the end of the sentence.

- In a passive sentence, the direct object of the corresponding active sentence usually functions as the subject of the sentence. Verbs that cannot occur with a direct object in an active sentence can also not occur in passive sentences.

  e.g.,   **Active:** The chef prepared the meal.
  Passive: The meal was prepared. / The meal was prepared by the chef.

- Passive sentences are formed using **NP Movement**, another type of Move. NP Movement transports an object from its deep structure position as a complement of the verb to an empty subject position.

> **NP Movement:**   Move an NP into the specifier position of TP.
>   e.g., **D-structure:** was prepared the meal
>   **S-structure:** *the meal* was prepared *t*

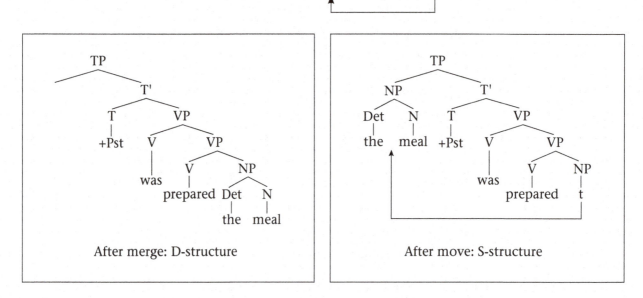

See Figures 5.31 and 5.32 in the text for another example of a tree diagram of the D-structure and S-structure of a passive sentence.

VP Internal Subjects

In a passive sentence, the subject starts out as the complement of a verb and moves to the subject position via NP Movement. This may also be true for active sentences: the subject starts out in the specifier position under VP and moves to the specifier position under TP using NP Movement. The following example illustrates this movement.

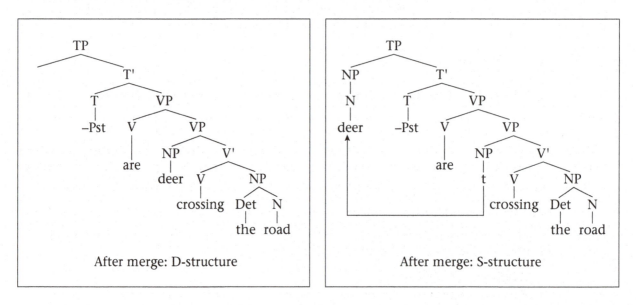

Having the subject originate in the VP may help explain:

- Sentences such as *There are deer crossing the road*, in which the subject *deer* remains in the verb phrase. In these sentences, the subject cannot move to the specifier position under T, since this position is already filled: it contains *there* (for example). See Figure 5.35 in the text for another example.

- Languages whose basic word order pattern has the verb before the subject. In these languages, the subject remains within the verb phrase (as the specifier of the verb), and the verb raises to T (Verb Raising). See Figure 5.36 in the text for an example from Welsh.

If the subject always starts out as the specifier of the verb, what happens to preverbal adverbs? Remember these function as the specifer of a verb. How would preverbal adverbs have to be analyzed in a sentence such as *The deer always cross the road*?

PRACTICE 5.12: Identifying other structures

The following exercises will give you some practice with identifying modifier phrases, relative clauses, and passives.

1. Each of the following sentences contains at least one modifier phrase. Identify all the modifier phrases. For each modifier phrase determine if it is modifying a noun or a verb. Identify the noun or verb that is being modified.

   a. Those musicians often play music loudly.
   b. The really awful movie won top prize.
   c. The gigantic waves pounded the shore fiercely.

2. Each of the following phrases contains a relative clause. Identify the relative clause and write its deep structure.

   a. the roads which the snowplows have finished clearing
   b. the roads which were plowed yesterday
   c. the staff who answered the phones

3. Decide if each of the following sentences is active or passive. Remember: A passive sentence does not necessarily include an agent. If the sentence is passive, write the deep structure.

   a. Those tigers were trained.
   b. The company should make a donation.
   c. That lamp could be fixed.

Review Exercise

Draw a tree diagram for each of the following sentences. You will need to use what you have learned about simple sentences, sentences with complement clauses, and various types of movement. If movement has occurred, draw arrows from the trace to the moved element.

1. The castle fell into the sea.

2. Dogs sometimes swim in the river.

3. The teacher believed that the student was honest.

4. Sally lives right in the middle of Chicago.

5. The kitten was hiding under a bush.

6. The unicorn might be eating the lilies.

7. Can the band play that song?

8. The tourist has reported that a thief stole her passport.

9. Who might want these books?

10. Which color has Jamie chosen?

11. That jerk who stole my car is crazy.

12. The archaeological site was excavated.

☑ **RECAP**

If you can do the following, then you've conquered syntax. (See also the Key Terms at the end of Chapter 5 of the main text.)

- describe the differences between lexical and nonlexical categories
- assign words to their syntactic category
- determine whether a group of words is a phrase
- identify and diagram phrases
- diagram simple sentences and complement clause structures
- determine complement options
- understand how the Merge operation builds sentences
- find the deep structure of a sentence
- understand Move operations
- draw tree diagrams to show Inversion, *Wh* Movement, and Verb Raising
- recognize modifiers, relative clauses, and passives

Questions? Problems?

six

Semantics: The Analysis of Meaning

Semantics is the study of meaning in human language. **Meaning** refers, very generally, to the content of an utterance.

Important concepts and topics in this chapter include:

Semantic relations	Lexical and structural ambiguity
Meaning	Thematic roles
Concepts	Pronoun interpretation
Constructional meaning	Role of pragmatics
Lexicalization and grammaticalization	Conversation

Semantic Relations (Sections 1.1–1.2)

Determining the semantic relations that exist among words, phrases, and sentences constitutes one of the basic notions used in evaluating meaning.

Relations between words:

- **Synonyms**—two words that have similar meanings
    e.g., *filbert / hazelnut*

- **Antonyms**—two words that have opposite meanings
    e.g., *hot / cold*

- **Polysems** (homonyms)—one word that has two or more related meanings
    e.g., *bright* (shining or intelligent)

- **Homophones**—two words with the same pronunciation but two distinct meanings
    e.g., *pen* (a writing instrument or an enclosure)

Note that homophones do not have to have the same spelling. *Two* and *too* are homophones since they are pronounced as [tu].

See Tables 6.1 to 6.4 in the text for some English examples of the above relations.

Polysemy and homophony can result in lexical ambiguity—a single form that has two or more meanings. Try and think of some examples. Keep in mind:

- Different words with the same spelling are called homographs.
- Homophones may or may not have the same spelling.
- Homographs, therefore, may or may not be homophones.

Relations between sentences:

- **Paraphrases**—two sentences that have different forms but the same meaning
    e.g.,   The cat ate the mouse.
             The mouse was eaten by the cat.

- **Entailment**—two sentences in which the truth of the first implies the truth of the second, but the truth of the second does not necessarily imply the truth of the first
    e.g.,   George killed the spider.
             The spider is dead.

- **Contradiction**—two sentences such that if one is true, the other must be false
    e.g.,   The coelacanth is extinct.
             A fisherman has just caught a coelacanth.

PRACTICE 6.1: Identifying semantic relations

For each of the following, identify the relation that exists between either the words or the sentences. The first one is done for you.

1. test
    exam   _____ synonyms _____

2. Mary sang a solo.
    The solo was sung by Mary.   _____

3. bug (insect)
    bug (microphone)   _____

4. Sam is a widower.
    Sam's wife is alive.   _____

5. The shark bit a swimmer.
    The swimmer is injured.   _____

6. parent
    offspring   _____

7. George gave Sally the book.
    George gave a book to Sally.   _____

8. Pat just became an aunt.
    Pat is the father of three children.   _____

9. hungry
    famished   _____

10. steak (a piece of meat)
    stake (a sharp piece of wood)   _____

Meaning (Section 1.3)

As native speakers of a language, we all know the meaning of a great many words in our language, but it may be difficult to describe precisely what a word means. Linguists and philosophers have explored how the following can help us understand meaning.

Connotation

This theory states that the meaning of a word is simply the set of associations that the word evokes. For example, a *desert* has associations of heat, dryness, and sand, even though some deserts do not have sand or are in cold areas.

Denotation

This theory states that the meaning of a word is not the set of associations it evokes, but rather the entity to which it refers—its denotation or referent in the real world. Accordingly then, the word *desert* would refer to that set of regions in the world characterized by barrenness and lack of rain.

Extension and Intension

This theory attempts to combine the first two. Extension refers to the set of referents of a word, and intension to the associations it evokes. Thus, the extension of *desert* would correspond to the set of barren, arid regions in the world, such as the Gobi, the Sahara, and the Kalahari. The intension would correspond to the concepts of barrenness and aridity, not necessarily to a specific existing desert. Thus, the meaning of a word includes both its extension and its intension.

Componential Analysis

This theory is based on the idea that meaning can be decomposed into smaller semantic units. These units of meaning are called semantic features. Semantic features can be combined to delineate a class of entities. For example, the semantic features [+living, +human, –adult] give us the category of children.

Componential analysis is useful for making generalizations, especially where verbs are concerned. For example, the verb *read* would typically have a human subject, and the verb *drink* would require an object that is a liquid.

PRACTICE 6.2: Meaning

1. For each of the following expressions, attempt to define its meaning according to the theories of connotation, denotation, and extension and intension discussed above.

   a. summer   b. a linguistics instructor   c. grass

2. Identify the types of phrases with which the verbs in A and B can occur. What difference in meaning between the verbs in A and the verbs in B determines the type of complement the verbs require?

A	B
sweep	crawl
kick	fall

3. Examine the following two groups of words and determine the semantic feature(s) each group has in common. What semantic feature(s) are different among members of each group? What about between the two groups?

   Group A: grandmother / mother / daughter / widow
   Group B: grandfather / father / son / widower

4. Now try doing a componential analysis for:
   - ewe and lamb
   - mare, filly, and colt

5. What difficulties do connotation, denotation, extension, intension, and componential analysis have in determining what meaning is?

Concepts (Section 2)

Linguists use the term **concepts** to refer to the system we use to identify, classify, and organize all elements of our many and varied experiences. Our conceptual system reveals how meaning is expressed through language.

Fuzzy Concepts (Section 2.1)

Fuzzy concepts are concepts that can differ from person to person. They have no clear-cut boundaries. Think about how much something has to cost before you would consider it expensive.

Graded Membership (Section 2.1)

Concepts have internal structure. Members of a concept can be graded according to how typical they are within that concept. The most typical member is selected as the **prototype**. Other members are arranged around the prototype. Members having more properties in common with the prototype occur closer to the prototype, and members sharing fewer properties occur farther away from the prototype. Figure 6.2 in the text illustrates members in the concept BIRD.

Metaphor (Section 2.2)

The concepts expressed by language do not exist in isolation, but are interconnected and associated. Metaphors, the understanding of one concept in terms of another, can be used to make these connections. Metaphors can be based on our perceptions, our physical experiences, our culture, and our shared feelings. For example, as Table 6.6 in the text illustrates, emotions are often compared to spatial terms such as *up* or *down* (e.g., *George is feeling down today*). A number of metaphors attribute animal-like properties to people.

Lexicalization (Section 2.3)

Lexicalization refers to the process whereby concepts (e.g. SNOW, LIGHT) are encoded into the meanings of words. Languages may differ in terms of how many words they use to convey a concept. How concepts are encoded also varies from language to language. See Tables 6.9–6.11 in the text for some examples of systematic differences in how motion is encoded into English, French, and Atsugewi verbs.

Grammaticalization (Section 2.4)

Grammaticalization refers to concepts that are expressed as affixes or functional categories. See Table 6.12 in the text for some examples of concepts in English that have been grammaticalized. Concepts that are grammaticalized can vary from language to language. See Table 6.13 in the text for an example in Hidatsa in which evidence for the truth of a statement has been grammaticalized. Think about the different ways in which negation has been grammaticalized in English.

PRACTICE 6.3: Concepts

1. For each of the following concepts, determine whether they are fuzzy, are graded, or have been grammaticalized.

   a. CATS   c. TIME
   b. MOUNTAINS   d. VEGETABLES

   For any of the above that exhibit a graded membership, determine the member that is prototypical for you. How might this differ from person to person?

2. **Menomini.** Quite often, languages contain different forms of grammaticalized affixes or functional categories whose use depends on some semantic characteristic of a stem or complement. Consider the data below from Menomini, a Native American language of Wisconsin. There are three different types of nouns depending on what forms they appear in. What are the three types of nouns, and what is the semantic basis for this?

	Unpossessed	'a person's—'	'my—'	Gloss
1.	oːs	_____	netoːs	'canoe'
2.	_____	meseːt	neseːt	'foot'
3.	_____	_____	nemeːh	'elder sister'
4.	atuːhpwaniːk	_____	netaːtuːhpwaniːk	'tablecloth'
5.	_____	_____	nekiah	'mother'
6.	_____	mɛhkaːt	nɛhkaːt	'leg'
7.	_____	metɛːʔtʃjak	netɛːʔtʃjak	'soul'
8.	_____	_____	nekiːʔs	'son'
9.	toːwahkɛh	_____	netoːwahkɛh	'water drum'
10.	ahkɛːh	_____	netahkɛːh	'kettle'
11.	_____	_____	neniːh	'maternal aunt'
12.	_____	meːs	neːs	'head'

3. **Kiswahili.** The data below from Kiswahili (an African language) can be divided into three noun classes, as revealed in the inflection of singular and plural. There is a semantic basis for the three noun classes represented here. What are the three noun classes, and how is each inflected for singular and plural? What is the semantic basis that determines which class a noun belongs to?

	Singular	Plural	Gloss		Singular	Plural	Gloss
1.	mtu	watu	'person'	6.	mgeni	wageni	'guest'
2.	mlima	milima	'mountain'	7.	kitanda	vitanda	'bed'
3.	kiti	viti	'chair'	8.	mke	wake	'wife'
4.	mto	mito	'river'	9.	kifungo	vifungo	'button'
5.	kitana	vitana	'comb'	10.	mti	miti	'tree'

4. **German.** In German, some prepositions assign either accusative or dative case, based on semantic grounds. In the data below, the article *das* marks the accusative case, while the article *dem* marks the dative case. What is the semantic basis for the case assignment shown here? What concept is contained in the German articles that is not found in English articles?

1. Der Doktor geht in das Zimmer.   'The doctor goes into the room.'
   Der Doktor sitzt in dem Zimmer.   'The doctor sits in the room.'

2. Das Auto fährt vor das Haus.   'The car drives to the front of the house.'
   Das Auto wartet vor dem Haus.   'The car waits in front of the house.'

3. Sie setzt sich neben das Kind.   'She sits down near the child.'
   Sie sitzt neben dem Kind.   'She sits near the child.'

4. Sie legt die Feder unter das Buch.   'She puts the pen under the book.'
   Die Feder ist unter dem Buch.   'The pen is under the book.'

Syntax and Sentence Interpretation (Section 3)

Not only do the words and phrases that make up a sentence contribute to its meaning, but the position of words and phrases in the syntactic structure also has a role.

The contribution of syntax to sentence interpretation includes constructional meaning, structural ambiguity, thematic roles, and pronoun interpretation.

Constructional Meaning

The meaning of a sentence goes beyond the meaning of the individual words and phrases that it is composed of. The syntactic structure, or construction, also contributes to the meaning of the sentence.

Two common constructions are

- The caused-motion construction: X causes Y to go somewhere
- The ditransitive construction: X causes Y to have Z

Ambiguity (Section 1.1; Section 3.2)

A sentence is ambiguous when it has more than one meaning. There are two main types of ambiguity.

- **Lexical ambiguity.** This type of ambiguity results from one word in the sentence having more than one meaning. Polysemy and homophony give us lexical ambiguity. For example, the sentence *The glasses are on the table* has two meanings: (1) the drinking glasses are on the table, and (2) the eyeglasses are on the table. The ambiguity arises because the word *glasses* has two possible meanings.

- **Structural ambiguity.** Structural ambiguity occurs when a group of words in a sentence can be combined in more than one way. Each different combination is associated with a different meaning. Ambiguity can be found in both noun and verb phrases.

  Noun Phrases. In the sentence *The surface was painted with red flowers and leaves,* the noun phrase *red flowers and leaves* can be combined in two ways. Each combination corresponds to a particular syntactic structure and meaning.

  Meaning One: red [flowers and leaves]: Both the flowers and the leaves are red.

  Meaning Two: [red flowers] and [leaves]: Only the flowers are red.

  Verb Phrases. In the sentence *Sam ate the cake in the kitchen,* the verb phrase *ate the cake in the kitchen* can be grouped together in two ways. As with noun phrases, each grouping corresponds to a particular syntactic structure and meaning.

  Meaning One: ate [the cake in the kitchen]: Sam ate the cake that was in the kitchen.

  Meaning Two: ate [the cake] [in the kitchen]: Sam was in the kitchen eating cake.

SOME HINTS FOR IDENTIFYING AMBIGUITY

1. Determine if the ambiguity is coming from one word in the sentence (lexical) or from more than one possible combination of the words in the sentence (structural).
2. For lexical ambiguity, identify the word that is ambiguous and determine the two (or more) possible meanings of the word.
3. For structural ambiguity, determine the phrase containing the ambiguity (usually noun or verb) and the possible meanings. Match each meaning with a different syntactic structure.

PRACTICE 6.4: Identifying constructional meaning and ambiguity

1. What constructional meaning is found in each of these sentences?

   a. Joe sold Sabrina the car.

   b. Dan flew the airplane to Harrisburg.

   c. Jen swept the papers aside.

   d. The donor wrote the charity a hefty check.

2. Each of the following sentences is ambiguous. For each sentence, state whether the ambiguity is lexical or structural and provide an unambiguous phrase or sentence for each possible meaning.

    a. Cool beer and wine are what we want.

    b. Fred was cool.

    c. I met the woman standing by the water cooler.

    d. Congress passed a dangerous drug bill.

    e. George and Harry or Fred will draw the picture.

    f. I want to look at the pictures in the attic.

    g. The instructor left his key in the office.

Thematic Roles (Section 3.3)

To interpret any sentence, we need to know who is doing the action, what is undergoing the action, the starting point of the action, etc. **Thematic**, or theta, **roles** capture the relations between a sentence and the situation the sentence describes.

There are three important properties of thematic roles.

- **Common thematic roles.** Some of the common thematic roles include:

  Agent (actor)—The entity performing an action
  Theme—The entity undergoing an action
  Source—The starting point of a movement
  Goal—The end point of a movement
  Location—The place where an action occurs

  For example, in the sentence *The gardener planted flowers by the front door*, *the gardener* is the agent, *the flowers* is the theme, and *the front door* is the location.

- **Thematic role assignment.** Thematic roles are assigned to noun phrases based on their position within the sentence. Typically, verbs and prepositions assign thematic roles.

  Verbs   Assign the agent role (if it has one) to its subject noun phrase.
                   Assign the theme role (if it has one) to its complement noun phrase.

  Prepositions Assign a thematic role to its complement noun phrase. The specific role depends on the preposition.

  Knowledge of the thematic roles that verbs and prepositions assign is stored in our mental lexicon.

  In the sentence, *John drove the car to Portland*, the verb *drove* assigns the agent role to the noun phrase *John* and the theme role to the noun phrase *the car*, while the preposition *to* assigns the goal role to the noun phrase *Portland*. See Figures 6.4–6.6 in of the text for other examples.

- **Thematic roles and deep structure.** Thematic roles are assigned at deep structure.

  - The Merge operation determines the position of the noun phrase within the syntactic structure (i.e., the D-structure). It is the noun phrase's position as a result of Merge that determines its thematic role.

  - The operation Move can move noun phrases to other positions in the structure.

  - If Move has transported the noun phrase to another position in the structure, this operation must be undone to determine how the noun phrase received its thematic role. That is, the noun phrase must be returned to its originating position.

  - The sentence *What should George make?* has the D-structure *George should make what.* In the D-structure, the verb *make* assigns the agent role to *George* and the theme role to *what.* See Figure 6.7 in the text for an example of thematic role assignment in a *wh* question.

PRACTICE 6.5: Identifying thematic roles

For each of the following sentences, identify all the noun phrases and the thematic role assigned to each noun phrase.

1. Sarah drove that bus from Indianapolis to Terre Haute.
2. The children are eating their ice cream in the kitchen.
3. Which shoes did you buy at the store?
4. Alyssa came from work.
5. The boys walked to the park.
6. Sally mailed a parcel to her nephew.
7. What did Bill leave at your house?
8. The letter was sent.
9. Ginger scribbled her address on the paper.
10. The minister in the pulpit was ordained recently.

Go back through each sentence and for each thematic role, determine the verb or preposition that assigned the role. Make sure you put any sentences in which Move has applied into D-Structure first. Remember: D-Structure is the result of Merge.

Pronoun Interpretation (Section 3.4)

Pronouns replace, or stand for, a noun phrase. This noun phrase is called the antecedent, and it is this antecedent that determines how the pronoun is interpreted.

- What is the antecedent of the pronoun *she* in the sentence *Janice's sister bought the dress that she liked*? Could *she* refer to *Janice*? How about *Janice's sister*? Could *she* refer to someone else not mentioned in the sentence?

- Consider the pronoun *herself* in the sentence *Janice's sister wondered if Fiona liked herself?* Does *herself* refer to *Fiona*, *Janice*, or *Janice's sister?* Can *herself* refer to someone not mentioned in the sentence?

It is the syntactic structure of the sentence that helps determine which noun phrase can or cannot function as the antecedent of a pronoun. The following concepts are important in understanding how the syntactic structure does this for pronominals and reflexive pronouns.

- **Pronominals and Reflexives.** English pronominals and reflexives vary in terms of number (singular and plural), person (first, second, and third), and gender (masculine, feminine, and neuter) in the third person. See Table 6.16 in the text for a complete list of the pronominals and reflexives found in English. For example, *she* is a pronominal (third person, singular, feminine) and *herself* is a reflexive (third person, singular, feminine).

- **C-Command.** The interpretation of pronominals and reflexive pronouns is based on the idea of c-command. A noun phrase c-commands another noun phrase if it is found in the following structure.

NP_a c-commands NP_b since the first category above NP_a (as indicated by A) contains NP_b. NP_b does not c-command NP_a since the first category above NP_b is B, and B does not contain NP_a.

- **Principles.** Two principles of interpretation are relevant. The first applies to reflexive pronouns, and the second to pronominals. Notice that these principles are opposite to each other.

  - **Principle A.** This principle applies to reflexive pronouns, and states that a reflexive pronoun must have an antecedent that c-commands it in the same clause (TP).

See Figure 6.9 in the text for an illustration of how this principle determines which NP can and cannot serve as an antecedent for a reflexive pronoun. Essentially, if an NP c-commands a reflexive, the NP can serve as the reflexive's antecedent. Conversely, if an NP does not c-command a reflexive, the NP cannot serve as the reflexive's antecedent.

  - **Principle B.** This principle applies to pronominals, and states that a pronominal cannot have an antecedent that c-commands it in the same clause (TP).

See Figure 6.10 in the text for an illustration of how this principle determines which NPs can and cannot serve as antecedents for a pronominal. Essentially, if an NP c-commands a pronominal, the NP cannot serve as the pronominal's antecedent. If an NP does not c-command a pronominal, the NP can serve as the pronominal's antecedent.

PRACTICE 6.6: Pronouns

For each of the following sentences:

- draw a tree diagram of the TP containing the underlined pronomial or reflexive.

- name the antecedent, and explain why it is the antecedent based on c-command and Principles A and B.

Use the following structure for the NP *Janice's sister*:

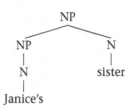

a. Janice's sister likes <u>herself</u>.

b. Janice's sister liked <u>her</u>.

c. Janice wondered if Fiona liked <u>herself</u>.

d. Janice's sister bought the dress which <u>she</u> liked.

REMINDER

The interpretation of a sentence involves many factors. Both the syntactic structure and the meaning of the words in that structure contribute to the meaning of a sentence. The construction in which words occur may also contribute to the meaning of the sentence. As well, the role each NP in a sentence plays must be interpreted. And, when words in a sentence can be combined in more than one way, ambiguity results.

Pragmatics (Sections 4.1–4.3)

Besides the structure of a sentence and the thematic roles assigned to the noun phrases within a sentence, there are many other factors involved in sentence interpretation. **Pragmatics** is the study of the role other necessary information has in sentence interpretation.

Beliefs and Attitudes

Nonlinguistic knowledge can be used to interpret elements within a sentence. For example, in the sentence *The city council denied the demonstrators a permit because they advocated violence*, we assume that the pronoun *they* refers to the demonstrators and not the council members because of our beliefs about demonstrators. If we change the verb from *advocate* to *abhor*, we now assume that *they* refers to the council and not the demonstrators. Again, this is based on our beliefs about the world.

Presupposition

Presupposition refers to the assumption or belief implied by the use of a particular word. For example, in the sentence *John admitted that the soccer team had cheated*, the use of the verb *admit* presupposes or implies that the team had actually cheated. A similar implication is not present in the sentence *John said that the soccer team had cheated*.

Setting/Deictics

The form and interpretation of some words depend on the location of the speaker and listener within a particular **setting**. These words are called **deictics**. Some examples of English deictics include *here/there* and *this/that*. *Here* and *this* are used to refer to items close to the speaker, while *there* and *that* are used to refer to words close to the listener. See Table 6.17 in the text for examples of how deictic distinctions can vary across languages.

Discourse/Topic

Many sentences can only be interpreted in reference to information contained in preceding sentences. **Discourse** is the term used to describe a connected series of utterances (e.g., in a conversation, lecture, or story). **Old (given) information** refers to knowledge that is known to the participants, while **new information** refers to knowledge that is introduced into the discourse for the first time. The **topic** is what a sentence or portion of the discourse is about. Some languages use a special affix to indicate the topic of the discourse (e.g., the affix *-wa* in Japanese).

PRACTICE 6.7: Sentence interpretation

How do we interpret the following sentences based on the underlined expressions? How does the underlined expression influence our interpretation?

1. a. At the wedding, every friend of the bride cried when she <u>walked down the aisle</u>.
   b. At the wedding, every friend of the bride cried when she <u>saw the couple together</u>.

2. a. Karen was <u>killed</u> in a car wreck.
   b. Karen was <u>murdered</u> in a car wreck.

3. a. Kevin <u>declared</u> that the accusation was false.
   b. Kevin <u>acknowledged</u> that the accusation was false.

4. a. When I <u>come</u> back to China, I'll climb the Great Wall.
   b. When I <u>go</u> back to China, I'll climb the Great Wall.

5. a. <u>A</u> priest is at <u>the</u> hospital.
   b. <u>The</u> priest is at <u>a</u> hospital.

Conversation (Section 4.4)

We use words and sentences to convey messages. And we often do this by having a conversation with someone. Conversations have rules. These rules refer to our understanding of how language is used to convey messages. Our knowledge of these rules also contributes to our interpretation of utterances.

- **Cooperative Principle**—This is the general principle guiding all conversation. It requires participants to make their contributions appropriate to the conversation.

- **Conversational maxims.** Conversations also have more specific guidelines (i.e., **maxims**). If we follow these maxims, then we have adhered to the Cooperative Principle. These maxims can be violated for specific purposes.

  Maxim of Relevance—Make your contribution relevant to the conversation.

  Maxim of Quality—Make your contribution truthful.

  Maxim of Quantity—Make your contribution only as informative as required.

  Maxim of Manner—Make your contribution unambiguous, clear, and logical.

- **Conversational implicature.** During the course of a conversation, we are often able to make inferences about what is meant but was not actually said. Consider, for example, the following interaction:

  > Mike: How did you do on the last exam?
  > Jim: Want to come with me to the Registrar's Office?

  In the above example, Jim violates the Maxim of Relevance, and even though he doesn't actually say how he did on the exam, it can be inferred from his response that he did rather badly.

PRACTICE 6.8: Violations of conversational maxims

You've just missed your bus and are standing at the bus stop waiting for the next one. The time is 2 p.m. and the next bus is due at 2:15 p.m., but you don't know that. You ask people at the bus stop when the next bus is due, and receive several replies. Each reply you receive may or may not violate one or more conversational maxims. For each reply, identify which maxim(s), if any, have been violated.

1. When's the next bus?

   At 2:30. (He's lying.)

   _____

2. When's the next bus?

   When I was little, I was obsessed with buses. I wanted to be a bus driver. I had hundreds of different kinds of buses. Little buses, big buses, red buses, blue buses, and even double-decker buses. Did you know that in England, many buses are double-decker? I have made a study of buses. I think the next bus will be here in 15 minutes. Did you know I wanted to be a bus driver? Did you know . . .

   _____

3. When's the next bus?

   Let me think! If the last bus was here at 1:50 and if they run every 20 minutes or so, then the next bus should be here at 2:10. (He has no idea.)

   _____

4. When's the next bus?

   At 2:15, but if we were in Denver that would be 3:15.

   _____

5. When's the next bus?

   I don't know. (She's telling the truth.)

   _____

Review Exercises

1. **Relations between words:** For each pair of words, write the term that indicates the relationship between the words:

   a. *bank* 'financial institution'   _____
      bank 'sloping land adjoining a body of water'

   b. *thick/thin*   _____

   c. *thin/slim*   _____

   d. *mammoth* 'extinct elephant'   _____
      mammoth 'something of great size'

   e. *offense/defense*   _____

   f. *safe* 'secure from danger'   _____
      safe 'container for storing valuables'

   g. *pale* 'light or whitish in color'   _____
      pail 'bucket'

   h. *bucket/pail*   _____

2. **Relations between sentences:** For each pair of sentences, write the term that indicates the relation:

   a. Tina has just had a baby.
      Tina is a mother.   _____

   b. Giza is the site of the Great Pyramids.
      The Great Pyramids are located in Giza.   _____

   c. Tonight is overcast.
      We can see the stars clearly tonight.   _____

   d. Mark Twain wrote a book called *Tom Sawyer*.
      The author of *Tom Sawyer* is Mark Twain.   _____

   e. Jimmy has a 4.0 grade point average.
      Jimmy is on the Dean's List.   _____

3. **Theories of meaning:** For each of the following sets of items, write the term or terms related to theories of meaning that the underlined words in the set exemplify. You should also be able to explain why the items exemplify the term(s).

   a. Prince Charles is the <u>Prince of Wales.</u>
      The <u>Prince of Wales</u> is next in line to the British throne.

   _____

   b. An international student from Vietnam describes 70-degree fall weather as <u>cold</u>.

   _____

   c. Mr. Burns lives in a <u>mansion</u>.
      Mr. Burns lives in a <u>large house</u>.

   _____

   d. You need to <u>push</u> the door open.
      You need to <u>pull</u> the door open.

   _____

   e. During their comprehensive exam, the graduate students were <u>sweating bullets</u>.

   _____

   f. Concept TREE: <u>maple</u> vs. <u>palm</u> tree

   _____

4. **Grammaticalized concepts:** Look at the data from Burmese. What concept is grammaticalized in Burmese that is usually not grammaticalized in English? How is this concept indicated?

   [̥] below a sound indicates that it is voiceless.
   Tones are marked as diacritics above the vowels.

1.	mjô	'be floating'	m̥jô	'set afloat'
2.	nôu	'be awake'	n̥ôu	'waken'
3.	láʔ	'be bare'	l̥áʔ	'uncover'

5. **Thematic roles:** Write three sentences of your own, and label thematic roles for each NP. You should have at least one example of each of the following:

agent
theme
source
goal
location

---

6. **Pragmatics and sentence interpretation:** Look at each snippet of conversation, and answer the questions that follow.

    a. Prosecution lawyer to defense witness: *Have you stopped taking drugs? Just answer with a simple yes or no.*

        If the witness has never taken drugs, can she answer the question? Why or why not?

    b. Doctor to patient with bursitis: *Can you reach the top shelf?*
        Short student to tall student in the library: *Can you reach the top shelf?*

        Is the implicature the same for both questions? Why or why not?

    c. A letter of recommendation for a student applying to graduate school: *I am writing to recommend Joe Blow for graduate study. He was my advisee, and I have always found him unfailingly polite and punctual. Also, he dresses extremely well. Sincerely . . .*

        What maxims are being violated? What is the implicature of the letter?

☑ **RECAP**

Make sure you know how to do the following. (See also the Key Terms at the end of Chapter 6 in the main text.)

- identify the semantic relations between words
- identify the semantic relations between sentences
- define connotation, denotation, extension, and intension
- do componential analysis
- recognize fuzzy concepts, grammaticalized concepts, and lexicalized concepts
- recognize constructional meanings
- recognize lexical ambiguity
- recognize and represent structural ambiguity
- identify noun phrases, their thematic roles, and how these are assigned
- determine how pronominals and reflexives are interpreted
- identify the effect of world knowledge in sentence interpretation
- identify when presupposition occurs in sentence interpretation
- recognize the different forms of deictic terms
- identify conversational principles, maxims, and implicatures

Questions? Problems?

_____

_____

_____

_____

_____

_____

_____

_____

_____

_____

_____

_____

_____

_____

seven

The Classification of Languages

Language classification involves arranging languages into groups based on shared characteristics. Important topics and concepts found in this chapter include the following:

Language universals
Markedness theory
Structural classification
Phonological classification
Morphological classification
Syntactic classification
Genetic classification
The Indo-European family of languages

Terms and Concepts (Sections 1.1, 1.2)

The following terms and concepts are important in understanding how linguists classify languages:

Term	Definition
mutual intelligibility	Mutual intelligibility is a criterion used to determine whether language varieties are dialects of the same language or are different languages altogether. Essentially, if speakers can understand each other, the varieties are considered dialects of the same language, and if the speakers cannot understand each other, they are considered different languages.
language death	Languages can die (become extinct) over time. An extinct language is not a language that evolves over time into one or more languages (e.g., Latin), but a language that ceases to be spoken altogether. For example, Manx (in 1974) and Bo (in 2010) disappeared completely: They have no speakers and no descendant languages.
classic pattern of language shift	Language loss through shift typically takes three generations. Parents are monolingual speakers of a language; their children adopt a new language and become bilingual speakers; and their children's children grow up monolingual in the new language.

149

Typological Classification (Section 2)

Linguistic typology groups languages together based on their structural characteristics. This type of classification can be done using phonological properties, morphological systems, and grammatical structures. Typological studies are carried out to uncover universal characteristics of language.

Linguistic Universals. Linguistic universals are structural characteristics that occur in all or most languages.

- An **absolute universal** is a structural characteristic that is found in all languages.

- A **universal tendency** is a structural characteristic that is found in most languages.

- An **implicational universal** outlines a particular relationship between two structural characteristics.
  - The presence of characteristic A (e.g., nasal vowels) implies that the language will also have characteristic B (e.g., oral vowels).
  - The presence of B (e.g., oral vowels) does not imply that the language will also have A (e.g., nasal vowels).

Implicational universals can be used to determine possible and impossible characteristics of language. If A (e.g., nasal vowels) implies B (e.g., oral vowels), then:

- it is possible for a language to have both B and A, and

- it is possible for a language to have B without having A, but

- it is impossible for a language to have A without having B. This is because if a language has A, it also has to have B.

Markedness Theory. Markedness theory is another way to analyze linguistic universals. Structural characteristics can be identified as being more or less marked in relation to each other.

- **Unmarked** characteristics are characteristics that are more common in world languages.

- **Marked** characteristics are characteristics that are less common in world languages.

Markedness is closely related to implicational universals. Where the presence of A implies the presence of B, this means that a language cannot have A unless it also has B. B is less marked than is A. Languages will typically not have the more marked characteristic unless they also have the corresponding less marked characteristic.

PRACTICE 7.1: Typological classification

1. The vowel phoneme /a/ is found in almost all world languages. This is a statement of (choose one):

   a. an absolute universal

   b. a universal tendency

   c. an implicational universal

Why did you choose the answer you did? _____

The vowel phoneme /a/ is (choose one):

a. marked   b. unmarked

Why did you choose the answer you did? _____

2. If a language has inflectional affixes, it will also have derivational affixes. This is a statement of (choose one):

a. an absolute universal

b. a universal tendency

c. an implicational universal

Why did you choose the answer you did? _____

Inflectional affixes are:

a. marked   b. unmarked

Why did you choose the answer you did? _____

Derivational affixes are:

a. marked   b. unmarked

Why did you choose the answer you did? _____

3. Is each of the following possible or impossible? Why?

<u>A language has:</u>   <u>possible or impossible?</u>

a. derivational and inflectional affixes   _____

   because _____

b. inflectional affixes, but no derivational affixes   _____

   because _____

c. derivational affixes, but no inflectional affixes   _____

   because _____

Phonological Classification (Section 2.1)

Phonological classification is based on the phonemes found in a language.

Vowel Systems. Languages can be classified according to the size and pattern of their vowel system. The most common system has five vowels: /i, u, e, o, a/. Other common vowel systems have three, four, six, seven, eight, or nine different vowels. See Figure 7.2 in the text for examples of some of the common vowel systems.

Some universal tendencies include:

- /a/ is the most commonly occurring vowel phoneme. /i/ and /u/ are almost as common.

- Front vowels are generally unrounded, while nonlow back vowels are generally rounded.

- Low back vowels are generally unrounded.

How many vowel phonemes are found in English? Is this more or less than the average number found across languages? Does English follow each of the universal tendencies shown above?

Some implicational universals include:

- If a language has contrastive nasal vowels, then it will also have contrastive oral vowels.

- If a language has contrastive long vowels, then it will also have contrastive short vowels.

See Table 7.4 in the text for some examples of contrastive long and short vowels in Finnish.

PRACTICE 7.2: Typology and vowel systems

1. Circle the more marked in each pair:

    a. nasal vowels   oral vowels

    b. short vowels   long vowels

    c. unrounded front vowels   rounded front vowels

    d. the vowel phoneme /i/   the vowel phoneme /ɛ/

2. Assume that a language contains the following vowels: /eː, oː, uː, iː, aː, ã/. Use your knowledge of implicational universals to predict which other vowels might be found in this language.

Consonant Systems. Languages are not usually classified according to the size of their consonant inventories. This is because there is a great deal of variation in the number of consonant inventories found in the world's languages. Some languages (e.g., Rotokas, spoken in Papua New Guinea) have as few as six, while others (e.g., !Kung, spoken in Namibia and Angola) have as many as 96.

Some absolute universals and universal tendencies include:

- All languages have stops, but not all languages have fricatives.

- The most common stop phonemes are /p, t, k/, with /t/ being the most common.

- The most commonly occurring fricative is /s/, followed by /f/.

- Most languages have at least one nasal phoneme.

- If a language has only one nasal phoneme, it is most likely /n/. If a language has contrasting nasal phonemes, they are most likely /m/ and /n/.

- Most languages have at least one phonemic liquid. (Some languages have none.)

How many consonant phonemes are found in English? Does English follow the universals outlined above?

Some universal implications include:

- If a language has voiced obstruent phonemes, then it will also have the corresponding voiceless obstruent phonemes.

- If a language has voiceless sonorant phonemes, then it will also have the corresponding voiced sonorant phonemes.

- If a language has fricative phonemes, then it will also have stop phonemes.

- If a language has affricate phonemes, then it will also have fricative and stop phonemes.

PRACTICE 7.3: Typology and consonant systems

1. Circle the least marked in each pair or group:

   a. fricatives   affricates

   b. voiced obstruents   voiceless obstruents

   c. the phoneme /t/   the phoneme /ð/

   d. voiced sonorants   voiceless sonorants

   e. stops   fricatives   affricates

2. Bulgarian has the consonant phonemes /b, d, g, ʤ/.

   a. From this information, circle the other types of sounds Bulgarian must have, based on implicational universals:

   voiceless obstruents   voiceless sonorants   fricatives   glides

b. Based on universal tendencies, which sounds would we expect the language to have (although it might not actually have them)?

1. /t/
2. /n/
3. /s/

4. the voiceless labiovelar glide /ʍ/
5. /l/ or /r/
6. the voiceless velar fricative /x/

Suprasegmentals. Suprasegmentals are prosodic characteristics of a sound independent of the sound's individual articulation.

Tone

• Tone languages (languages in which differences in pitch are used to indicate differences in meaning) can have two, three, or four contrastive level tones. Most tone languages have two levels.

• If a tone language has contrastive contour tones, then it will also have contrastive level tones. A contour tone is a tone that involves moving pitch.

Stress

• In a fixed stress system, the stress is predictable: for example, always on the first syllable, like Hungarian, or always on the last syllable, like Modern Hebrew.

• In a free stress system, stress is not predictable; it must be learned for every word. In these languages (e.g., Russian), a difference in stress placement can cause a meaning difference. See Table 7.13 in the text for some examples of the relationship between stress and meaning in Russian.

Syllable Structure

• All languages have CV and V syllable types. This means that all languages allow syllables that begin with an onset, but not all languages have syllables with codas.

• If a language allows sequences of consonants in an onset (i.e., a complex onset), then it will allow onsets with only one consonant (i.e., a simple onset). Similarly, if a language allows sequences of consonants in a coda (i.e., a complex coda), then it will allow codas with one consonant (i.e., a simple coda).

PRACTICE 7.4: Typology and suprasegmentals

1. Circle the more marked in each pair:

a. VCC syllable   VC syllable

b. level tones   contour tones

c. language with two tones   language with five tones

d. CCVC syllable   CVC syllable

e. CV syllable   CVC syllable

2. Examine the data below and answer the questions that follow. (Note: The data are from a hypothetical language.)

/drong/	"basket"	/sas.gnu/	"foot"
/ben/	"stove"	/gle/	"sun"
/a.dupt/	"chicken"	/brit.e.aks/	"chair"

   a. Identify the syllable types present in each of the words. Remember that a period indicates a syllable boundary.

   b. Does this language allow sequences of consonants in an onset? In a coda?

   c. Which other syllable type would be found in this hypothetical language?

   d. Which syllable structure universals (including implicational universals) are evident in the data?

3. Examine the following data and answer the questions below. (Note: The data are from a hypothetical language.)

```
    H  M              H  LH             HL  M
    |  |              |   \/            \/  |
/t i k u/ "man"   /t i k u/ "woman"   /t i k u/ "child"
```

   a. Identify the tones as either level or contour.

   b. Use your knowledge of implicational universals to predict which other tones this hypothetical language might have.

PRACTICE 7.5: Phonological classification

1. Using your knowledge of implicational universals, decide whether each of the following corresponds to a possible or impossible combination of sounds in language.

   a. contrastive long vowels without contrastive short vowels   _____

   b. voiced sonorants without voiceless sonorants   _____

   c. affricates without fricatives   _____

   d. contrastive oral vowels without contrastive nasal vowels   _____

   e. voiceless obstruents without voiced obstruents   _____

   f. level tones without contour tones   _____

   g. syllables with complex onsets and syllables with simple onsets   _____

   h. closed syllables without open syllables   _____

2. The consonant inventory of Farsi (Persian) is given below. Examine the inventory, and fill in the blanks of the implicational universals that Farsi illustrates.
   Note: [x] represents a voiceless velar fricative; [ɣ] represents a voiced velar fricative; [r] represents a trill

	LABIAL	**CORONAL**	**DORSAL**	**GLOTTAL**
Stops	p b	t d	k g	ʔ
Affricates		tʃ dʒ		
Fricatives	f v	s z ʃ ʒ	x ɣ	h
Nasals	m	n		
Liquids		r		
		l		
Glides	j			

   a. The most common stop, fricative, and nasal are present. These are (stop)

   _____ ; (fricative) _____ ; and (nasal)

   _____ .

   b. The presence of affricates implies the presence of _____ and

   _____ .

   c. The presence of voiced obstruents implies the presence of _____ .

   d. What universal tendency is illustrated by the liquids? _____

   _____

3. The vowel inventory of Hungarian is given below. Examine the inventory, and fill in the blanks of the implicational universals that Hungarian illustrates.
   Note: [y] represents a high tense front rounded vowel; [ø] represents a mid front tense rounded vowel; [ː] after a vowel represents a long vowel.

	Short vowels			**Long vowels**		
High	i y		u	iː yː		uː
Mid		ø	o	eː øː		oː
	ɛ					
Low			ɑ			aː

a. Two of the three most common vowels are present, and they are: _____

and _____ .

b. The presence of long vowels implies _____

_____ .

c. An unmarked feature of the Hungarian back vowels is that _____

_____ .

d. A marked feature of the Hungarian inventory of front vowels is that _____

_____ .

Morphological Classification (Section 2.2)

Morphological classification is based on the different ways in which languages combine morphemes to form words. There are four types of morphological systems.

- **Isolating.** In an isolating language, words consist only of free morphemes. There are no affixes. Information such as tense or plural is contained within separate free morphemes.

  ○ Mandarin is an example of a language with an isolating morphology.

- **Agglutinating.** In an agglutinating language, words contain many affixes. Each affix typically corresponds to a single piece of grammatical information (e.g., number, tense, possession, etc.).

  ○ Turkish is an example of a language with an agglutinating morphology.

- **Fusional.** In a fusional (or inflectional) language, words also contain many affixes. However, each affix may contain several pieces of grammatical information at the same time. That is, one affix may contain information on gender, number, case, and so on.

  ○ Russian is a good example of a language with a fusional morphology.

- **Polysynthetic.** In a polysynthetic language, a single word consists of a number of roots and affixes. These words often express meanings that are associated with entire sentences in other languages.

  ○ Inuktitut is a good example of a language with a polysynthetic morphology.

Consider the information found in English pronouns such as *he, she, him*, and *her*; in English derived words such as *activation, optionality*, and *denationalize*; and in English phrases such as *John will sing*. What type of system do each of these structures correspond to? Is the same type of system found in each structure? If not, what conclusion can you make about the type of morphological system found in English?

Some universals include:

- If a language has inflectional affixes, then it will also have derivational affixes.

- If a word has both a derivational and an inflectional affix, the derivational affix will be closer to the root. See Table 7.16 in the text for some examples of the ordering of inflectional and derivational affixes in English and Turkish.

- If a language has only suffixes, it will have only postpositions (e.g., Turkish). A postposition is the equivalent of a preposition. The difference between the two is that a preposition occurs before its noun phrase complement, while a postposition occurs after its noun phrase complement.

PRACTICE 7.6: Morphological classification

1. Identify the morphological system evident in each of these. Note that the words are divided into their morphemes (indicated with a hyphen). The meaning of each morpheme is given in English directly underneath. The equivalent English translation is given on the third line.

   a. Blackfoot: maːt-jaːk-waːxkaji -waːtsiksi
      not -will-go home-he
      'He is not going home.'

   b. Chinese: tā   qù zhōngguó xué zhōngguó huà
      s/he go China learn China painting
      'S/he went to China to learn Chinese painting.'

   c. Turkish: bülbül   -ler -imiz -in
      nightingale-PL -1PL -GENITIVE
      'belonging to our nightingales'

   d. Latin: trib -us   trib -ibus
      tribe-F SG NOMINATIVE   tribe-F PL DATIVE
      'tribe' (SUBJECT)   [to, for] 'tribes'

2. Considering the implicational universals and tendencies, answer the questions about what you would expect for each of these languages:

   a. Modern Greek has inflectional affixes to mark gender, case, number, and tense. Does

      Greek have derivational affixes? Why or why not? _____

      _____

   b. French has inflectional affixes for tense, person, and number, but none to mark case.

      What would you expect about derivational affixes and why? _____

      _____

   c. Thai has no inflection for case, gender, tense, or number. What would expect about

      derivational affixes and why? _____

      _____

Syntactic Classification (Section 2.3)

Much of syntactic classification is based on the word order patterns found in basic declarative sentences (e.g., *The boy kicked the ball*). The three most common word order patterns are:

- **SOV.** In this word order pattern, the subject (S) comes first, followed by the object (O) and then the verb (V). Using this pattern, the English sentence *The boy kicked the ball* would have the order *The boy the ball kicked*.

    ○ Turkish and Japanese are examples of languages that follow this pattern.

- **SVO.** In this word order pattern, the subject (S) comes first, followed by the verb (V) and then the object (O). This pattern corresponds to the English sentence *The boy kicked the ball*.

    ○ English and French are examples of languages that follow this pattern.

- **VSO.** In this word order pattern, the verb (V) comes first, followed by the subject (S) and then the object (O). Using this pattern, the English sentence *The boy kicked the ball* would have the order *Kicked the boy the ball*.

    ○ Welsh is an example of a language using this pattern.

What do the three word order patterns have in common? Why might this be so? Are there other word order patterns found in the world's languages that do not follow this generalization? Which word order pattern is the most common?

There are also some universal tendencies regarding word order. These are related to whether a language places the verb before the object (VO) or after the object (OV).

VO languages

- have prepositions (e.g., *in* the park, *with* his foot)
- place prepositional phrases after the verb (e.g., The boy <u>ran</u> *in the park*)
- generally place adverbs after the verb (e.g., The boy <u>ran</u> *quickly*)
- generally (though not always) place the noun before its possessor (e.g., *the dog* <u>of the boy</u>)

OV languages

- have postpositions (e.g., the park *in*, his foot *with*)
- place postpositional phrases before the verb (e.g., The boy *the park in* <u>ran</u>)
- place adverbs before the verb (e.g., The boy *quickly* <u>ran</u>)
- place the possessor before the noun (e.g., <u>the boy's</u> *dog*)

REMINDER

VO languages tend to be right-branching languages, meaning that the complement occurs after the head. In contrast, OV languages tend to be left-branching languages, meaning that the complement occurs before the head. Figure 7.6 in the text illustrates this structural difference.

PRACTICE 7.7: Syntactic classification

1. Determine the word order in each of the following sentences. The English translation for each word is given on the line underneath. The equivalent English sentence is given on the third line. (Yuwaalaraay is an Australian language.)

<u>Word order</u>

a. Spanish: Los soldados quebraron las ventanas.   _____
the soldiers broke   the windows
'The soldiers broke the windows.'

b. Yuwaalaraay: duyugu nama dayn yiy   _____
snake that man bit
'The snake bit that man.'

2. Would you expect Spanish to have prepositions or postpositions? What about Yuwaalaraay? Would the phrase containing the preposition or postposition come before or after the verb in Spanish? What about in Yuwaalaraay?

3. What is the difference in the ordering of nouns and demonstratives in the following phrases? (Tinrin is an Austronesian language; Limbu is a Sino-Tibetan language spoken in Nepal.)

Tinrin: moo horro ha   Limbu: khɛy nɛpphu cum ha
Det prayer this   that two friend PLURAL
'this prayer (going on right now)'   'those two friends'

Explaining Universals (Section 2.4)

Why are some patterns found in language? Why are other patterns not found in language? Why are some structural characteristics more common than others? There are no definitive answers to such questions, although some possible explanations have been given:

- Some phonological universals may have a perceptual basis. Others may be motivated by articulatory possibilities (e.g., that languges tend to have more obstruents than sonorants).

- Some morphological universals may be linked to language change (see Chapter 8). Others may be related to the internal structure of words (see Chapter 4).

- Syntactic patterns may be linked to how we process language (see Chapter 11).

Genetic Classification (Section 3)

Genetic classification groups languages together based on common ancestry. These groups of languages are called "families," since all members of the group are descended from the same ancestor.

There can be many difficulties in doing genetic classification. One is the amount of data that is needed to be sure of the genetic status of a language. Some others are given below.

- **Language Contact.** When languages come into contact with each other, they often borrow sounds, words, morphemes, and syntactic structures from one another. The result is that languages that are unrelated may end up being similar in many ways.

- **Sound Change.** Sound changes over time can make it difficult to find relationships between languages, since sound changes may render words in related languages very different from one another. The result is that languages that are related may not look similar.

- **Vocabulary Change.** Words that are often good indicators of a genetic relationship between two languages may be lost from the lexicon over time.

The Indo-European Family (Section 3.1)

English belongs to the Indo-European family of languages. These languages are found in Europe as well as in the Middle East and India. The Indo-European language family currently has nine branches.

- **Albanian.** Albanian, the only member of this family, is spoken in Albania and in parts of the former Yugoslavia, Greece, and Italy.

- **Armenian.** Armenian, the only member of this family, is spoken in the Republic of Armenia as well as in Turkey, Iran, Syria, Lebanon, and Egypt.

- **Baltic.** Latvian and Lithuanian are the two Baltic languages. They are spoken in Latvia and Lithuania (west of Russia and northeast of Poland).

- **Celtic.** The Celtic languages are divided into the Insular and Continental branches. The Insular branch is further divided into the Brythonic and Goidelic (or Gaelic) sub-branches. Celtic languages are spoken in the British Isles as well as in northwestern France.

- **Germanic.** The Germanic languages are divided into East, North, and West branches. North Germanic languages are spoken in Scandinavia, while the West Germanic languages are spoken in Germany, the Netherlands, Belgium, South Africa, England, and, of course, North America.

- **Hellenic.** This branch has only one member: Greek.

- **Indo-Iranian.** This branch is divided into Indic and Iranian languages. Iranian languages are spoken in Iran, Afghanistan, Iraq, Turkey, the former Yugoslavia, and China. Indic languages are spoken in northern India, Pakistan, and Bangladesh.

- **Italic.** The Italic languages are divided into four branches: Ibero-Romance, Gallo-Romance, Italo-Romance, and Balkano-Romance.

- **Slavic.** The Slavic languages are divided into East, West, and South branches. These languages are spoken in Russia, the Ukraine, Belarus, and the former Yugolsavia.

See Figure 7.8 in the text for the approximate locations of the different Indo-European languages.

Some interesting facts about Indo-European:

- The ancestor of the Indo-European language family is a reconstructed language called Proto-Indo-European (PIE).

- The reconstruction of PIE is based on Old English, Old Norse, Latin, Sanskrit, and Attic Greek, among other languages.

- Lithuanian has a case system thought to be similar to that found in PIE.

- English descended from the languages spoken by the Germanic tribes: the Angles, Jutes, and Saxons.

- Frisian is the closest relative to English.

- Some Indo-European languages are extinct. For example, Gothic is an extinct East Germanic language and Cornish is an extinct Celtic language.

REMINDER

There are many other language families, including Uralic, Altaic, and Austronesian. You can find more information on these families (and others) online at LaunchPad Solo on **launchpadworks.com**.

PRACTICE 7.8: The Indo-European family

Study the Tables 7.20 to 7.25 in the text, and construct a diagram of the Indo-European language family by filling in the chart. Provide (1) the names of the sub-branches in the different branches and (2) the languages of each branch or sub-branch. Extinct languages and their branches have been omitted from the diagram.

PRACTICE 7.9: Indo-European relationships

1. Name a language that is a sister (i.e., a member of the sub-branch, or branch if the language has no sub-branch) to each of the following languages.

LANG	SISTER	LANG	SISTER
Italian	_____	Polish	_____
Swedish	_____	Russian	_____
Yiddish	_____	Latvian	_____
Catalan	_____	Bulgarian	_____

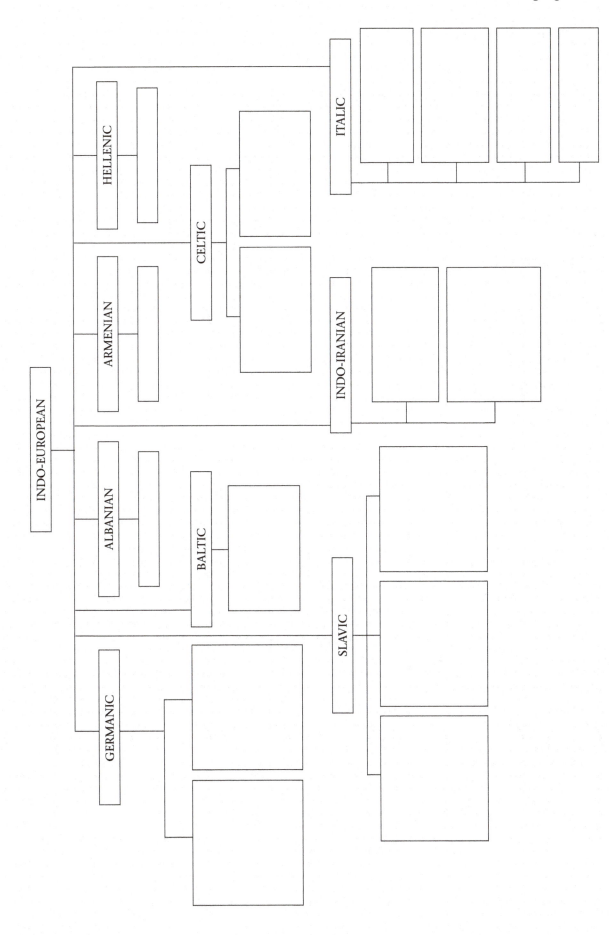

2. Circle the language that does not fit.

a.	Greek	Danish	Frisian
b.	Russian	Hungarian	Polish
c.	Persian	Bengali	Romany
d.	Portuguese	Macedonian	Sardinian
e.	Albanian	Romanian	Catalan
f.	Italian	German	Spanish

3. Give the sub-branch (and branch if applicable) for each of the following languages.

   a. Danish _____

   b. Scots Gaelic _____

   c. Sardinian _____

   d. Kurdish _____

   e. Bengali _____

   f. Slovene _____

   g. Bulgarian _____

   h. Czech _____

   i. Greek _____

   j. Yiddish _____

REMINDER

There is a third type of classification: areal. This type of classification groups languages according to shared characteristics based on geographical contact. Languages that are geographical neighbors often borrow sounds, morphemes, words, and even syntactic structures from each other. This means that neighboring languages may resemble each other even though they are not genetically related.

Review Exercises

1. **Consonants:** Of the two possible consonant inventories below, one is from a real language, and one is not.

    Note: [ts] represents a voiceless alveolar affricate; [dz] represents a voiced alveolar affricate; [ʲ] represents palatalization; [ɲ] represents a palatal nasal; [β] represents a voiced bilabial fricative; [ɣ] represents a voiced velar fricative

	Inventory A			Inventory B			
	LABIAL	CORONAL	DORSAL	LABIAL	CORONAL	DORSAL	LARYNGEAL
Stops				p b	t d tʲ dʲ	k g	ʔ
Affricates		dz dʒ			ts tʃ		
Fricatives	β v	ð z ʒ	ɣ	f	s ʃ		h
Nasals	m		ŋ	m	n	ɲ ŋ	
Liquids					l lʲ r		
Glides	ʍ		j ʍ	w		j w	

Which one is real? _____

Justify your conclusion by commenting on the following:

a. expected, unmarked obstruent phonemes: _____

b. implicational universals concerning obstruents: _____

c. expected, unmarked sonorant phonemes: _____

2. **Vowels:** Of the two possible vowel inventories below, one is from a real language, and one is not. Note: The symbol [ɒ] is a low back rounded vowel. A tilde over a vowel means the vowel is nasalized.

Inventory A		Inventory B	
i	u		ũ
e	o	ɜ̃	ʊ̃
æ	ɒ	ʌ̃	ɔ̃

a. Which one is real? _____

b. In what ways is the real vowel inventory more consistent with universal tendencies than the made-up one? Comment in terms of:

use of phonological space: _____

_____

adherence to implicational universals: _____

_____

3. For each language below, specify the word order for subject (S), verb (V), and object (O). Data not in square brackets are in the orthography of the source.

   a. Hindi: [radʒu ne   kɪtab pəɾhi]   _____
                         Raju AGENT book read
                         'Raju read the book.'

   b. Warao: Erike   hube abun-ae   _____
                         Enrique snake bite-PAST
                         'A snake bit Enrique.'

   c. Classical Arabic: [ʔiʃtaraː   rradʒulaːni kitaːban]   _____
                         bought-3 SG the-men-two book-ACC
                         'The two men bought a book.'

   (Note: 3 SG = third person singular; ACC = accusative for the direct object)

   d. Thai: [kʰaw àan nǎŋsɨ̆ dǐawníi]   _____
                         he   read book now
                         'He is reading a book now.'

   e. Hixkaryana: Toto yonoye kamara.   _____
                         man ate   jaguar
                         'The jaguar ate the man.'

   f. Toba Batak: Manghindat poti i   baoa i.   _____
                         lift   case the man the
                         'The man lifted the case.'

4. **Lakhota:** Examine these data in Lakhota (a Native American language). Under each sentence is a word-by-word gloss. At the side is the translation in English. Then based on the glosses, translations, and sentence patterns, you should be able to complete the questions below. Data are in phonetic transcription.

   a. [wakpala   aglagla]   'near [the] creek'
       creek   near

   b. [tʃ'ăpagmijăpi   ogna   ijaje]   'He went in [a] wagon.'
       wagon   in   he-went

   c. [xe   kĩ   ohomni   japi]   'They went around the mountain.'
       mountain   the   around   they-went

Now write in the word-by-word glosses under the phrases below. The translation of each phrase is given at the side.

d. [wakpala   opʰaja]   'along [the] creek'

     _____   _____

e. [wa   ohã   ijaje]   'He went through [the] snow.'

     _____   _____   _____

f. [tʰpi   kĩ   okʃã   enaʒĩ]

     _____   _____   _____   _____

                                                    'They stood around/about the house.'

What is the order of P and its complement NP in Lakhota? _____

What is the order of Det and N in the NP? _____

Now look at these full sentences. What do you predict the order will be of the V and O? Why?

_____

g. [wakʰãtʰãka makʰa   kĩ   kage]   'God made the earth.'
     God   earth   the   he-made

h. [ʃũka he   kʰokʰajexʻãla   tʰebje]   'That dog ate [a] chicken.'
     dog   that chicken   he-ate

i. [ʃũkamanitu wã   hokʃila kĩ   kte]   'A wolf killed the boy.'
     wolf   a   boy   the   he-killed

What is the order of S, V, and O in Lakhota? _____

☑ **RECAP**

Make sure you know how to do the following. (See also the Key Terms at the end of Chapter 7 in the main text.)

- define mutual intelligibility
- explain the difference between the three types of classification
- understand the different types of language universals
- understand the difference between marked and unmarked characteristics
- determine possible and impossible phonological, morphological, and syntactic systems
- know the common phonological systems found across the world's languages
- know the four types of morphological systems found across the world's languages
- identify the three most common word order patterns found across the world's languages
- specify the phonological, morphological, and syntactic universals
- identify the branches of the Indo-European language family and the languages of each branch

Questions? Problems?

_____

_____

_____

_____

_____

_____

_____

_____

_____

_____

_____

_____

_____

_____

eight

Historical Linguistics: The Study of Language Change

Historical linguistics studies the principles governing language change. This branch of linguistics is concerned with both the description and the explanation of language change. Following are some of the important topics and concepts covered in this chapter. Make sure you are familiar with them.

Phonetic sound change
Phonological change
Morphological change
Syntactic change
Lexical change
Semantic change
Language reconstruction
Naturalness and typology

Language Change (Section 1)

Some important points concerning language change include:

- Language is always changing. However, for a particular change to take hold, it must be accepted by the language community as a whole.

- Language change is regular and systematic. Some changes affect all words without exception. Other changes begin in a small number of words in the speech of a small number of speakers. These changes may gradually spread through both the vocabulary and the population.

- Languages change because of the way language is acquired. Children are not born with a complete grammar, but must construct a grammar based on the language they are exposed to. Therefore, changes will occur from one generation to the next, and because all children have the same genetic capabilities for language and construct their grammars in similar fashions, the same patterns of change repeat both within and across languages.

- Causes of language change include **articulatory simplification**, **reanalysis**, **analogy**, and **language contact**.

Sequential Sound Change (Section 2.1)

While all aspects of a language's structure can change, sound change is often the most noticeable. There are many types of sound change that can occur, but most sound changes involve sequences of segments. The major types of sequential sound changes are outlined below.

- **Assimilation.** Assimilation involves sounds changing to become more like nearby sounds. Assimilation increases the efficiency of the articulations involved in producing the sequence of sounds. Such an increase in efficiency can result in articulatory simplification. See Tables 8.3–8.4 in the text for more examples of the following types of assimilation.

Some common examples include:

Types of assimilation

a. **Place of articulation assimilation**
   A sound becomes similar to a nearby sound in terms of place of articulation.

   Palatalization

   A nonpalatal sound becomes more palatal. This usually occurs near a sound that is made with the tongue at or near the hard palate—usually [j] or [i].

   Palatalization is often the first step in the creation of an affricate. The type of change in which a palatalized stop becomes an affricate is called **affrication**. Like palatalization, affrication is often induced by front vowels or [j].

b. **Manner of articulation assimilation**
   A consonant changes its manner of articulation to be like a nearby sound.

c. **Voicing assimilation**
   A sound assimilates to the voicing of neighboring sounds.

d. **Nasalization**
   A vowel becomes nasal near a nasal sound.

e. **Total assimilation**
   A sound assimilates totally to a following sound.

- **Other types of sound change.** There are other types of sound changes as well, many of which will be familiar to you from the phonology chapter. These types of sound changes are not as frequent as assimilation, but like assimilation, they also tend to have the overall effect of making sequences of sounds easier to articulate. Also like assimilation, these changes can affect adjacent segments or segments at a distance.

Some common examples include:

Types of sound change

a. **Dissimilation**
   A sound becomes less like a nearby sound. This often occurs so that a sequence of sounds is easier to articulate or perceive.

b. **Epenthesis**
A sound is inserted. This sometimes occurs to break up a consonant cluster that is hard to pronounce.

c. **Metathesis**
The position of two sounds has changed relative to each other.

- **Weakening and deletion.** Both vowels and consonants tend to weaken over time. They can also delete. Deletion is often the end result of the weakening process.

Vowel weakening: See Table 8.8 in the text for examples.

Types of weakening

a. **Vowel reduction**
An unstressed vowel reduces to schwa.

b. **Vowel deletion**
A vowel is deleted word-finally (apocope) or word-internally (syncope).

Consonant weakening: See Tables 8.9–8.11 in the text for examples.

Consonants tend to weaken along a path determined by the following hierarchy.

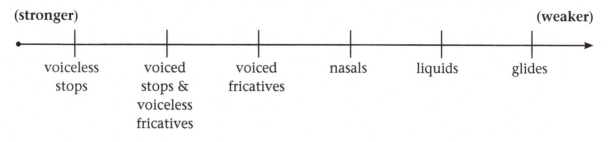

Geminate (long) consonants are stronger than their nongeminate counterparts. The tendency over time is for consonants to weaken along this path.

Types of weakening

a. **Degemination**
A doubled consonant is shortened to a single consonant.

b. **Voicing**
A voiceless obstruent weakens to a voiced obstruent.

c. **Frication**
A stop weakens to a fricative, often between vowels.

d. **Rhotacism**
This is when [z] weakens to [r].

e. **Deletion**
A consonant often deletes when it occurs in a consonant cluster or as the final consonant in the word.

- **Strengthening.** Consonants can also strengthen. Glides often strengthen to an affricate. This process is called **glide strengthening** and is common in word-initial position.

PRACTICE 8.1: Identifying types of sound change

Each of the following exemplifies one or more sound changes. The older form is on the left, and the newer, more recent form on the right. Identify the sound change that has taken place for each of the underlined sounds.

1. Proto-Slavic [k̲emerai] > Russian [t͡ʃemer]

    _____

2. Old English [kno̲tta] > Modern American English [n̲ɑt]

    _____

3. Early Latin [i̲npossibili̲s̲] > Latin [i̲mpossibilis]

    _____

4. Proto-Bantu [mu̲k̲ki̲:pa] > Swahili [mʃipa]

    _____

5. Middle Indo-Aryan [ka̲m̲pa-] > Hindi [kã̲:p-]

    _____

6. Vulgar Latin [fā̲bu̲lare̲] > Spanish [ablar]

    _____

7. Early Greek [t̲ʰrikʰós] > Later Greek [trikʰós]

    _____

8. Old English [θy:mel] > Modern English [thim̲b̲le]

    _____

9. Quechua [suq̲ta] > Cuzco Quechua [soχ̲ta]

    _____

10. Old English [hro̲s] > Modern English [ho̲r̲se]

    _____

11. Latin [lupu̲] > Spanish [lob̲o]

    _____

12. Old Norse [gestr̲] > Swedish [gest]

    _____

13. Proto-Dravidian [tap̲u]   >   Kannada [tav̲u]

---

14. Proto-Baltic Finnic [luɣettiin]   >   Vote [lugə̲tiː]

Other Types of Sound Change (Sections 2.2–2.3)

The changes considered so far have all involved segments changing under the influence of nearby, though not necessarily adjacent, segments. However, this is not true of all sound change that occurs in language. There are two other common types of sound change: segmental and auditory.

- **Segmental change.** Segmental change involves a change within a segment itself. Segmental change often involves affricates. Affricates are considered a complex segment, since they consist of a stop and a fricative.

  One common example is given below:

Deaffrication	**Example**
An affricate becomes a fricative by eliminating the stop portion of the affricate.	Old French [t͡s]ent > French [s̲]ent

- **Auditorily based change.** In addition to the articulatory considerations typically involved in sound change, auditory factors can also have an influence.

  One common example is given below:

Substitution	**Example**
One segment is replaced with a similar-sounding segment.	Middle English lau[x̲] > English lau[f̲]

PRACTICE 8.2: Other types of sound change

1. The underlined phones in the following list of words from Lebanese colloquial Arabic are all pronounced as [dʒ] in Modern Standard Arabic. Lebanese Arabic has undergone a second change. Name the process that is responsible.

ʒdiːd	'new'	maʒnuːn	'crazy'
ʒɪbni	'cheese'	rʒaːl	'men'
ʒariːdi	'newspaper'		

2. The Latin word *caput* [k] 'head' became the Old French word *chef* [tʃ] and the modern French word *chef* [ʃ].

    a. List the changes that took place from Latin to modern French, and where possible, name the processes.

    b. The English words *chief* and *chef* were borrowed at different times from French. When in the process was each borrowed?

Phonological Change (Sections 2.4–2.5)

The sound changes described in the previous sections can influence a language's phonological inventory. That is, they can add, eliminate, or rearrange the phonemes within a language.

*   **Phonological splits.** A phonological **split** adds phonemes to a language's phonological inventory. In a phonological split, allophones of the same phoneme come to contrast with each other. This is often caused by a loss of the conditioning environment. That is, sounds that were once predictable are no longer predictable and are, therefore, phonemic.

Consider the following example in the development of English.

Old English:	In Old English, /n/ had two allophones: • [ŋ] occurred before velar stops • [n] occurred elsewhere So a word like *sing* was pronounced as [sɪŋg].
Middle English:	Consonant deletion applied to remove [g] at the end of a word (after a nasal consonant). This created a minimal pair between *sing* now pronounced as [sɪŋ] and *sin* pronounced as [sɪn]. And minimal pairs tell us that sounds contrast. [ŋ] and [n] are now separate phonemes.

This split can be diagrammed as follows:

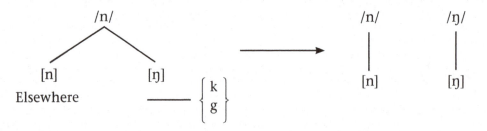

Remember: Spelling often lags behind sound change. We still spell *sing* with the final *g* even though it is now silent. Many silent letters in our English spelling system are a reflection of older pronunciations.

*   **Phonological mergers.** While a phonological split adds phonemes to a language, a phonological **merger** reduces the number of contrasts.

A phonological merger occurred in the development of German. At one time, /s/ and /z/ were contrastive sounds: They could occur in the same environments. Later [z] was only found between vowels. This merger can be diagrammed as follows:

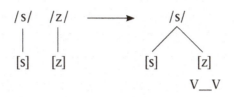

- **Phonological shifts.** A phonological **shift** does not add to or diminish a language's phonemic inventory. Rather, some of the phonemes are reorganized with respect to each other.

  The **Great English Vowel Shift**, beginning in Middle English, is a well-known example of this. The chart below gives the Middle English long vowels before the vowel shift occurred.

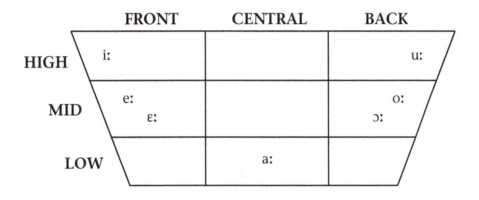

PRACTICE 8.3: The Great English Vowel Shift

Look at the words in Middle English and their pronunciation in Modern English. On the vowel chart that follows the list, draw arrows to show how the pronunciation of the vowel changed. Number each arrow to correspond to the number in the data set. The first one is done for you.

Middle English	Modern English			Middle English	Modern English	
1. [tiːd]	/tajd/	'tide'		5. [goːs]	/gus/	'goose'
2. [nuː]	/naw/	'now'		6. [gɔːst]	/gost/	'ghost'
3. [seːd]	/sid/	'seed'		7. [taːlə]	/tel/	'tale'
4. [sɛː]	/si/	'see'				

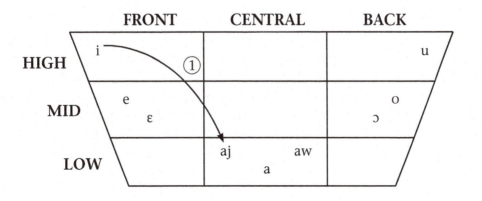

The Great English Vowel Shift probably began with the changes shown in 1 and 2 of the data set. The creation of the diphthongs [aj] and [aw] reduced the number of simple vowels from seven to five. The remaining vowels then shifted upward in their articulation.

Fill in the blanks to summarize the vowel shifts:

1. Long [i] became the diphthong _____ .

2. Long [u] became the diphthong _____ .

3. Long [e] became _____ .

4. Long [ɛ] became _____ .

5. Long [o] became _____ .

6. Long [ɔ] became _____ .

7. Long [a] became _____ .

As the vowels shifted, length was lost. After the Great English Vowel Shift, the long vowels now looked like this:

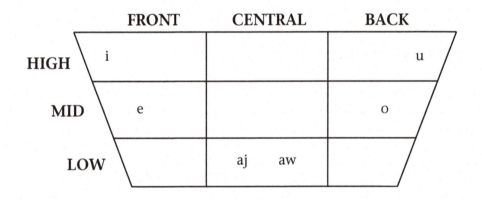

As is evident by comparing the before and after charts, the overall effect of the vowel shift was a reduction in the number of vowels, thereby lessening the crowdedness of the phonological space. Note: Middle English also contained short (lax) vowels, which have not been included on the preceding charts.

Remember: Many of our vowel spellings reflect Middle English pronunciation. For example, *goose* is spelled with *oo* because this orthographic symbol represented [oː]. The word *goose* continues to be spelled this way, even though as a result of the Great English Vowel Shift, Middle English [oː] is now pronounced as [u], changing the pronunciation of goose from Middle English [goːs] to Modern English [gus]. One reason for this mismatch between spelling and pronunciation is that spelling was standardized before the vowels had finished shifting.

Morphological Change (Section 3)

Morphological change affects the structure of words within a language. This type of change involves the addition or loss of affixes. Recall from morphology that affixes are bound morphemes that attach to a base, and either provide grammatical information (inflection) or are used to create new words (derivation).

- **The addition of affixes.** Affixes can be added to a language through

  - borrowing

  - grammaticalization (creating new grammatical forms from lexical forms)

  - fusion (developing an affix from two words that are frequently adjacent to each other)

- **The loss of affixes.** Affixes can also be lost, through

  - lack of use

  - sound change

- **The effect of adding or losing affixes.** The loss of affixes can result in a synthetic morphological system becoming more analytic, while the addition of affixes can result in an analytic morphological system gradually becoming more synthetic. An **analytic language** has very few inflectional affixes. In contrast, a **synthetic language** has many inflectional affixes.

- **Reanalysis and analogy** can also affect the morphological structure of a language. Reanalysis can add new morphemes to a language. Analogy can change an existing morphological pattern. Sometimes, reanalysis is based on a false identification of component morphemes of a word; in such cases, this is known as **folk etymology**.

Practice 8.4: Morphological change

1. Compare the Old English plurals with the Modern English plurals. What happened to the plural morpheme between Old English and Modern English?

Old English	Modern English
handa	hands
gear	years
ēagan	eyes
stānas	stones

2. Look at the data from Welsh. Where did Welsh get the morpheme that is used to reinforce the plurality of a collective noun?

[sɛren]	'star'
[seːr]	'stars' (collectively)
[seːrs]	'stars' (plurally)

3. How did the English forms below arise from the French? What is this process called?

French		English
Bois Brulé	'burnt wood'	Bob Ruly (place name in Michigan)
Purgatoire	'purgatory'	Picketwire (River, in southeastern Colorado)
L'eau Froide	'cold water'	Low Freight (stream in Arkansas)
L'ours	'bear'	Loose (Creek, in Missouri)

4. Examine the data from Latin and Italian. What morphological change has taken place? How has this affected syntax?

Latin

Marcellus Sophiam amat.	'Marcello loves Sophia.'
Marcellus amat Sophiam.	'Marcello loves Sophia.'
Amat Marcellus Sophiam.	'Marcello loves Sophia.'
Sophiam amat Marcellus.	'Marcello loves Sophia.'

Italian

Marcello ama Sophia.	'Marcello loves Sophia.'
Sophia ama Marcello.	'Sophia loves Marcello.'

Syntactic Change (Section 4)

Change can also affect the syntactic component of a language's grammar. Change often affects the word-order patterns found in a language. It can also affect the transformations found within a language.

- **Word order.** Languages can change their basic word-order pattern. One common change involves the change from an SOV (subject-object-verb) order to an SVO (subject-verb-object) order. This is a change that happened in the development of English. English descended from a Germanic language having an SOV order.

- **Inversion.** *Yes-no* questions in English are formed using inversion. In Old English, both main verbs and auxiliary verbs could be inverted. In Modern English, though, only auxiliary verbs can be inverted. Now, any sentence that does not contain an auxiliary must be made into a *yes-no* question using *do*.

PRACTICE 8.5: Syntactic change in English

Here are some sentences from early seventeenth-century English along with their modern counterparts. How were negatives formed then? How does this differ from today's English?

1. They hearkened not to the voice of their father.
   'They did not listen to their father.'

2. Hide it not from me.
   'Do not hide it from me.'

3. Look not on his countenance or on the height of his stature.
   'Do not look at his appearance or height.'

4. If thou save not thy life, tomorrow thou shalt be slain.
   'If you do not save your life, tomorrow you will be killed.'

5. He cometh not to the king's table.
   'He does not come to the king's table' (i.e., he does not eat with the king).

The Effect of Change

Changes can have far-reaching effects. A change that affects the phonology of a language can eventually affect the morphology, which in turn can affect the syntax.

Consider an example (somewhat simplified) of three stages in the development of English:

1. Old English was a highly inflected language. Old English inflectional affixes included:

   - Case: nominative, accusative, dative, genitive
   - Number: singular, dual, plural
   - Person: first, second, third
   - Gender: masculine, feminine, neuter
   - Tense: past, present

   Inflectional affixes were found on pronouns, nouns, articles, adjectives, verbs, etc. As in many inflected languages, Old English had a fairly free word order. Sentences with SVO, VSO, and SOV orders were all used.

2. During Middle English, sound changes started happening in unstressed syllables. These sound changes included three that affected word-final sounds:

   - m → n / _____#
   - n → Ø / _____#
   - a, o, u, i, e → ə / _____#

   These three sound changes affected the inflectional system, since inflectional affixes in Old English were suffixes, and suffixes are typically not stressed. The following examples illustrate the application of the above rules and their effect on the inflectional system.

   <u>Old English</u>   <u>Middle English</u>

   | foxum | > | foxun | > | foxu | > | foxə |
   | helpan | > | helpan | > | helpa | > | helpə |

   As a result of these sound changes, all the affixes became the same: [ə]. Since it was now impossible to tell what information was contained in an affix, the Old English affixes were dropped, and the language became more analytic.

3. But speakers still needed to know what the subject of a sentence was, what the object of a sentence was, and what noun an adjective referred to. To get this information, speakers of English began to:

- rely on prepositions
- rely on fixed word order (SVO)

So sound changes can have drastic effects on a language's development over time.

REMINDER

Just as with phonological rules, sound changes often require an order to their application. For example, the three changes presented in the last section require some ordering. [m] has to first change to [n] before it can be deleted. If this change does not occur first, then [n] would not delete and the affixes would not all become [ə]. (Note that it doesn't matter when the vowel reduction rule applies.)

Lexical Change (Sections 5.1–5.2)

Lexical change involves modifications to the lexicon. There are two main types of lexical change: addition and loss.

Addition of Lexical Items

New lexical items are typically added to a language's vocabulary in one of two ways.

- **Word formation.** Some of the word-formation processes found in the morphology chapter are frequently used to add new words to a language. These new words often fill a lexical gap resulting from technological innovations. Compounding and derivation are frequently used word-formation processes for this purpose, and Old English examples are given in Tables 8.24–8.25 in the text. Acronyms, backformation, blending, clipping, and conversion can also be used to add new words to a language.

- **Borrowing.** As languages come into contact with each other, they often borrow words from each other. There are three types of influences that languages can have on each other.

  - **Substratum influence.** This is the influence of a politically or culturally nondominant language on the dominant language in the area. Typically, the dominant language borrows place names as well as names for unfamiliar objects or items from the nondominant language. English borrowed place names such as Thames, London, and Dover from Celtic.

  - **Superstratum influence.** This is the influence of a politically or culturally dominant language on a nondominant language in the area. For example, Middle English borrowed many words from French, which was the dominant language after the Norman Conquest.

• **Adstratum influence.** This refers to a situation where two languages are in contact, but neither is politically or culturally dominant. Adstratum influence often results in the borrowing of common, everyday words. Such a relationship existed between English and Scandinavian speakers during the Old English period.

Loss of Lexical Items

Words can also be lost from the vocabulary of a language. Loan words, nonloan words, compounds, and derived words can also be lost. The most common reason for the loss of a lexical item is some societal change that has rendered an object, and therefore its name, obsolete. See Table 8.25 in the text for some examples.

PRACTICE 8.6: Lexical change

1. One of the reasons new and borrowed words are interesting is that they reflect a speech community's history—past conflicts, contacts, and advances. For this exercise, you will need to consult a good dictionary that gives etymologies for words. For each of the following words, find out from what language it is derived and when it entered the English language. Try to figure out why or how English added the word to the language.

Word	Origin	When/Why/How Added
1. plaid	_____	_____
2. shepherd	_____	_____
3. cherubim	_____	_____
4. skin	_____	_____
5. residence	_____	_____
6. algebra	_____	_____
7. portico	_____	_____
8. theory	_____	_____
9. moccasin	_____	_____
10. jungle	_____	_____
11. banana	_____	_____
12. automobile	_____	_____
13. boondocks	_____	_____

2. For each recent word, write the word-formation process responsible.

Facebook   _____

BOGO   _____

tase   _____

LOL   _____

spork   _____

app   _____

(to) friend   _____

sudoku   _____

photobomb   _____

dashcam   _____

Semantic Change (Section 5.3)

Along with the addition and loss of lexical items, the meanings of existing words can also change over time. There are seven main types of semantic change. See Tables 8.30–8.32 in the text for examples.

TYPE	DEFINITION
Broadening	The meaning of a word becomes more general or inclusive over time.
Narrowing	The meaning of a word becomes less general or inclusive over time.
Amelioration	The meaning of a word changes to become more positive or favorable.
Pejoration	The meaning of a word changes to become less positive or favorable.
Weakening	The meaning of a word weakens over time.
Semantic Shift	A word loses its former meaning and takes on a new, but related, meaning.
Metaphor	A word with a concrete meaning takes on a more abstract meaning, without losing the original meaning.

PRACTICE 8.7: Semantic change

For each of the following words, identify which of the processes in the preceding table best captures the semantic change that has occurred.

(Language) Word	Earlier meaning	Later meaning	Change
1. (Spanish) *pájaro*	(Latin) 'sparrow'	'bird'	_____
2. (English) *horribly*	'in a manner that creates horror'	'unpleasantly'	_____
3. (Spanish) *casa*	(Latin) 'hut'	'house'	_____
4. (French) *soldat*	'paid person'	'person paid for military service'	_____
5. (Spanish) *ramera*	'innkeeper's wife'	'prostitute'	_____
6. (English) *bless*	(Old English) 'to mark with blood' (for pagan sacrifice)	'to sanctify'	_____
7. (Spanish) *sierra*	'saw' [tool]	'mountain range'	_____
8. (Finnish) *raha*	'animal pelt' > 'pelt used as medium of exchange'	'money'	_____
9. (English) *stud*	'male horse used for breeding'	'good-looking, sexy male'	_____
10. (English) *dilettante*	'devoted amateur with love of a subject'	'dabbler with superficial knowledge of a subject'	_____
11. (English) *starve*	'to die'	'to die from hunger'	_____
12. (Spanish) *calle*	(Latin) 'cattle path'	'street'	_____

Comparative Reconstruction (Sections 7.1–7.2)

By comparing languages with each other, it can be determined whether they are genetically related. **Genetically related languages** are languages that have descended from a common ancestor. Using the **comparative method**, this ancestor can be reconstructed. This is typically done by comparing later forms to determine what the earlier form must have looked like. Although it is possible to reconstruct all aspects of a language's grammar, the focus here is on phonological reconstruction.

Some important terms:

- **Cognates** are phonetically and semantically similar words that have descended from a common source. Cognates are compared to reconstruct what this common source must have looked like.

- A **protolanguage** is a language that has been reconstructed using a comparative method. Written evidence of what this language actually looked like typically doesn't exist.

- A protolanguage consists of **protoforms**. These are the individual reconstructed words of the protolanguage. Protoforms are usually indicated with an asterisk (*).

Some important strategies:

- The **phonetic plausibility strategy** requires that any change posited to account for the differences between the protoform (the ancestor) and the cognates must be phonetically plausible. That is, a sound change that has been found to occur in the course of language development must be able to account for these differences. For our purposes, the sound changes listed under the heading *sequential change* as well as under *segmental* and *auditorily based change* are all plausible.

- The **majority rules strategy** operates in the absence of a phonetically plausible sound change. This strategy states that when no phonetically plausible sound change can be determined, we may reconstruct the segment that occurs in the majority of the cognates. This strategy should be used as a last resort.

PRACTICE 8.8: Reconstructing phonemes

The following problems will give you practice in seeing systematic correspondences among phonemes of different languages and will guide you toward reconstruction of protoforms.

1. **Finno-Ugric: word-initial [k], [h]**

   Examine the first sound in each word of the data set, and fill in the correspondence chart after the data set. The data are in phonetic transcription.
   [ʲ] represents a palatalized sound.
   [ɨ] represents a high central unrounded vowel.
   [y] represents a high front rounded vowel.
   [ø] represents a mid front rounded vowel.
   [ž] represents a voiced alveopalatal fricative.

	Finnish	Hungarian	Udmurt (Votyak)	Gloss
1.	kamara	haːm-	kəm	'peel'
2.	kolme	haːrom	kuinʲm-	'three'
3.	kuole-	hɔl	kul-	'to die'
4.	kusi	huːdʲ	kɨẓ	'urine'
5.	kunta	hɔd	—	'community' (F); 'army' (H)
6.	kæte-	keːz	ki	'hand'
7.	keri	keːr	kur	'(tree-) bark'
8.	kivi	kø	kə	'stone'
9.	kyːnek	kønnj	-kɨlʲi-	'tear' (noun)
10.	kyː	kiːdʲoː	kɨj	'adder' (F); 'snake' (H, U)

Fill in the correspondence chart:

Finnish	Hungarian	Udmurt

What is/are the protoform/s? _____

Why? (Hint: Look at the phonetic environment.) _____

2. **Proto-Algonquian: consonant clusters**

Examine the following data and look for regular alternation patterns in the underlined consonant clusters. Note: None of the languages make a phonemic distinction between voiced and voiceless obstruents. In addition, in Menomini, [s] and [ʃ] are allophones of the same phoneme.

First, sort the data so that you can see the four alternation patterns. Then, write the alternations in the list below the data set.

	Fox	Ojibwa	Menomini	Gloss
1.	kiːʃkahamwa	kiːʃkaʔank	keːskaham	'he chops it through'
2.	netehkoma	nintikkom	neteːhkom	'my louse'
3.	ahteːki	atteːk	aʔtek	'when it is there'
4.	nehtoːːwa	nittoːt	nɛʔtaw	'he kills it'
5.	iʃihtoːwa	iʃittoːt	eseːhtaw	'he makes it so'
6.	neʃkiːʃekwi	niʃkiːnʃik	neskeːhsek	'my eye'
7.	ahkohkwa	akkikk	ahkɛːhkok	'kettle'
8.	mehtekwi	mittik	mɛʔtek	'stick'
9.	aʃkoteːwi	iʃkoteː	eskoːtɛːw	'fire'
10.	noːhkomesa	noːkkomiss	noːhkomɛh	'my grandmother'
11.	poːnihtoːwa	poːnittoːt	poːnehtaw	'he ceases from it'
12.	—	nantottank	natoːhtam	'he listens for it'

The four consonant cluster alternation patterns are:

Fox	Ojibwa	Menomini	Evidence
————	————	————	————————————
————	————	————	————————————
————	————	————	————————————
————	————	————	————————————

Now fill in the chart with the correct pattern beside the protoform:

*PA	Fox	Ojibwa	Menomini
*ʔt			
*ʃk			
*hk			
*ht			

3. **Arabic:** [t], [d], [θ], [ð]

In the following data from Syrian and Iraqi colloquial Arabic, examine the alternations in [t], [d], [θ], and [ð]. First look for regular patterns; then determine what the protoforms were. Fill in the chart to help you. Assume phonetic transcription.

[ɣ] represents a voiced velar fricative.

[ʕ] represents a voiced pharyngeal fricative.

[sˤ] represents a pharyngealized [s].

	Syrian	**Iraqi**	**Gloss**
1.	daftar	daftar	'notebook'
2.	tneːn	θneːn	'two'
3.	ɣada	ɣada	'lunch'
4.	ʔaxad	ʔaxað	'he took'
5.	waʔət	wakɪt	'time'
6.	taːlɛt	θaːlɪθ	'third'
7.	dahab	ðahab	'gold'
8.	ʔaktar	ʔakθar	'more'
9.	maktab	maktab	'office'
10.	haːda	haːða	'this'
11.	tɪsʕa	tɪsʕa	'nine'
12.	duːd	duːd	'worm'
13.	sanduːʔ	sˤanduːg	'box'
14.	matal	maθal	'example'

a. Which of the four sounds does each language have in the following positions? Fill in the chart.

Position	Syrian	Iraqi	Evidence
word-initial			
word-final			
between vowels			
after a consonant			

b. How are Syrian and Iraqi different in the use of the four sounds?

c. What were the protoforms?

d. What phonological changes have taken place to lead to the differences between Syrian and Iraqi? **Remember:** Phonological change can involve splits or mergers.

4. **Ponosakan**

Ponosakan is a nearly extinct language of northeastern Sulawesi in Indonesia. It belongs to the Malayo-Polynesian branch of the Austronesian language family. Languages of Sulawesi belong to a subbranch of Mongondow-Gorontalo languages. In the following exercise, examine the data from Proto Mongondow-Gorontalo (PMoGo) and determine three phonological changes that have occurred in consonants between PMoGo and Ponsakan (Pon).

	*PMoGo	Pon	Gloss
1.	bulawan	bulaan	'gold'
2.	?awak	aak	'body'
3.	kolawag	kolaah	'turmeric'
4.	kawag	kaah	'crow'
5.	tontolawa?	tontolaa?	'spider'
6.	ginawa	ginaa	'breath, breathe'
7.	?ugat	uhat	'vein'
8.	bogas	bohas	'uncooked rice'
9.	?ulag	ulah	'snake'
10.	ba?ag	ba?ah	'loincloth'
11.	dugu?	duhu?	'blood'

What are three changes that have occurred in consonants between PMoGo and Ponsakan? Write each change as a rule:

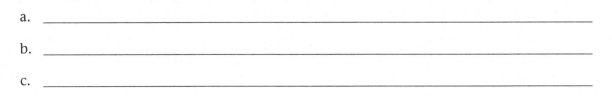

a. _____

b. _____

c. _____

Reconstructing Words in a Protolanguage

We can move from a consideration of specific phonemes to more general reconstruction of words in the protolanguage. We can see it best through an example.

An example:

Reconstruct the protoforms for the data below.

Language A	Language B	Language C
1. hauda	hauta	hauta
2. sav	ʃive	sav

1. Determine the number of sounds that need to be reconstructed. This is straightforward for data set 1 in that all the cognates have the same number of sounds: five. The situation is different in 2. In 2, two of the cognates contain three sounds, and one contains four. If four sounds are reconstructed, then deletion must have occurred in languages A and C. If three sounds are reconstructed, then epenthesis must have occurred in language B. It is more plausible for deletion rather than epenthesis to occur at the end of words. Data set 2, therefore, requires the reconstruction of four sounds.

2. Look for any total correspondences. These are sounds that have not changed; they are the same for all the cognates. Reconstruct these sounds. The protoforms after this step are: *hau?a and *??v?. (The question marks indicate sounds we're not yet sure about.)

3. Examine alternations between the different languages, and determine phonetic plausibility.

   • Data set 1 exhibits an alternation between [t] and [d]. Either [t] or [d] can be reconstructed in the protoform.

      ○ If [d] is reconstructed, then the change from the protoform to the form in languages B and C ([d] > [t]) does not correspond to a sound change. Therefore, this has a low phonetic plausibility.
      ○ If [t] is reconstructed, then the change from the protoform to language A ([t] > [d]) can be explained as an instance of weakening (a voiceless stop weakens to a voiced stop). This has a high phonetic plausibility.
      ○ Reconstruct the change that has the highest phonetic plausibility. The protoform becomes *hauta.

   • Data set 2 exhibits three alternations. First, consider the alternation between [s] and [ʃ].

      ○ If [ʃ] is reconstructed, then the change [ʃ] > [s] in languages A and C has low phonetic plausibility since there is no motivation for it.
      ○ If [s] is reconstructed, then the change [s] > [ʃ] in language B can be explained as palatalization. This has high phonetic plausibility, so [s] is reconstructed.

   Second, consider the presence or absence of a word-final vowel in the cognates. Recall from above that it is more plausible for a sound to delete than be epenthesized in this position. Therefore, [e] is reconstructed.

Third, consider the vowel alternation between [a] and [i].

- ○ If [a] is reconstructed, then the change [a] > [i] occurs in language B.
- ○ If [i] is reconstructed, then the opposite change [i] > [a] occurs in languages A and C.

Neither corresponds to a sound change, so both have a low phonetic plausibility. This strategy, therefore, cannot be used to reconstruct this segment. The protoform, after this step, is *s?ve.

4. If no phonetically plausible sound change could be identified for a sound, then use the majority rules strategy. In data set 2, the alternation between [a] and [i] cannot be accounted for using a sound change; therefore, [a] is reconstructed since it occurs in the majority of the cognates. The protoform becomes *save. Notice that this protoform does not correspond to any of the cognates. This is okay.

5. Put together a summary of the sound changes that have occurred since the different languages split from the protolanguage. Remember that the form you have just reconstructed is older than the cognates from the descendent languages. Both voicing and apocope occurred in the development of language A, while only apocope occurred in the development of language C. Palatalization occurred in the development of language B.

- • Sound changes that tend to occur across languages are often referred to as natural. Sound changes that are phonetically plausible are more natural than those that are not. **Naturalness** is important to think about when doing reconstruction, since language change is regular and systematic.

- • It is also important to think about universal properties of language when doing reconstruction. This is often referred to as **typological plausibility**.

REMINDER

In order to do language reconstruction, you need to be able to identify phonetically plausible sound changes. And in order to do that, you need to know the different types of sequential, segmental, and auditory sound changes. Make sure you are very familiar with them.

PRACTICE 8.9: Reconstructing words

To ease into reconstruction, try a couple of examples from hypothetical languages first. Then move on to real languages for the next exercises.

Each of the following data groups contains some cognate sets. Assume that all the cognates are in phonetic transcription and that all members of the cognate set have the same meaning. Reconstruct the protoforms, and list all the sound changes that have taken place in each language. Remember that for some languages there may be no sound changes, while for others there may be multiple sound changes.

While the data are from hypothetical or highly regularized data, they exemplify processes found in actual languages.

1. **Hypothetical Language Group One**

Language A	Language B	Protoform
1. mũtə	mudo	*_____
2. fumə	vumo	*_____
3. pippon	bipona	*_____
4. nõk	noga	*_____
5. wus	juza	*_____
6. fitə	vido	*_____

Summary of Sound Changes:

Lang A	
Lang B	

Remember: The reconstructed form does not have to be the same as any of the forms found in one of the descendant languages.

2. **Hypothetical Language Group Two**

[x] represents a voiceless velar fricative.
[dz] represents a voiced alveolar affricate.

Language A	Language B	Language C	Language D	Protoform
1. puxa	buga	puka	puk	*_____
2. nizudz	nizuz	nizu	nir	*_____

Summary of Sound Changes:

Lang A	
Lang B	
Lang C	
Land D	

3. **Austronesian**

The Austronesian languages under investigation here are located in southeast Asia. Malay is spoken on the Malay peninsula and is closely related to Chamic languages. Chamic is a branch of the Austronesian language family brought to southeast Asia about two thousand years ago. Written Cham is the written form of Phan Rang Cham, a Chamic language of Vietnam. Tsat is a Chamic language spoken on the Chinese island of Hainan, off the south coast of China.

Your job is to reconstruct the Proto-Austronesian (*PAN) word for each of the words in the data set. Then below, summarize the sound changes.

	Malay	Written Cham	Tsat	Gloss	*PAN
1.	anak	anəʔ	naʔ	'child'	_____
2.	sakit	hakiʔ	kiʔ	'sick, painful'	_____
3.	ikat	ikaʔ	kaʔ	'to tie'	_____
4.	urat	uraʔ	zaʔ	'vein, tendon'	_____

Summary of Sound Changes:

Malay:	
Written Cham:	
Tsat:	Tsat has also developed into a tone language (tones were not shown here). Why do you think Tsat has developed phonemic tones?

4. **German dialects**

The following data are from two dialects of German. Reconstruct the protoforms for each word, and describe the changes that have occurred in the obstruents (stops and fricatives). You may not be able to reconstruct all the vowels accurately based on the amount of data here. Assume phonetic transcription.

[x] represents a voiceless velar fricative.
[pf] represents a voiceless labiodental affricate; it is a single segment.
[ts] represents a voiceless alveolar affricate; it is a single segment.

	Northern dialect	Southern dialect	Gloss	Protoform
1.	maːkə	maxən	'make'	_____
2.	ik	ix	'I'	_____
3.	slaːpə	ʃlaːfən	'sleep'	_____
4.	pʊnt	pfʊnt	'pound'	_____

5. bejtə	bajsən	'bite'	_____
6. dat	das	'that'	_____
7. tuː	tsuː	'to'	_____

Summary of Sound Changes:

Northern dialect:	
Southern dialect:	

Review Exercises

The items below provide a review of various topics covered in this chapter, particularly the history of the English language and comparative reconstruction on the basis of sound change.

1. **The Great English Vowel Shift:** For each of the Middle English words below, state the vowel change that would have occurred as a result of the Great English Vowel Shift, and then give the spelling of the corresponding Modern English word.

	Middle English	Vowel Change	Modern English Word
a.	[noːn]	_____	_____
b.	[liːfə]	_____	_____
c.	[sweːt]	_____	_____
d.	[bɔːst]	_____	_____
e.	[guːn]	_____	_____

2. **Changes in English since Shakespeare:** The quotations on the left are all from Shakespeare. Some parts of the quotations are in boldface. To the right are modern "translations" of the boldfaced elements. Compare the early Modern English of Shakespeare's time with contemporary English in:

    - the word order of statements (think in terms of subject, verb, and object)
    - the word order in negatives
    - the word order in questions
    - the use of pronouns and verbs that agree with them

    Examine the data and answer the questions after the data.

    1. From *Romeo and Juliet:*

    Romeo: By a name
    I know not how to tell thee who I am.   I do not know how to tell you
    My name, dear saint, is hateful to myself
    Because it is an enemy **to thee.**   to you
    Had I it written, I would tear the word.   If I had written it

    2. From *Hamlet:*

    Ghost: But, howsoever **thou pursuest** this act,   you pursue
    Taint not thy mind, nor let thy soul contrive   Do not taint your mind or let your soul contrive

    Against thy mother aught.   Anything against your mother.

    3. From *Macbeth:*

    Macb: I have done the deed. **Didst thou not   Did you not hear/Didn't you hear
         hear** a noise?
    Lady: I heard the owl scream and the crickets
         cry. **Did not you speak?**   Did you not speak?/Didn't you speak?

    4. From *Macbeth:*

    Macb: **Saw you** the weird sisters?   Did you see
         . . . **Came they not** by you?   Did they not come/Didn't they come

    a. What is the order of subject (S), verb (V), and object (O) in English today?

        What order of S,V, and O did Shakespeare use? Did he always use the same order? Cite evidence.

    b. Where do we put the negator *not* in sentences today?

        Where did Shakespeare put *not*? Did he always put it in the same place? Cite evidence.

What does Shakespeare's use of negation suggest about the time of the change in negation patterns?

c. What is the word order of *yes-no* questions in English today?

What word order did Shakespeare use? Did he always use the same order? Cite evidence.

d. What pronouns did Shakespeare use that have fallen out of use today?

What verb forms have fallen out of use along with these pronouns?

3. **Sound changes in Romance:** For the following languages, which have all descended from Latin, describe the changes that have taken place in consonants and in vowels on the edges of words. Given the small data set, you will not be able to account for every change, especially in internal vowels; however, you should be able to detail the process of change, including intermediate steps. Note: Latin is the protolanguage here, so you are not expected to reconstruct it but merely to list changes that have occurred.
[ɥ] represents a palatal glide articulated with rounded lips.
[β] represents a voiced bilabial fricative.

	Latin	Italian	Spanish	French	Gloss
1.	spina	[spina]	[espina]	[epin]	'thorn'
2.	scutella	[skodɛlla]	[eskuðija]	[ekɥɛl]	'bowl'
3.	scribere	[skrivere]	[eskriβir]	[ekriːr]	'write'
4.	schola	[skwɔla]	[eskuela]	[ekɔl]	'school'

Summary of changes from Latin to:

Italian:

Spanish:

French:

4. **Austronesian:** Reconstruct the protoform for each word in the data set. Before you reconstruct the protoforms, though, fill in the correspondence chart to help you focus on some of the systematic differences. The column for Tagalog has already been filled in for you.

Note: Tagalog is spoken in the Philippines. Rapanui is spoken on Easter Island.

	Tagalog	Javanese	Fijian	Samoan	Rapanui	Gloss
1.	lima	limo	lima	lima	rima	'five'
2.	manok	manuʔ	manumanu	manu	manu	'bird'
3.	mata	moto	mata	mata	mata	'eye'
4.	tēŋa	—	daliŋa	taliŋa	tariŋa	'ear'
5.	lāŋit	laŋit	laŋi	laŋi	raŋi	'sky'
6.	bato	watu	vatu	—	—	'stone'
7.	kūto	kutu	kutu	ʔutu	kutu	'head louse'

Correspondence table

	Tagalog	Javanese	Fijian	Samoan	Rapanui
word-final	t				
word-final	k				
word-initial	t				
word-initial	b				
word-final	a				
2nd syllable	o				

Now write the protoforms for each word, and beside each reconstruction, note the rationale for your reconstruction. (Note: the protolanguage did not have long vowels.)

Gloss	Protoform	Rationale
1. 'five'	*_____	_____
2. 'bird'	*_____	_____
3. 'eye'	*_____	_____
4. 'ear'	*_____	_____
5. 'sky'	*_____	_____
6. 'stone'	*_____	_____
7. 'head louse'	*_____	_____

☑ **RECAP**

Make sure you know the following material. (See also the Key Terms at the end of Chapter 8 in the main text.)

- the nature and causes of language change
- how change spreads through a language and its speakers
- the different types of sound change
- the different types of morphological change
- the different types of syntactic change
- the different types of lexical change
- the different types of semantic change
- how to reconstruct protoforms and identify sound changes
- the role of naturalness and typology in language change

Questions? Problems?

Sources

The following references provide background information for exercises that are new to the American edition of the *Study Guide.*

Chapter 2

Facial diagrams. Adapted from:
Ladefoged, Peter. 1982. *A Course in Phonetics.* 2nd ed. San Diego: Harcourt Brace Jovanovich.

Chapter 3

Practice 3.1, Cofan. Data from:
Borman, M. B. 1962. "Cofan phonemes." In *Ecuadorian Indian Languages.* Edited by Benjamin Elson. Norman: SIL of the University of Oklahoma, 45–59.

Practice 3.4, #3, Japanese. Data derived from a number of sources:
Fromkin, Victoria, and Robert Rodman. 1993. *An Introduction to Language.* 5th ed. New York: Harcourt Brace, 267.
Okada, Hideo. 1999. "Japanese." In *Handbook of the International Phonetic Association.* Cambridge: Cambridge University Press, 117–119.
Takahashi, Naoko. Personal communication.

Practice 3.5, #1, Sawai. Data from:
Whisler, Ronald. 1992. "Phonology of Sawai." In *Phonological Studies of Four Languages of Malaku.* Edited by Donald Burquest and Wyn Laidig. Dallas: SIL, 7–32.

Practice 3.5, #2, Biblical Hebrew. Data from:
Holladay, William L. 1971. *A Concise Hebrew and Aramaic Lexicon of the Old Testament.* Leiden: Brill.
Weingreen, J. 1959. *A Practical Grammar for Biblical Hebrew.* 2nd ed. Oxford: Clarendon.

Practice 3.5, #3, German. Data from:
Cowan, W., and J. Rakušan. 1998. *Source Book for Linguistics.* Amsterdam: John Benjamins, 7, 31.
Kohler, Klaus. 1999. "German." In *Handbook of the International Phonetic Association.* Cambridge: Cambridge University Press, 86–89.
Kurtz, John W., and Heinz Politzer. 1966. *German: A Comprehensive Course for College Students.* New York: W.W. Norton, 8.

Practice 3.5, #4, Zinacantec Tzotzil. Data from:
www.zapata.org/Tzotzil/Audio/index.html.
www.zapata.org/Tzotzil/Chapters/Chapt1.html.

Practice 3.6, #2, Siona. Data from:

Wheeler, Alva, and Margaret Wheeler. 1962. "Siona Phonemics (Western Tucanoan)." In *Studies in Ecuadorian Indian Languages*. Edited by Benjamin Elson. Norman: SIL of the University of Oklahoma, 96–111.

Practice 3.6, #3, Inuktitut. Data from:

www.shindale.com/inuktitut. *Note:* This link no longer connects to Inuktitut material.

Practice 3.6, #5, Yakut. Adapted from:

O'Grady, William, Michael Dobrovolsky, and Mark Aronoff. 1989. *Contemporary Linguistics*. 1st ed. New York: St. Martin's Press, 85.

Practice 3.6, #6, Italian. Data from:

Love, Catherine E. 1985. *Collins Concise Italian Dictionary*. London: Collins.

Practice 3.7, #1–2, Mon. Data from:

Zandt, Deanna. "Phonemes." Accessed at www.albany.edu/anthro/fac/broadwell/mon/.

Practice 3.7, #3, Hausa. Data from:

"Hausa consonant sounds." Accessed 2016 through aflang.humnet.ucla.edu/Hausa/hausa .html.

Schuh, Russell G., and Lawan D. Yalwa. 1999. "Hausa." In *Handbook of the International Phonetic Association*. Cambridge: Cambridge University Press, 90-95.

Practice 3.10, #1a, Japanese. Data from:

Okada, Hideo. 1999. "Japanese." In *Handbook of the International Phonetic Association*. Cambridge: Cambridge University Press, 117–119.

Practice 3.10, #1b, Akan. Data from:

Dolphyne, Florence Abena. 1988. *The Akan (Twi-Fante) Language: Its Sound System and Tonal Structure*. Accra: Ghana Universities Press.

Practice 3.10, #1c, Bemba. Data from:

Spitulnik, Debra, Josh Walker, and Hal Odden. "Phonology: Bemba." Accessed 2009 at www.linguistics.emory.edu/POLYGLOT/phonology.html#bemba.

Practice 3.10, #1d, Persian. Data from:

Majidi, Mohammad-Reza, and Elmar Ternes. 1999. In *Handbook of the International Phonetic Association*. Cambridge: Cambridge University Press, 124–125.

Some glosses have been supplied by Jackie Khorassani, personal communication. Syllable structure constraints are given in: Windfuhr, Gernot. 1990. "Persian." In *The World's Major Languages*. Edited by Bernard Comrie. New York: Oxford University Press, 529.

Practice 3.11, #1, Korean. Data from:

Lee, Hyun Bok. 1999. "Korean." In *Handbook of the International Phonetic Association*. Cambridge: Cambridge University Press, 120–123.

Some glosses supplied by Zeping Bai and Sunwoo Choi, personal communication.

Practice 3.11, #2, Larike. Data from:

Laidig, Carol. 1992. "Segments, Syllables, and Stress in Larike." In *Phonological Studies of Four Languages of Malaku*. Edited by Donald Burquest and Wyn Laidig. Dallas: SIL, 67–126.

Practice 3.14, #1, Polish. Data from:

Cohn, Abigail. 2001. "Phonology." In *The Handbook of Linguistics*. Edited by Mark Aronoff and Janie Rees-Miller. Oxford: Blackwell, 206–209.

Practice 3.14, #3, Fante. Data from:

Dolphyne, Florence Abena. 1988. *The Akan (Twi-Fante) Language: Its Sound Systems and Tonal Structure*. Accra: Ghana Universities Press.

Practice 3.15, #2, Standard Spanish and Andalusian Spanish. Data from:

Danford, Richard. Personal communication.

Review Exercise, #1, French. Data from:

Fagyal, Zsuzsanna, Douglas Kibbee, and Fred Jenkins. 2006. *French: A Linguistic Introduction*. Cambridge: Cambridge University Press.

French pronunciations available through www.wordreference.com.

Isabelli, Casilde. "French Phonological Rules." Accessed 2011 at www.unr.edu/cla/fll/people /faculty/Pages/isabelli/FLL455655?455-7.pdf.

Review Exercise, #2, Kpelle. Data from:

Welmers, Wm. E. 1973. *African Language Structures*. Berkeley: University of California Press, 30.

Review Exercise, #3, Ḥausa. Data from:

"Hausa." Accessed 2016 through aflang.humnet.ucla.edu/Hausa/hausa.html.

Schuh, Russell G., and Lawan D. Yalwa. 1999. "Hausa." In *Handbook of the International Phonetic Association*. Cambridge: Cambridge University Press, 90–95.

Review Exercise, #4, Bemba. Data from:

Spitulnik, Debra, and Mubanga Kashoki. 1998. "Bemba: A Brief Linguistic Profile." Accessed at www.emory.edu/COLLEGE/ANTHROPOLOGY/FACULTY/ANTDS/Bemba/profile.html.

Review Exercise, #5, Syrian Arabic. Data from:

Cowell, Mark W. 1964. *A Reference Grammar of Syrian Arabic*. Washington, DC: Georgetown University Press, 6–7.

Stowasser, Karl, and Moukhtar Ani. 1964. *A Dictionary of Syrian Arabic*. Washington, DC: Georgetown University Press.

Review Exercise, #6, Mandarin. Data from:

Sun, Chaofen. 2006. *Chinese: A Linguistic Introduction*. Cambridge: Cambridge University Press.

Review Exercise, #7, Brazilian Portuguese. Data from:

Perini, Mário A. 2002. *Modern Portuguese: A Reference Grammar*. New Haven: Yale University Press, 18.

Chapter 4

Practice 4.12, #3, French and German. Data from:

Fagan, Sarah. 2009. *German: A Linguistic Introduction*. Cambridge: Cambridge University Press.

Fagyal, Zsuzsanna, Douglas Kibbee, and Fred Jenkins. 2006. *French: A Linguistic Introduction*. Cambridge: Cambridge University Press.

Practice 4.13, #1, Kisar. Data from:

Christensen, John, and Sylvia Christensen. 1992. "Kisar Phonology." In *Phonological Studies of Four Languages of Malaku*. Edited by Donald Burquest and Wyn Laidig. Dallas: SIL, 33–65.

Practice 4.13, #2, Kiswahili. Data from:

Erikson, Helen, and Marianne Gustafsson. "Kiswahili Grammar Notes." Accessed 2009 at https://kamusi.org/content/noun-classes.

"Kiswahili: Lesson 6 Nouns—Singular and Plural." Accessed 2009 at victorian.fortunecity .com/louvre/88/swahili/lessons6.htm.

Practice 4.13, #3, Toba Batak. Data from:

Crowhurst, Megan. 1998. "*Um* Infixation and Prefixation in Toba Batak." *Language* 74, no. 3: 595.

Practice 4.13, #4, Danish. Data from:

"DK Headlines: Learn Danish." 2005. Accessed at www.dkheadlines.com/learndanish.htm #grammar.

Madsen, John. 1998–2005. "Danish Grammar." Accessed at www.hjem.tele2adsl.dk /johnmadsen/Danish.

Practice 4.14, #1, Bahasa Indonesian. Data from:

"Tata Bahasa: Indonesian Grammar." Seasite Indonesia. Accessed 2005 at www.seasite.niu.edu /Indonesia/TataBahasa.

Practice 4.14, #2, Turkish. Data from:

Bender, Byron. Accessed through http://www2.hawaii.edu/~bender/toc.html.

Lewis, G. L. 1953. *Teach Yourself Turkish*. London: The English Universities Press.

Practice 4.14, #3, Classical Nahuatl. Data from:

Jordan, D. K. 1997. "Inadequate Nahuatl Reference Grammar" and "Nahuatl Lessons." Accessed through http://weber.ucsd.edu/~dkjordan/nahuatl.

Karttunen, Frances. 1983. *An Analytical Dictionary of Nahuatl*. Austin: University of Texas Press, xxvi–xxvii.

Practice 4.15, #2, Turkish. Data from:

O'Grady, William, Michael Dobrovolsky, and Mark Aronoff. 1997. *Contemporary Linguistics*. 3rd ed. New York: St. Martin's Press, 242–243.

Practice 4.15, #3, Dutch. Data from:

King, Peter, and Margaretha King. 1958. *Concise Dutch and English Dictionary*. London: Teach Yourself Books, Hodder and Stoughton.

www.sr.net/srnet/InfoSurinam/dutch.html.

Review Exercise, #1, Ancient Egyptian. Data from:

Allen, James P. 2000. *Middle Egyptian: An Introduction to the Language and Culture of Hieroglyphs*. Cambridge: Cambridge University Press, 36–37.

Review Exercise, #2, Luganda. Data from:

www.buganda.com/ggulama.htm#noun.

Review Exercise, #4, Twi. Data from:

Dolphyne, Florence Abena. 1988. *The Akan (Twi-Fante) Language: Its Sound System and Tonal Structure*. Accra: Ghana Universities Press, 84–90.

Yeboa-Dankwa, J. 2008. *Basic Twi for Learners (Asante)*, rev. ed. Trans. by Patricia Kyeremateng Berchie. Accra: Sebewie Publishers, 37.

Review Exercise, #6, Iraqi Arabic. Data from:

Erwin, Wallace. 2004. *A Short Reference Grammar of Iraqi Arabic*. Washington, DC: Georgetown University Press, 84–88.

Chapter 6

Practice 6.3, #2, Menomini. Data from:

Bloomfield, Leonard. 1962. *The Menomini Language.* Edited by Charles F. Hockett. New Haven: Yale University Press.

Practice 6.3, #3, Kiswahili. Data from:

Erickson, Helen, and Marianne Gustafsson. "Kiswahili Grammar Notes: Nouns." Accessed at www.cis.yale.edu:80/swahili/grammar/Noun_Classes.htm.

"Kiswahili: Lesson 6 nouns." Acccessed 2009 at victorian.fortunecity.com/louvre/88/Swahili /lessons6.htm.

Practice 6.3, #4, German. Data from:

Buckley, R. W. 1965. *Living German.* London: Hodder and Stoughton, 75–77.

Review Exercise, #3, Burmese. Data from:

Ladefoged, Peter, and Ian Maddieson. 1996. *The Sounds of the World's Languages.* Cambridge, MA: Blackwell, 69.

Chapter 7

Practice 7.3, #2, Bulgarian. Data from:

Ternes, Elmar, and Tatjana Vladimirova-Buhtz. 1999. "Bulgarian." In *Handbook of the International Phonetic Association.* Cambridge: Cambridge University Press, 55–57.

Practice 7.5, #2, Persian (Farsi). Data from:

Majidi, Mohammad Reza, and Elmar Ternes. 1999. "Persian (Farsi)." In *Handbook of the International Phonetic Association.* Cambridge: Cambridge University Press, 124–125.

Practice 7.5, #3, Hungarian. Data from:

Szende, Tamás. 1999. "Hungarian." In *Handbook of the International Phonetic Association.* Cambridge: Cambridge University Press,104–107.

Practice 7.6, #1–2, Various languages. Data from:

Comrie, Bernard (ed.). 1990. *The World's Major Languages.* New York: Oxford University Press.

Review Exercise #1, Consonants. Data from:

Lindskoog, John N., and Ruth M. Brend. 1962. "Cayapa Phonemics." In *Studies in Ecuadorian Indian Languages.* Edited by Benjamin Elson. Norman, OK: SIL.

Review Exercise #2, Vowels. Data from:

Majidi, Mohammad Reza, and Elmar Ternes. 1999. "Persian (Farsi)." In *Handbook of the International Phonetic Association.* Cambridge: Cambridge University Press, 124–125.

Review Exercise, #3, Word order. Data from:

Comrie, Bernard (ed.). 1990. *The World's Major Languages.* New York: Oxford University Press.

Davis, Philip. 2008. "Chapter 8 Focus: Warao and Urarina." Accessed 2016 at www.owlnet .rice.edu/~pwd/index.html.

Keenan, Edward. 2014. "The syntax of Subject-Final Languages." In *Syntactic Typology: Studies in the Phenomenology of Language.* Edited by Winfred Lehmann. Accessed 2016 at www.utexas.edu/cola/centers/lrc/books/type06.html.

Review Exercise #4, Lakhota. Data from:

Buechel, Eugene. 1939. *A Grammar of Lakota*. St. Francis, SD: Rosebud Educational Society.

Karol, Joseph S., and Stephen L. Rozman (eds.). 1997. *Everyday Lakota: An English-Sioux Dictionary for Beginners*. 2nd ed. St. Francis, SD: Rosebud Educational Society.

Chapter 8

Practice 8.1, #6–15. Data from:

Campbell, Lyle. 2004. *Historical Linguistics: An Introduction*. Cambridge, MA: MIT Press, 27–49, 302.

Practice 8.4, #1, English. Data from:

Arlotto, Anthony. 1972. *Introduction to Historical Linguistics*. Lanham, MD: University Press of America, 132.

Practice 8.4, #2, Welsh. Data from:

Weinreich, Uriel. 1968. *Languages in Contact*. The Hague: Mouton, 32.

Practice 8.4, #3, Folk etymology. Data from:

Mencken, H. L. 1963 [1951]. *The American Language: An Inquiry into the Development of English in the United States*. 4th ed. Edited by Raven I. McDavid. New York: Alfred A. Knopf, 648–649.

Practice 8.4, #4, Latin and Italian. Data from:

Arlotto, Anthony. 1972. *Introduction to Historical Linguistics*. Lanham, MD: University Press of America, 151–152.

Practice 8.5, Seventeenth-century English. Data from:

All sentences from the book of I Samuel in the King James Version of the Bible.

Practice 8.7. Data from:

Campbell, Lyle. 2004. *Historical Linguistics: An Introduction*. Cambridge, MA: MIT Press, 254–264.

Practice 8.8, #1, Finno-Ugric. Data from:

Campbell, Lyle. 2004. *Historical Linguistics: An Introduction*. Cambridge, MA: MIT Press, 148–155.

Practice 8.8, #2, Proto-Algonquian. Data from:

Bloomfield, Leonard. 1946. "Algonquian." In *Linguistic Structures of Native America*. Edited by Harry Hoijer. New York: Viking Fund Publications in Anthropology, no. 6, 85–129.

Practice 8.8, #3, Syrian and Iraqi Arabic. Data from:

Clarity, Beverly E., Karl Stowasser, and Ronald Wolfe. 1964. *A Dictionary of Iraqi Arabic*. Washington, DC: Georgetown University Press.

Stowasser, Karl, and Moukhtar Ani. 1964. *A Dictionary of Syrian Arabic*. Washington, DC: Georgetown University Press.

Practice 8.8, #4, Ponosakan. Data from:

Lobel, Jason William. 2015. "Ponosakan: A Dying Language of Northeastern Sulawesi." *Oceanic Linguistics* 54.2: 396–435.

Practice 8.9, #3, Austronesian. Data from:

Thurgood, Graham. 1996. "Language contact and the directionality of internal drift: The development of tones and registers in Chamic." *Language* 72.1: 21.

Practice 8.9, #4, German dialects. Data from:

Bloomfield, Leonard. 1984 [1933]. *Language*. Chicago: University of Chicago Press, 342.

Review Exercise, #3, Romance. Data from:

Bloomfield, Leonard. 1984 [1933]. *Language*. Chicago: University of Chicago Press, 335.

Collins Concise Italian Dictionary. 1985. Glasgow: William Collins.

Danford, Richard. Personal communication.

Review Exercise, #4, Austronesian. Data from:

Bellwood, Peter. 2007. *Prehistory of the Indo-Malaysian Archipelago*, 3rd ed. Canberra: Australian National University Press. Table 4.1. Accessed at http://epress.anu.edu.au/pima /pdf/ch04.pdf.

Answer Key

Chapter 1

Practice 1.1

1–2. Possible sentences include:
   The early bird catches every worm.
   Every early bird catches the worm.
   Every bird catches the early worm.

3. Examples of unacceptable sentences:
   Worm early the bird catches every.
   Bird every early worm the catches.

4. One possible answer is that words must be in a specific order in a sentence; e.g., the subject comes before the verb, and the object follows the verb; adjectives come before the nouns they modify.

Practice 1.2

1. Possible English words: b, d, e, h
2. Possible English words: b, d
3. Possible English sentences: b, d, e

Practice 1.3

1. All are examples of prescriptive grammar.
2. a. The first is prescriptive, the second descriptive.
   b. The first is prescriptive, the second descriptive.
   c. The first is descriptive, the second prescriptive.
   d. The first is prescriptive, the second descriptive.

Review Exercise

a. 4 (answer supplied in text)
b. 1   c. 3   d. 2   e. 4   f. 4   g. 3   h. 2   i. 3   j. 4   k. 1

Chapter 2

Practice 2.1

1. Diphthongs are counted as single sounds.

    a. 3   d. 6
    b. 3   e. 3
    c. 5   f. 4

2. a. The letters *th* represent one sound.
    b. Three sounds are represented: [t], [θ], and [ð].
    c. One sound in *sung* [ŋ].
       Two sounds in *hunger* [ŋ] + [g]
    d. Depending on dialect, the letter *i* may represent four sounds in these words: [ɪ], [aj], [i], and [ə].
    e. *kite:* ache, architect, choir, common, kin, piccolo, queen
       choke: arch, batch, cello, chain, each
       There is not a one-to-one correspondence of sound and symbol.

Practice 2.2

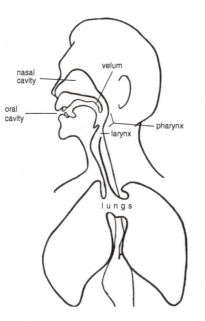

Practice 2.3

1. consonant (answer supplied in text)
2. vowel
3. consonant
4. glide
5. consonant
6. glide
7. vowel
8. consonant

Practice 2.4

1. labial sounds (answer supplied in text)
2. labiodental sounds
3. alveolar sounds
4. alveopalatal sounds
5. palatal sounds

6. velar sounds
7. uvular sounds
8. pharyngeal sounds
9. laryngeal sounds
10. glottal sounds

Practice 2.5

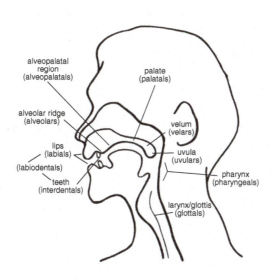

Practice 2.6

		GLOTTAL STATE	PLACE OF ARTICULATION							
			Bilabial	Labiodental	Interdental	Alveolar	Alveopalatal	Palatal	Velar	Glottal
M A N N E R O F A R T I C U L A T I O N	Stop	voiceless	p			t			k	ʔ
		voiced	b			d			g	
	Fricative	voiceless		f	θ	s	ʃ			h
		voiced		v	ð	z	ʒ			
	Affricate	voiceless					tʃ			
		voiced					dʒ			
	Nasal	voiced	m			n			ŋ	
	Liquid a. lateral	voiced				l				
	b. retroflex	voiced				ɹ				
	Glide	voiced	w					j	w	

Practice 2.7

1. a. [θ]
   b. [ʃ]
   c. [n]

   d. [w] or [ʍ]
   e. [f]
   f. [k]

2. a. [f]
   b. [ŋ]
   c. [s]

   d. [θ]
   e. [m]
   f. [s]

Practice 2.8

Words with aspirated voiceless stops:　2, 4, 6

Practice 2.9

1. Note: The distribution of clear and dark *l* varies according to dialect. In one dialect, clear *l* occurs at the beginning of stressed syllables and dark *l* elsewhere. The answers here reflect this dialect.
   Clear *l* is pronounced in:　a, c, e
   Dark *l* is pronounced in:　b, d, f
2. Syllabic liquid or nasal in:　b, d, e, f

Practice 2.10

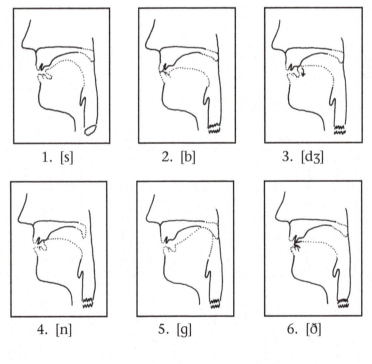

1. [s]　　　2. [b]　　　3. [dʒ]

4. [n]　　　5. [g]　　　6. [ð]

Practice 2.11

1. [k]
2. [m]

3. [z]
4. [θ]

5. [f]
6. [d]

Practice 2.12

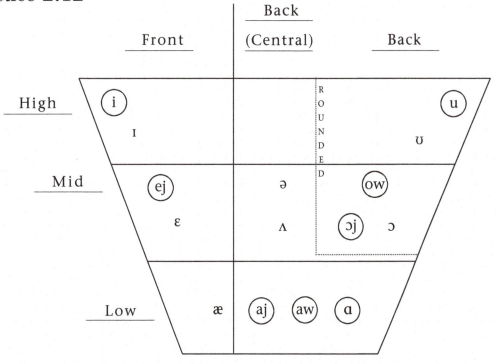

Practice 2.13

1. [u]
2. [aj]
3. [i]
4. [ɑ]
5. [ɪ]
6. [ʊ]

Practice 2.14

1. [æ̃]
2. [ɛ]
3. [ɔ]
4. [ĩ]

Practice 2.15

1. [kɹæft]
2. [saj]
3. [hɛlθ]
4. [bejʒ]
5. [fɹɔg], [fɹɑg]
6. [pʰædl̩]
7. [ejndʒl̩]
8. [ɹitʃ]
9. [tʰejp]
10. [vejg]
11. [ɹustɹ̩]
12. [ɪnstɛd]
13. [bɑɾm̩]
14. [tʃɚtʃ]
15. [θɔt], [θɑt]
16. [hæd]
17. [ɛgzɪt], [ɛksɪt]
18. [ʃʊgɹ̩]
19. [junɪt]
20. [kwɛstʃn̩]

Practice 2.16

1. [kʰi]
2. [du], [dju]
3. [lowf]
4. [mejd]
5. [tʃiz]
6. [ejt]
7. [wiz], [ʍiz]
8. [θɹu]
9. [bown]
10. [ist]
11. [bejbi]
12. [θɹow]

Practice 2.17 (Note: Answers are subject to dialectal variation.)

1. [tʃɪɹ], [tʃiɹ]
2. [kʰɑɹ]
3. [sɚ]
4. [ɔɹ], [oɹ]
5. [hɑɹt]
6. [ʃɑɹp]
7. [ðɛɹ]
8. [stɑɹ]
9. [hɚ]
10. [hɔɹs], [hoɹs]
11. [hɑɹd]
12. [ʃɚt]
13. [tʃɛɹ], [tʃejɹ]
14. [skɔɹ], [skoɹ]
15. [flɔɹ], [floɹ]
16. [kʰɔɹs], [kʰoɹs]
17. [hɑɹm]
18. [θwɔɹt]

Practice 2.18 (Note: Numbers 6, 13, 14 will be different for raising dialects.)

1. [vɔjs]
2. [awɾ]
3. [ajz]
4. [ʃejkɪŋ]
5. [pɹawl]
6. [najft]
7. [tɹejn]
8. [ɔjli]
9. [pɹajz]
10. [saj]
11. [kɹow]
12. [dawn]
13. [bajsɪkl̩]
14. [gowt]
15. [ɛmbɹɔjdɾ]
16. [lejzi]
17. [θɹown]
18. [dʒɔjnt]

Practice 2.19 (Note: Pronunciation of schwa is subject to dialectal variation.)

1. [slʌdʒ]
2. [kwɑləɹi]
3. [lʌk]
4. [nowɹəs]
5. [θʌndɾ]
6. [bəhejv]
7. [ɛmfəsɪs]
8. [ənawns]
9. [hʌŋ]
10. [ʌvn̩]
11. [stʌf]
12. [ʌndɚstænd]

Practice 2.20

1. leisure
2. axe
3. worthy
4. once
5. shade
6. shy
7. sweet
8. tube
9. choice
10. mutton
11. pipe
12. soften
13. phony
14. statue
15. square

Practice 2.21

1. a. voiced (oral) stops (answer supplied in text)
   b. voiced consonants
   c. strident consonants
   d. voiced sonorant consonants
   e. back vowels
   f. lax front vowels

2. a. m: fricatives;   ð: labials
   b. n: oral stops;   g: alveolar consonants;   t: voiced consonants
   c. ɪ: back vowels or tense vowels

Practice 2.22 (Note: There may be dialectal variation in vowels and syllabic consonants.)

1. [ˈskɹɪnd]
2. [dɪsˈkʰʌvɾ]
3. [ɛkˈsplowʒn̩]
4. [ˈdʒinjəs]
5. [mækəˈɹowni]
6. [ˈdupləkət] or [ˈduplə̩kʰejt]
7. [ˈdɪktejt] or [dɪkˈtʰejt]
8. [ˈɑkjəpajd]
9. [ɪnˈfɔɹməɹɪv]
10. [ajˈdɑlətɹi]

Practice 2.23

1. metathesis
2. assimilation (voicing, manner)
3. epenthesis
4. deletion, nasalization (of the vowel)
5. dissimilation
6. epenthesis

Review Exercises

1. a. The lungs provide the air necessary for making speech sounds.
   b. The larynx is responsible for different glottal states such as voicing.
   c. The velum is one place of articulation in the oral cavity. Also, opening and closing the velum allows or prevents air from passing through the nasal cavity, creating nasal or oral sounds.

2. a. [ʔ]
   b. [i]
   c. [m]
   d. [f]

3. a. low front unrounded lax vowel
   b. voiceless velar stop
   c. (voiced) palatal glide
   d. mid back (or central) unrounded lax vowel

4. a. vocal tract
   b. sound classes
   c. articulatory descriptions
   d. places of articulation
   e. American English consonants
   f. aspiration
   g. facial diagrams
   h. American English vowels
   i. segments
   j. transcription
   k. shared phonetic properties
   l. suprasegmentals
   m. articulatory processes

5. Note: There may be dialectal variations. Vowels in unstressed syllables may also vary.

   1. [dejz]
   2. [zɪɹɑks], [ziɹɑks]
   3. [gɛs]
   4. [jɛlow]
   5. [mɛɭ]
   6. [junəsajkl̩]
   7. [ɛkstɪŋgwɪʃ]
   8. [pʰapjəlɹ]
   9. [ajsəlejt]
   10. [fɹajtn̩], [fɹaj?n̩]
   11. [ædʒɪtʰejt]
   12. [ɹowst]
   13. [θiætɹɪkl̩]
   14. [baɹgn̩]
   15. [məʃin]
   16. [səɹawndəd]
   17. [kʰastjum]
   18. [pʰandɹ]
   19. [tʰajmtʰejbl̩]
   20. [jufəmɪzm̩]
   21. [nowm]
   22. [pɪnstɹajps]
   23. [mæskjəlɪn]
   24. [pɹɛʃəs]
   25. [fɔɹmjələ]
   26. [kʰa’mədi]
   27. [gɹædʒuejt], [gɹædʒuɪt]
   28. [ɹɹɪgejt]
   29. [ʌnfɔɹgɪvəbl̩]
   30. [kʰɔld], [kʰald]

6. a. epenthesis
   b. deletion, nasalization
   c. epenthesis, voicing
   d. deletion, epenthesis
   e. metathesis

Chapter 3

Practice 3.1

1. minimal pair
2. near-minimal pair
3. minimal pair
4. neither

5. minimal pair
6. near-minimal pair
7. neither: This looks like a minimal pair, but the one segment that is different does not make a difference in meaning.

Practice 3.2 (Sample answers are given; answers will vary.)

1. (answer supplied in text)
2. tuck: duck   wrote: rode
3. cut: gut   buck: bug
4. fine: vine   safe: save
5. sip: zip   bus: buzz
6. more: nor   sum: sun
7. red: led   litter: little
8. tank: thank   bat: bath
9. cheer: jeer   batch: badge
10. pine: fine   cup: cuff

Practice 3.3

1. a. [pʰ] occurs word-initially and at the beginning of a stressed syllable.
   [p˺] occurs before a consonant and word-finally.
   [p] occurs after [s] and at at the beginning of an unstressed syllable.
   b. [hɪpi], [pʰɑt], [lɛp˺t]

2. a. [l] occurs in the onset of a stressed syllable and word-initially.
   [ɫ] occurs right after a stressed vowel and word-finally after a vowel.
   [l̩] occurs word-finally after a consonant (in an unstressed syllable).
   b. [slajd], [miɫ], [hæsl̩]

Practice 3.4

1. Oneida: [z] occurs between vowels (V___V).
                  [s] occurs elsewhere.
   Since they do not occur in the same environment, they are in complementary distribution.

2. Oneida: [ʃ] occurs before [j].
                  [s] occurs elsewhere.
   Since they do not occur in the same environment, they are in complementary distribution.

3. Japanese: [ts] occurs before [u].

[tʃ] occurs before [i].

[t] occurs elsewhere.

Since they do not occur in the same environment, they are in complementary distribution.

Practice 3.5

1. Sawai: [e] and [ɛ] are separate phonemes.

Minimal pairs: 1–7; 2–9; 3–5; 8–14; 10–12

2. Biblical Hebrew: [ð] occurs after a vowel or between vowels here; [d] occurs elsewhere.

They are in complementary distribution and are allophones of the same phoneme.

3. German: [χ] occurs after a back vowel; [ç] occurs elsewhere.

They are in complementary distribution and are allophones of the same phoneme.

4. Zinacantec Tzotzil:

[p'] and [p] are separate phonemes.

Minimal pair: 5–12

Near-minimal pairs: 1–7; 4–10

[k'] and [k] are separate phonemes.

Minimal pair: 3–6

Near-minimal pair: 9–11

Practice 3.6

1. English

Note: We assume diphthongs are single sounds.

Corresponding short and long vowels are allophones of the same phoneme. They are in complementary distribution. Long vowels occur before word-final voiced obstruents; short vowels occur elsewhere.

Sample representation:

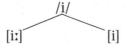

2. Siona

[ɾ] and [t'] are allophones of the same phoneme.

[ɾ] occurs intervocalically; [t'] occurs elsewhere.

Representation:

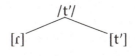

3. Inuktitut

[k] and [q] are separate phonemes that occur in similar environments (word-initially, word-finally, between front and back vowels).

4. English

All are allophones of one phoneme.

They are in complementary distribution: [gʷ] occurs before [u]; [gʲ] occurs before [i]; [g] occurs elsewhere.

Representation:

/g/

[g]   [gʷ]   [gʲ]

5. Yakut

All are separate phonemes.

Minimal pairs:

[i] : [ɨ]	3–7
[i] : [y]	1–10
[i] : [u]	4–12
[ɨ] : [y]	5–9
[ɨ] : [u]	6–13
[y] : [u]	9–14

Representations: /i/   /ɨ/   /y/   /u/

                       [i]   [ɨ]   [y]   [u]

6. Italian

[dʒ] and [g] are allophones of one phoneme.

[dʒ] occurs before front vowels; [g] occurs elsewhere.

Representation:

/g/

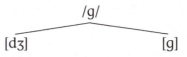

[dʒ]   [g]

Practice 3.7

Sample answers are provided:

Practice 3.6:

1. English
   2. /ɹɑbd/   (vowel length is not shown)
   4. /mod/   (vowel length is not shown)
2. Siona
   10. /saʔət'o/   (intervocalic flapping is not shown)
   11. /tut'upɨ/   (intervocalic flapping is not shown)
4. English
   6. /ɹægu/   (lip rounding of /g/ is not shown)
   12. /gis/   (fronting of /g/ is not shown)

Practice 3.8

1. Mon diphthongs:
    a. /i, e, ɛ/ take [j]. They are all front vowels.
    b. /u, o, ɔ/ take [w]. They are all back vowels.

2. Mon schwa insertions:
    a. /i, u, ɛ, o, ɔ/ take schwa. They are all nonlow vowels.
    b. /ɔ/ is diphthongized, in accordance with the answer to #1.

3. Hausa palatalization:
    a. They are front, nonlow vowels.
    b. /t/ → [tʃ]; /d/ → [dʒ]; /s/ → [ʃ]; /z/ → [dʒ]. The nonpalatal consonants are all alveolar.

Practice 3.9

1.	garden	/gɑɹ.dn̩/	2 syllables, both basic
2.	parks	/pɑɹks/	1 syllable, complex
3.	trained	/tɹejnd/	1 syllable, basic
4.	beauty	/bju.ti/	2 syllables, both basic
5.	twinkle	/twɪŋ.kl̩/	2 syllables, both basic
6.	lovely	/lʌv.li/	2 syllables, both basic
7.	understand	/ʌn.dɚ.stænd/	3 syllables, 2 basic, 1 complex
8.	triangle	/tɹaj.aŋ.gl̩/	3 syllables, all basic
9.	tent	/tɛnt/	1 syllable, basic
10.	angry	/æŋ.gɹi/	2 syllables, both basic
11.	cleanser	/klɛn.zɹ̩/	2 syllables, both basic
12.	splashdown	/splæʃ.dawn/	2 syllables, 1 complex, 1 basic

Practice 3.10

1. English

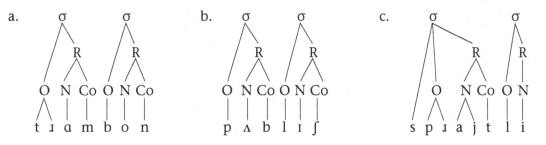

2. Japanese

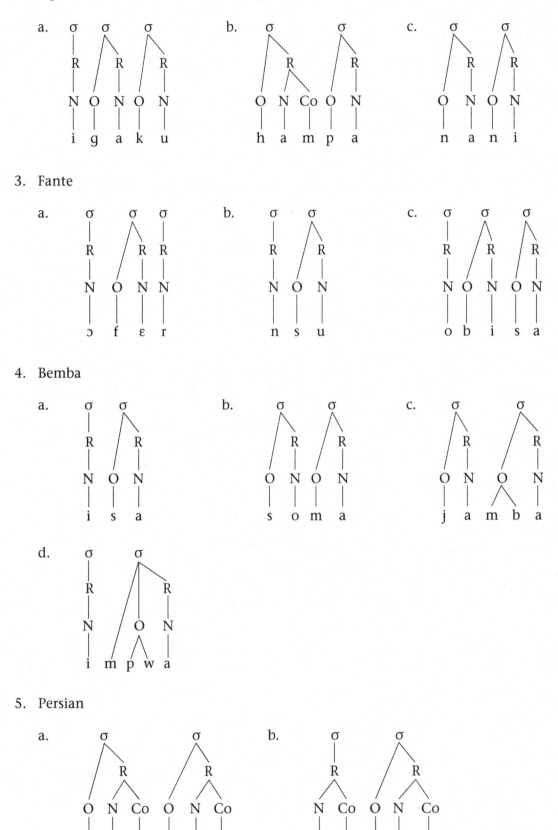

3. Fante

4. Bemba

5. Persian

c.

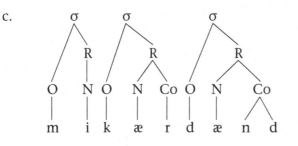

Practice 3.11

1. Korean: stress falls on the first syllable if the first syllable (1) has a long vowel or (2) is a closed syllable.
2. Larike: /i/ becomes [ɪ] in a closed syllable.

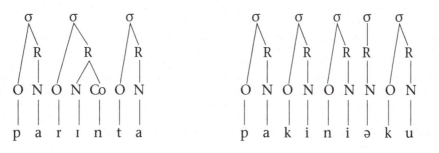

Practice 3.12

1. a. (answer supplied in text)
   b. [+/–continuant]
   c. [+/–strident]
   d. [+/–nasal], [+/–sonorant]
   e. [+/–continuant], [+/–delayed release]

2. Note: Sample answers are given. Other answers are possible.
   a. (answer supplied in text)
   b. [ʃ] [+continuant], [–voice]
   c. [o] [–low], [+tense]
   d. [d] [–continuant]
   e. [w] [+sonorant]
   f. [e] [–back]

3. a. glides
   b. voiced fricatives

4. a. [t] [+voice], or [v] [–continuant]
   b. [ɹ] [LABIAL], or [m] [–nasal]
   c. [j] [–continuant], or [t] [+voice]
   d. [u] [–back]

5. a. [p, f, m, w] are all LABIAL
      [k, ŋ, j] are all DORSAL and [+high]

   b. [p, t, k] are all [–sonorant, –continuant, –voice]
      [t, s, ʃ, ɹ] are all CORONAL
      [s, ʃ] are both [+strident]

    c. [ɪ, ɛ, æ] and all [–tense], [–back]
        [æ, a] are both [+low]

    d. [g, ŋ] are both DORSAL
        [m, n, ŋ] are all [+nasal]
        [f, z, tʃ] are all [–sonorant]

6. a. The sounds in the group share the following features:

$$
\begin{bmatrix}
\text{+consonantal} \\
\text{–sonorant} \\
\text{–syllabic} \\
\text{–nasal} \\
\text{+continuant} \\
\text{–lateral} \\
\text{–delayed release}
\end{bmatrix}
$$

The following features distinguish each sound:

[f]	[v]	[θ]	[ð]
[–voice]	[+voice]	[–voice]	[+voice]
LABIAL	LABIAL	CORONAL	CORONAL

    b. The sounds share the following features:

$$
\begin{bmatrix}
\text{+consonantal} \\
\text{–sonorant} \\
\text{–syllabic} \\
\text{–nasal} \\
\text{–continuant} \\
\text{–lateral} \\
\text{+voice}
\end{bmatrix}
$$

The following features distinguish each sound:

[g]	[dʒ]
[–delayed release]	[+delayed release]
DORSAL	CORONAL

    c. The sounds share the following features:

$$
\begin{bmatrix}
\text{–consonantal} \\
\text{+sonorant} \\
\text{+syllabic} \\
\text{+continuant} \\
\text{+voice} \\
\text{LABIAL} \\
\text{+round} \\
\text{DORSAL} \\
\text{–low} \\
\text{+back} \\
\text{+tense} \\
\text{–reduced}
\end{bmatrix}
$$

The following features distinguish each sound:

[u]   [o]
[+high]   [–high]

d. The sounds share the following features:

$$\begin{bmatrix} -\text{consonantal} \\ +\text{sonorant} \\ +\text{syllabic} \\ +\text{continuant} \\ +\text{voice} \\ \text{DORSAL} \\ -\text{back} \\ -\text{reduced} \end{bmatrix}$$

The following features distinguish each sound:

[i]	[ɪ]	[e]	[ɛ]	[æ]
+high	+high	–high	–high	–high
–low	–low	–low	–low	+low
+tense	–tense	+tense	–tense	–tense

Practice 3.13

1. **Rules and feature matrices:**

Note: Full feature matrices are not given; only those features that distinguish the particular sounds are included in the feature matrices. For the sake of brevity, we use V to mean any vowel [–consonantal, +syllabic] and C to mean any consonant [+consonantal, –syllabic].

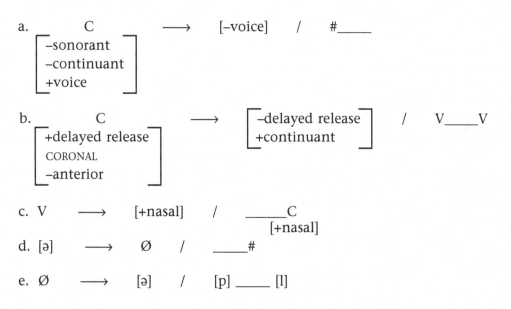

a.   C   ⟶   [–voice]   /   #____
$$\begin{bmatrix} -\text{sonorant} \\ -\text{continuant} \\ +\text{voice} \end{bmatrix}$$

b.   C   ⟶ $\begin{bmatrix} -\text{delayed release} \\ +\text{continuant} \end{bmatrix}$ / V____V
$$\begin{bmatrix} +\text{delayed release} \\ \text{CORONAL} \\ -\text{anterior} \end{bmatrix}$$

c. V   ⟶   [+nasal]   /   ____C
                             [+nasal]

d. [ə]   ⟶   Ø   /   ____#

e. Ø   ⟶   [ə]   /   [p] ____ [l]

2. **Statements:**

   a. A voiceless alveolar stop becomes glottalized following a glottal stop.

   b. Voiceless fricatives become voiced between vowels.

   c. Nonlow tense front vowels become lax word-finally.

   d. An alveolar stop becomes a flap between vowels.

Practice 3.14

1. Polish
   Voiced stops are devoiced word-finally.

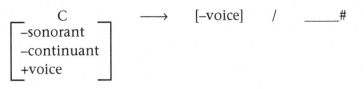

2. South Midland and Southern American English
   [ɛ] becomes [ɪ] before a nasal consonant.

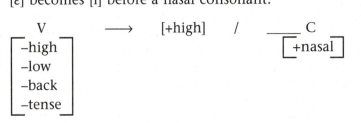

3. Fante
   Alveolar stops become affricates before a front vowel.

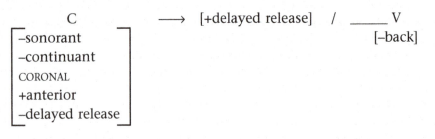

Practice 3.15

1. Tamil:
   The two members in each pair of stops are allophones of one phoneme. They are in complementary distribution. Voiceless stops become voiced intervocalically.

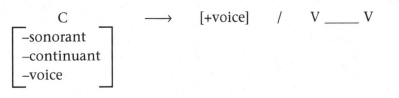

Derivation:

UR	#kappal#	#mukil#	#kuṭi#
Voicing	——	#mugil#	#kuḍi#
PR	#kappal#	#mugil#	#kuḍi#

2. Standard and Andalusian Spanish

Note that the answers given here are based on the data set. The situation is actually somewhat more complicated.

a.–b. In both Standard Spanish and Andalusian Spanish, [d] becomes [ð] after [r] and after a vowel.

We could write: [d] → [ð] / [+continuant] _____
But what is happening (manner assimilation) is clearer if we use features:

$$\begin{bmatrix} \text{C} \\ -\text{sonorant} \\ -\text{continuant} \\ +\text{voice} \\ \text{CORONAL} \\ -\text{strident} \end{bmatrix} \longrightarrow [+\text{continuant}] \ / \ [+\text{continuant}] \ \_\_\_\_\_$$

c. In Andalusian Spanish, [r] is deleted syllable finally: [r] → Ø _____$_\sigma$
(Note it is *not* just when it comes after a vowel—see #12 [floriːo].)

d. [ð] is deleted after a vowel.
[ð] → Ø / V _____

$$\begin{bmatrix} \text{C} \\ -\text{sonorant} \\ +\text{continuant} \\ +\text{voice} \\ \text{CORONAL} \\ -\text{strident} \end{bmatrix} \longrightarrow \text{Ø} \ / \ \text{V} \ \_\_\_\_$$

Note that in both cases of deletion, there is compensatory lengthening of the vowel. This may require a separate rule, but we will assume here for the sake of simplicity that it happens automatically.

e. Note: [ð] deletion must come before [r] deletion.

UR	#berdad#	#merkado#
[d] frication	berðað	merkaðo
[ð] deletion	berðaː	merkaːo
[r] deletion	beːðaː	meːkaːo
PR	#beːðaː#	#meːkaːo#

Review Exercise

1. French
   Liquids and nasals become voiceless after a voiceless consonant.

   $$\begin{bmatrix} \text{+consonantal} \\ \text{+sonorant} \end{bmatrix} \longrightarrow \quad [\text{–voice}] \quad / \quad \underset{[\text{–voice}]}{C} \underline{\quad\quad}$$

2. Kpelle
   Nasalized and oral vowels are separate phonemes.
   Minimal pair: 4–8

3. Hausa
   [r] and [ɽ] are separate phonemes.
   Near-minimal pairs: 2–8; 3–7

4. Bemba
   [s] and [ʃ] are in complementary distribution.
   [ʃ] occurs before [i]; [s] occurs elsewhere. This is a case of palatalization.

   [s] $\longrightarrow$ [–anterior] / ____ [i]

5. Syrian Arabic
   The plain and pharyngealized consonants are separate phonemes.
   Minimal pair: 4–9
   Near-minimal pairs: 2–14; 6–16

6. Mandarin: Each pair of velar and palatal obstruents represents two allophones of one phoneme. The velars become palatalized before a high vowel.

   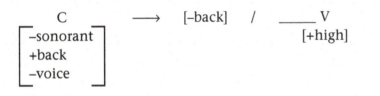

7. Brazilian Portuguese

   a.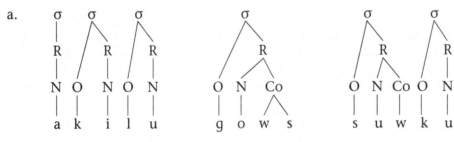

   b. /l/ does not change when it is in the onset.

   c. /l/ becomes [w] when it is in the coda.

Chapter 4

Practice 4.1

1. desert = 1
2. memory = 1
3. format = 1
4. flowchart = 2
5. bug = 1
6. debug = 2
7. supply = 1
8. supplies = 2
9. supplier = 2
10. faster = 2
11. power = 1
12. processor = 2

Practice 4.2

	# of Morphemes	Free	Bound
1.	(answer supplied in text)		
2.	1	wicked	
3.	2	valid	in-
4.	1	invalid	
5.	2	Jack	-s
6.	4	opt	-tion, -al, -ity
7.	2	furnish	re-
8.	4	able	in-, -ity, -s
9.	4	nation	de-, -al, -ize
10.	1	deride	
11.	4	act	-ive, -ate, -tion

Practice 4.3

	# of Morphemes	Root	Root Category	Word Category
1.	(answer supplied in text)			
2.	2	amaze	verb	noun
3.	3	use	verb	adjective
4.	2	honest	adjective	adjective
5.	1	Baltimore	noun	noun
6.	3	love	noun	adjective
7.	2	history	noun	adjective
8.	3	control	verb	adjective
9.	3	person	noun	adjective
10.	2	tree	noun	noun
11.	2	fast	adjective	adjective
12.	3	read	verb	verb
13.	2	beauty	noun	adjective
14.	1	child	noun	noun

Practice 4.4

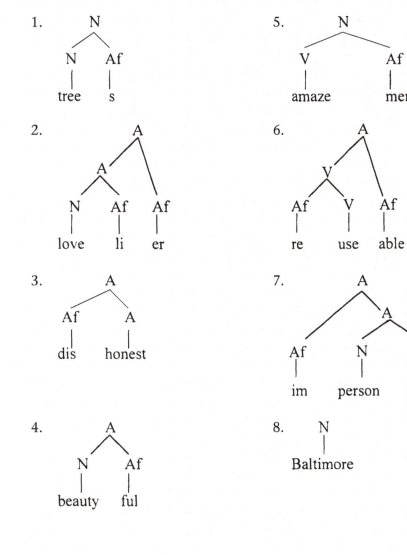

1. N
   N — Af
   tree — s

2. A
   A — Af
   N — Af — Af
   love — li — er

3. A
   Af — A
   dis — honest

4. A
   N — Af
   beauty — ful

5. N
   V — Af
   amaze — ment

6. A
   V — Af
   Af — V — able
   re — use

7. A
   Af — A
   N — Af
   im — person — al

8. N
   Baltimore

Practice 4.5

1. a. V
     Af — V
     dis — appear

   b. A
      N — Af
      home — less

   c. N
      A — Af
      electric — ity   Class I

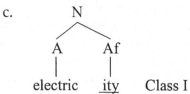

   d. A
      Af — A
      V — Af
      un — break — able

e.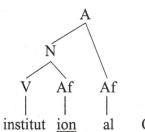

f.

2.

1.	-able	V → A
2.	-ial	N → A
3.	-ness	A → N
4.	dis-	V → V
5.	-ize	N → V
	-ation	V → N
6.	-ive	V → A
7.	-ous	N → A
8.	-ity	A → N

9.	re-	V → V
10.	-ian	N → A (or N)
11.	-ize	N → V
12.	-ate	A → V
13.	-en	A → V
14.	un-	A → A
	-ant	V → A
15.	un-	V → V

Practice 4.6

1. **Compound**   **Lexical Categories**

   a. bathroom (answer supplied in text)

   b. scarecrow   V   +   N

   c. skin-deep   N   +   A

   d. bittersweet   A   +   A

   e. upstairs   P   +   N

(Note: Sample examples are given in the tree diagrams; answers will vary.)

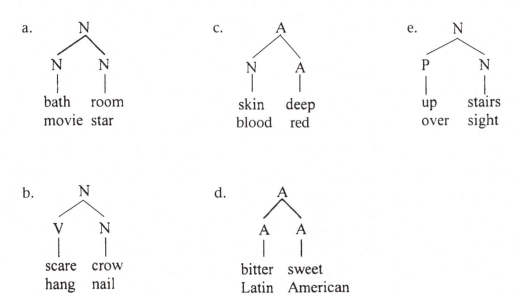

2. a.

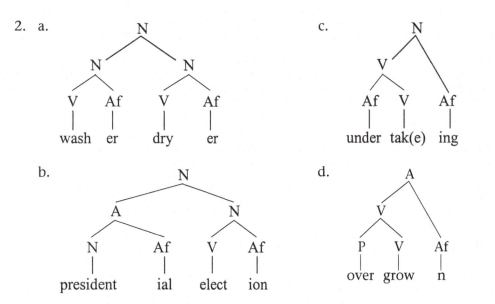

Practice 4.7

	Lexical Category	Inflectional Information
1.	(answer supplied in text)	
2.	V	third-person singular nonpast *or*
	N	plural
3.	A	superlative
4.	N	plural
5.	V	progressive
6.	V	past participle
7.	A	comparative

Practice 4.8

	Affix	Infl/Deriv
1.	(answer supplied in text)	
2.	-ion, -al	derivational
3.	re-	derivational
4.	-'s	inflectional
5.	-er	inflectional
6.	-ful	derivational
7.	-al, -ize	derivational
8.	-ed	inflectional
9.	mis-	derivational
10.	un-, -i-, -est	derivational, derivational, inflectional

Practice 4.9

(Note: The affix is supplied.)

1. (answer supplied in text)

2. -y S
   -y N
   -y D
   -y S

3.   N
   -en S
   -en D
   -en S

4. -er S
   -er D
     N
   -or S

5. -er S
   -er D
   -er S
     N

6. -ly D
   -ly S
   -ly S
     N

7.   N
   in- D
   in- S
   in- S

8. -ed D
   -ed S
   -ed S
     N

Practice 4.10

1. inflection

2. compound inflection

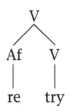

3. derivation

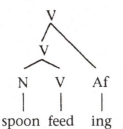

4. derivation, inflection

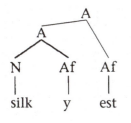

5. derivation, inflection

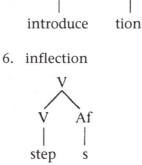

6. inflection

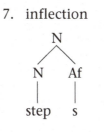

7. inflection

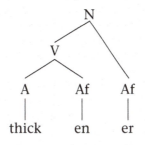

8. derivation, inflection

9. derivation, inflection

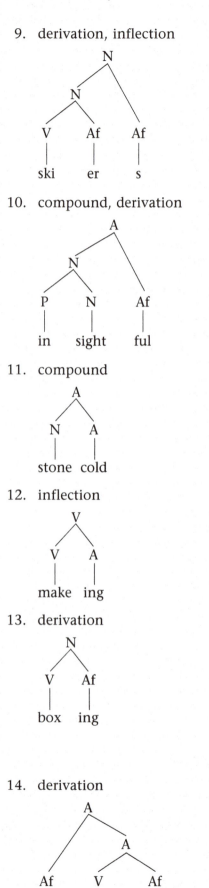

10. compound, derivation

11. compound

12. inflection

13. derivation

14. derivation

15. derivation

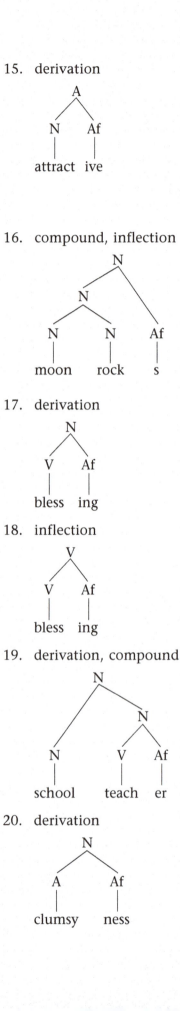

16. compound, inflection

17. derivation

18. inflection

19. derivation, compound

20. derivation

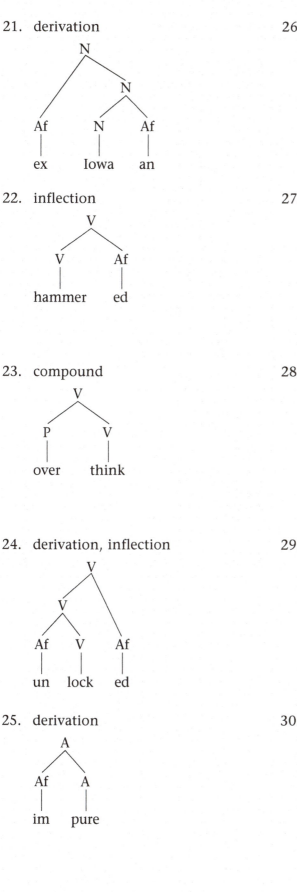

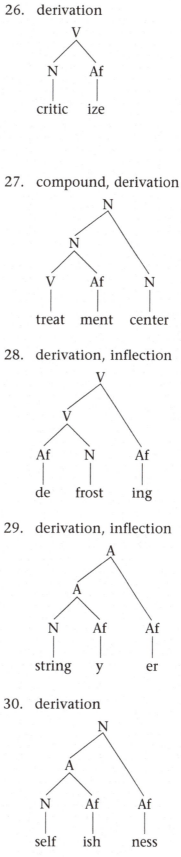

21. derivation

22. inflection

23. compound

24. derivation, inflection

25. derivation

26. derivation

27. compound, derivation

28. derivation, inflection

29. derivation, inflection

30. derivation

Practice 4.11

1. (answer supplied)
2. suppletion
3. affixation
4. (full) reduplication
5. suppletion
6. affixation
7. affixation
8. (partial) reduplication
9. internal change

Practice 4.12

1.   1. (answer supplied in text)
     2. conversion
     3. inflection (internal change)
     4. compounding
     5. onomatopoeia
     6. inflection (affixation)
     7. derivation
     8. clipping
     9. derivation
    10. cliticization
    11. compounding
    12. onomatopoeia
    13. acronym
    14. blending
    15. borrowing

2.   Words from the passage:

Dave	clipping
brunch	blending
chirping	onomatopoeia
outside	compounding
buzz	onomatopoeia
infomercial	blending
TV	initialism
headache	compounding
hammering	conversion
eyeball	compounding
Kleenex	coinage
scuba	acronym
flu	clipping
fingered	conversion
med	clipping
enthused	backformation
off-putting	compounding

CAT	acronym
blood test	compounding
laser	acronym
laze	backformation
Coke	clipping of a coinage
sandwiches	eponym (from the Earl of Sandwich)
channel-surfing	compounding

3. French and German
   1. compound
   2. derivation (affixation)
   3. derivation (affixation)
   4. clipping
   5. conversion
   6. blend
   7. compound
   8. conversion (zero derivation)
   9. blend
   10. (full) reduplication
   11. compound
   12. clipping

Practice 4.13

1. Kisar

'day'	ler	'this'	-eni
'girl'	mawek	'that'	-onne
'father'	pap	'one'	-iṭa
'mouse'	ornoh		
'boy'	moʔon		
'banana'	muʔu		
'goat'	pipi		

2. Kiswahili
   a. SINGULAR ki-
   b. PLURAL vi-
   c. kiti
   d. vikombe

3. Toba Batak
   a. -um- indicates comparative
   b. infix (after the first consonant)
   c. [dumatu] 'wiser'
   d. [sumɔmal] 'more usual'
   e. [dʒɛppɛk] 'short'
   f. [lógo] 'dry'

4. Danish
   a.

'red'	rød	'man'	mand
'book'	bog	'hat'	hat
'color'	farve	'big'	stor
'black'	sort	'car'	bil
'door'	dør		
'is'	er	POSSESSIVE	-s

   b. 'a' en, free morpheme
   c. 'the' -en, bound morpheme

Practice 4.14

1. Bahasa Indonesian
   a. ber-
   b. -wan
   c. 'cause to be':   mem- BASE -kan
   d. abstract noun: ke- BASE -an

2. Turkish
   a. Morphemes

1.	'city'	[ʃehiɾ]	8.	'from'	-[den]
2.	'hand'	[el]	9.	'to'	-[e]
3.	'bridge'	[kœpɾy]	10.	'on, in'	-[de]
4.	'bell'	[zil]	11.	'my'	-[im]
5.	'house'	[ev]	12.	'your'	-[iniz]
6.	'voice'	[ses]	13.	PLURAL	-[leɾ]
7.	'bus'	[otobys]			

   b. Order of morphemes: ROOT + PLURAL + POSSESSIVE + POSTPOSITION

   c. English translation
      1. 'in a city'
      2. 'your hands'

   d. Turkish translation
      'to the buses' [otobysleɾe]

3. Classical Nahuatl
   a. Morphemes
      1. 'sing'   [kʷiːka]
      2. 'eat'   [kʷa]
      3. 'bathe'   [aːltia]
      4. you (SG) (subject)   [ti]-
      5. s/he (subject)   Ø (not marked)
      6. it (object)   [ki]-
      7. we (subject)   [ti]- (STEM)-[ʔ]
      8. you (PL) (subject)   [an]- (STEM)-[ʔ]
      9. they (subject)   -[ʔ]

   b. suffix marking plural subject in present: -[ʔ]

   c. customary present marked with lengthening of final vowel plus suffix: -[:ni]

Practice 4.15

1. English
   a. Three allomorphs: [ɪn], [ɪm], [ɪŋ]
   b. 1. [ɪm] occurs before labials.
      2. [ɪŋ] occurs before velars.
      3. [ɪn] occurs elsewhere.

2. Turkish
   a. [lɑɾ], [leɾ]
   b. [+/–back]
   c. [+/–back] If the last V in the root is [+back], the allomorph is [lɑɾ]. If the last V in the root is [–back], the allomorph is [leɾ].

3. Dutch
   a. -en
   b. ge-(STEM)-t/d
      -t is used when stem ends with a voiceless C.
      -d is used when stem ends with a voiced C or V.
   c. Both are pronounced as [t] because of word-final consonant devoicing.
   d. ge-
   e. *gestolen* is a strong verb. It has no -t/d suffix as would be expected with a weak verb.

Review Exercises

1. Ancient Egyptian
   a. Morphemes:

1. 'sibling'	sn		4. MASCULINE	Ø (not marked)	
2. 'deity'	ntʲr		5. DUAL	-j	
3. FEMININE	-t		6. PLURAL	-w	

   b. Order of morphemes:

1. M SG:	ROOT	4. F PL:	ROOT/PLURAL/FEMININE
2. F SG:	ROOT/FEMININE	5. M DU:	ROOT/PLURAL/DUAL
3. M PL:	ROOT/PLURAL	6. F DU:	ROOT/FEMININE/DUAL

2. Luganda

SG	PL	Stems	Gloss
mu-	ba-	-ntu (1, 20)	'person'
		-wala (12, 18)	'girl'
ka-	bu-	-ti (2, 16)	'stick'
		-tiko (9, 14)	'mushroom'
ki-	bi-	-tabo (3, 4)	'book'
		-ntu (10, 17)	'thing'
ku-	ma-	-gulu (5, 13)	'leg'
		-tu (8, 15)	'ear'
mu-	mi-	-ti (7, 6)	'tree'
		-sege (11, 19)	'wolf'

3. Fore
   a. Morphemes:

1. I	-[uw]		6. they (DUAL)	-[aːs]	
2. he	-[iy]		7. eat	-[na]	
3. we	-[un]		8. yesterday	-[t]	
4. they	-[aːw]		9. today	-[gas]	
5. we (DUAL)	-[us]		10. will	-[k]	

    b. QUESTION -[aw]
       STATEMENT -[i]

    c. Order of morphemes:
       V; adverb (tense); personal pronoun; question/statement marker

    d. Translations:
       1. 'He ate yesterday?'   [natiyaw]
       2. 'They (DUAL) will eat?'   [naka:saw]
       3. 'They ate today.'   [nagasa:wi]

4. Twi:

    a.

'America'	Amerika
'Ghana'	Ghana
'is/are'	(-)yɛ
'we'	yɛ-
'you' (SG)	wo-
'they'	wɔ-
'citizen of'	-ni
'citizens of'	-foɔ

    b. 'not'   (-)n-, placed in front of the verb

    c. 'We are not Ghanaians' Yɛnyɛ Ghanafoɔ

    d.

'I'	me-
'like'	-pɛ
'come from'	-firi

    e. 'not'   (-)m-
       This is different from the answer in question b because the negative morpheme (a nasal) assimilates to the place of the following sound.

5. **English** (names of dog breeds)

1.	eponym	6.	eponym
2.	compound	7.	compound
3.	blend	8.	eponym
4.	eponym, clipping	9.	blend
5.	blend	10.	borrowing

6. Iraqi Arabic (Past Tense)

    a.

1 SG	-it
1 PL	-na
2 M SG	-it
2 F SG	-ti
2 PL	-tu
3 M SG	Ø
3 F SG	-at
3 PL	-aw

    b. The 3 F SG and 3 PL forms have vowel deletion in the stem. (Actually it is a bit more complex than this since the root in Arabic is consonantal.)

    c. 'You (M SG) cooked'   tˤubaxit

Chapter 5

Practice 5.1

1.
   V   Deg   V   A   N
   beat   really   listened   intermittent   knocking

     N   P   N   P   V   N   V
   door   near   tracks   beside   thought   bum   heard

2.
   N   V   P
   leg   said   in

3.
   A   Con   A   V   Aux   Aux   V
   long   and   great   says   could   be   circumnavigated

4.
   V   N   N   Aux   Deg   A   Aux   V   N   Aux
   turned   key   my   would   very   dull   had   flopped   his   was

     A   Adv   V   V
   little   frantically   realized   bugged

5.
   Det   Deg   Con   A   N   P   Aux   V   Det   P
   a   rather   but   green   clarity   by   were   making   that   of

6.
   V   N   Adv
   hate   pineapples   dolefully

7.
   N   V   N   N   Aux
   fortune   buy   pigs   male   will

Practice 5.2

	Head (Lexical Category)	Specifier	Complement	Type of Phrase
1.	(answer supplied in text)			NP
2.	George (N)	—	—	NP
3.	in (P)	—	the barn	PP
4.	mean (A)	really	—	AP
5.	worked (V)	—	—	VP
6.	worked (V)	—	at the station	VP
7.	boring (A)	extremely	—	AP
8.	destruction (N)	that	of the city	NP
9.	walks (V)	never	to the park	VP
10.	small (A)	very	—	AP
11.	in (P)	—	the room	PP
12.	cute (A)	awfully	—	AP
13.	smiles (V)	seldom	—	VP
14.	swept (V)	—	the floor	VP
15.	poem (N)	the	about love	NP
16.	pancakes (N)	—	—	NP

Practice 5.3

Note: Sample answers are given. Some answers may vary.

1. Substitution test:
    1. [They] arrived [there] [then].
    2. *The cabbage [them] salty.
       Not a phrase.
    3. They moved [it].
    4. Little Andrew swallowed [them].
    5. Mike is [doing so].

2. Movement test:
    1. *[Army was surrounded] the by the enemy.
       Not a phrase.
    2. [Viennese waltzes and Argentinean tangos] Leona likes.
    3. [In the revolving restaurant], Shawn ate his lunch.
    4. *[Be merry for] eat, drink, and today will become yesterday.
       Not a phrase.
    5. *[Were swimming among] the polar bears the ice floes.
       Not a phrase.

3. Coordination test:

	Conjunction (sample answers)	Substitution	Type of Phrase
1.	[the new desk] and [the old chair]	they	NP
2.	[assembled the new desk] and [painted the old chair]	did so	VP
3.	[new] and [expensive]	(no proform)	AP
4.	[in a hole] or [under a rock]	there	PP
5.	[rather huge] but [somewhat ugly]	(no proform)	AP
6.	[worked on a movie] and [played in a band]	did so	VP
7.	[beside the fence] or [near the tree]	there	PP
8.	[really lovely] but [hideously expensive]	(no proform)	AP
9.	[talked to the girls] and [played with the boys]	did so	VP
10.	[a dentist] or [a lawyer]	she	NP

Practice 5.4

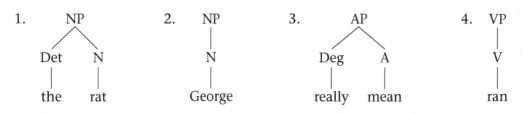

1. NP
    Det   N
    the   rat

2. NP
    N
    George

3. AP
    Deg   A
    really mean

4. VP
    V
    ran

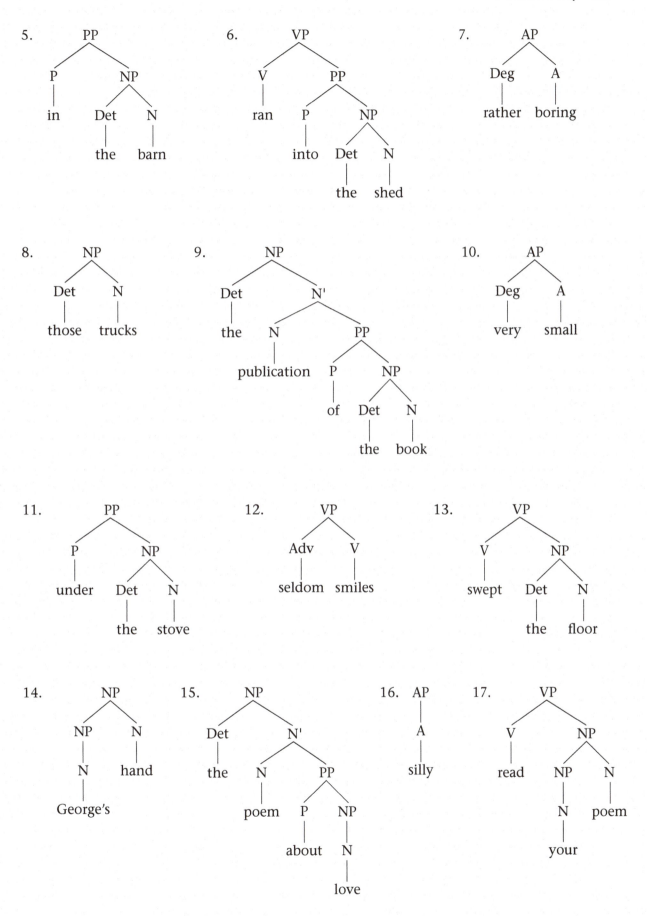

18.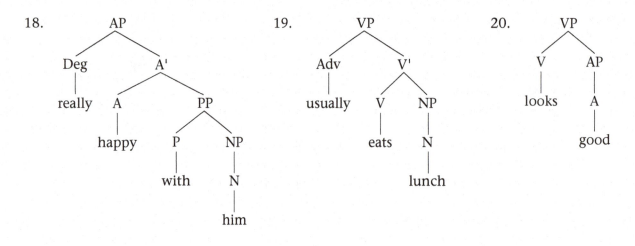

19.

20.

Practice 5.5

1.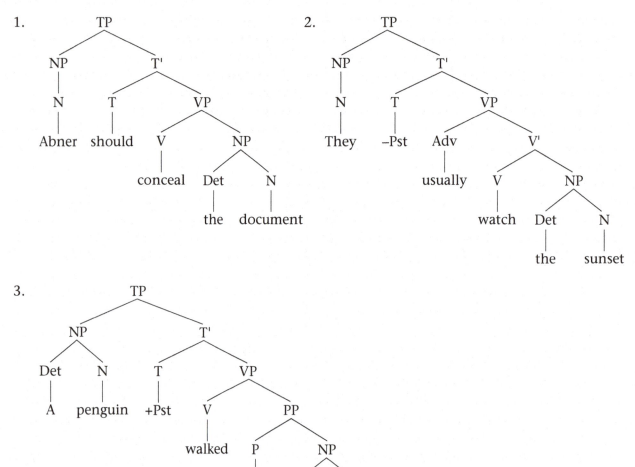

2.

3.

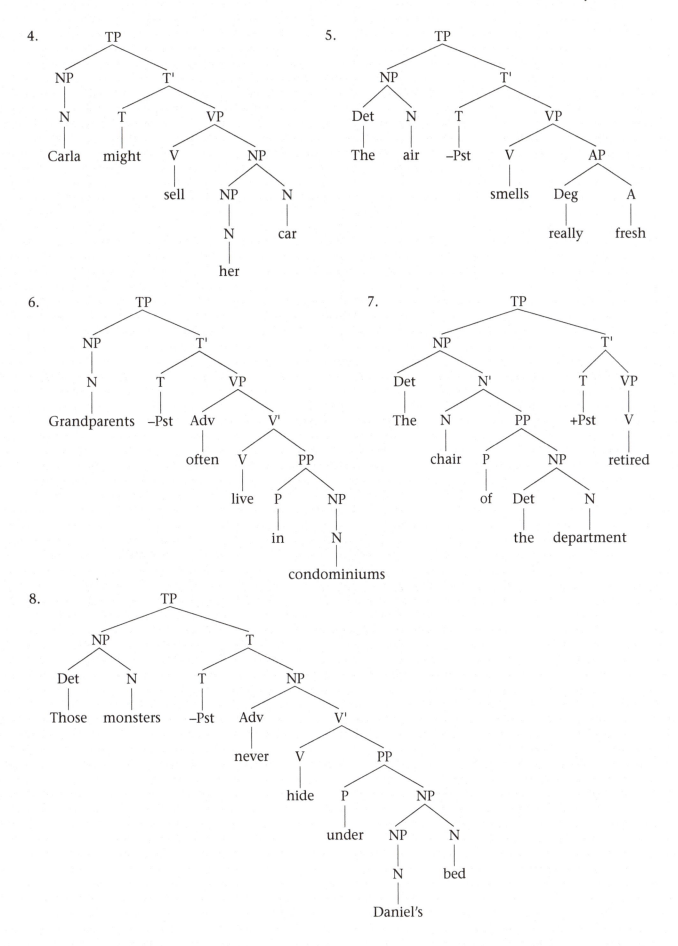

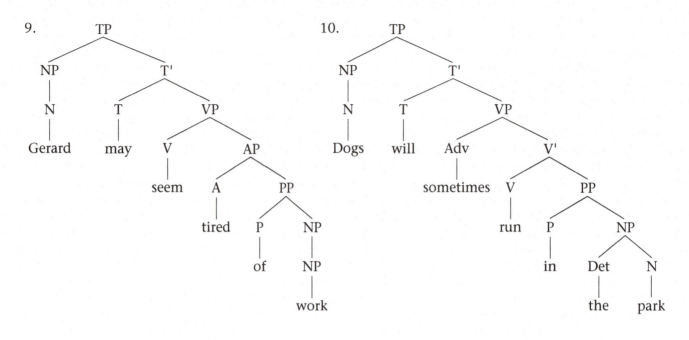

9.

10.

Practice 5.6

1. Complement options for verbs:
   (Note: Sample sentences are given, but answers will vary.)

Complement options	Sample sentences
1. No complement:	When we saw the price of the dinner, we panicked.
	*We panicked the price.
2. NP	We watched the show.
3. NP or	I can't imagine it.
CP	The child imagined that she was an astronaut.
4. NP or	Mark Twain wrote a book.
NP, PP or	He wrote a letter to his sister.
NP, NP	He wrote his sister a letter.
5. CP or	We wondered what was happening.
PP	They wondered about the story.
6. Ø or	The children played.
NP	The Cardinals play baseball.

2. Complement options for nouns, adjectives, prepositions:

   1. PP or CP or Ø   3. PP   5. NP
   2. NP   4. Ø   6. PP or Ø

Practice 5.7

1.

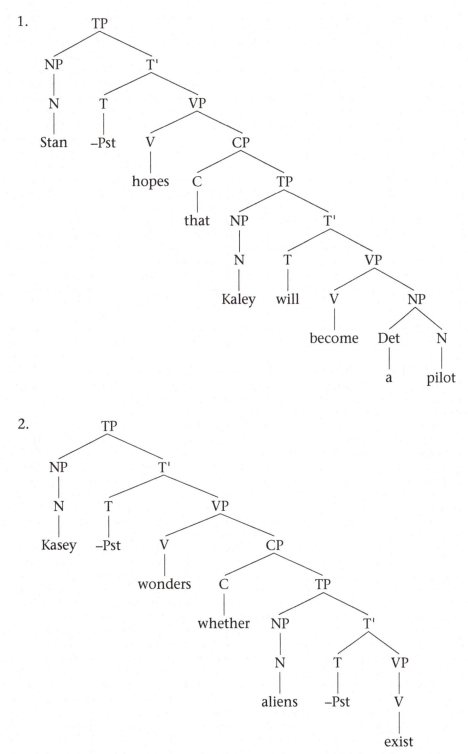

2.

3.

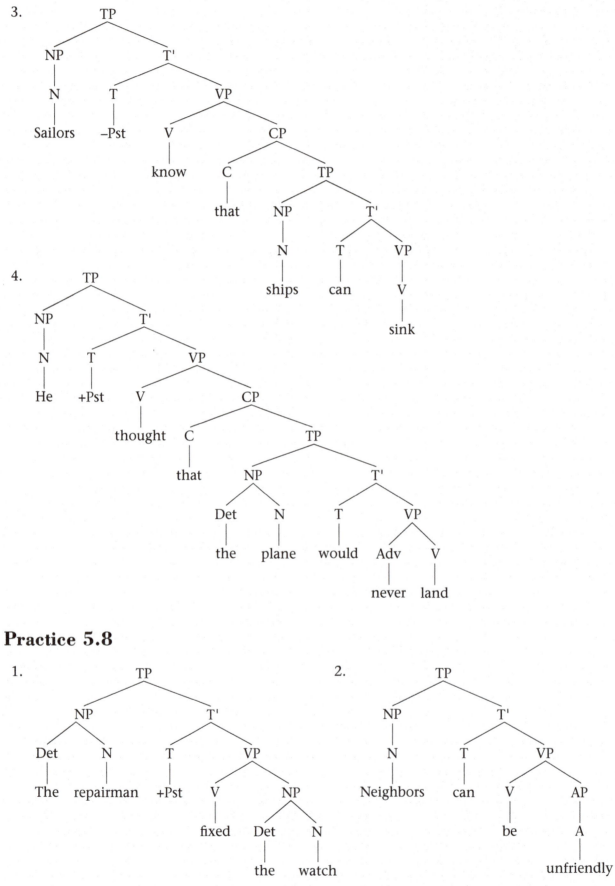

4.

Practice 5.8

1.

2.

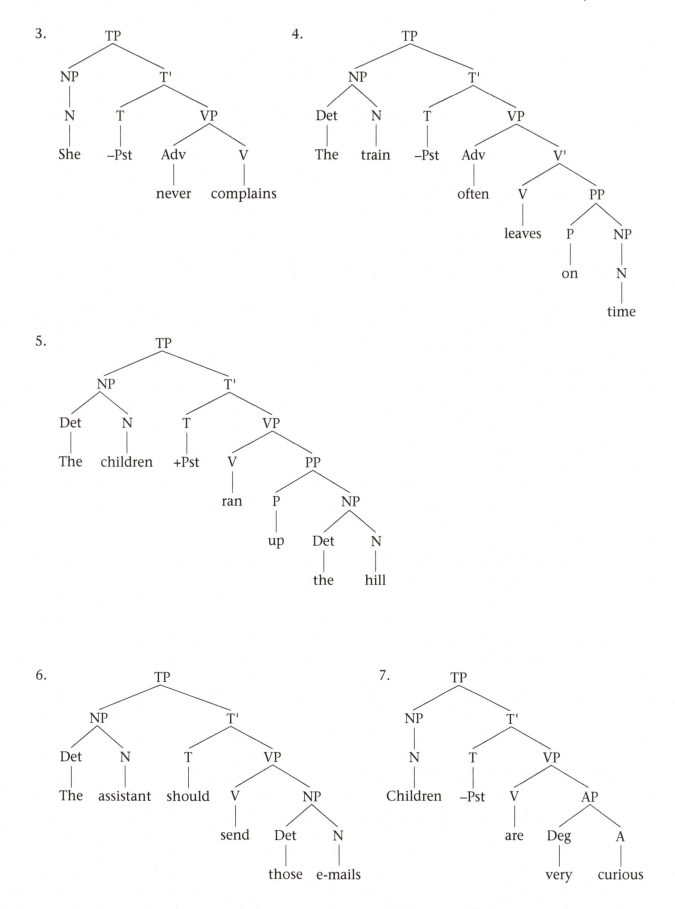

3.

TP
- NP
  - N
    - She
- T'
  - T
    - –Pst
  - VP
    - Adv
      - never
    - V
      - complains

4.

TP
- NP
  - Det
    - The
  - N
    - train
- T'
  - T
    - –Pst
  - VP
    - Adv
      - often
    - V'
      - V
        - leaves
      - PP
        - P
          - on
        - NP
          - N
            - time

5.

TP
- NP
  - Det
    - The
  - N
    - children
- T'
  - T
    - +Pst
  - VP
    - V
      - ran
    - PP
      - P
        - up
      - NP
        - Det
          - the
        - N
          - hill

6.

TP
- NP
  - Det
    - The
  - N
    - assistant
- T'
  - T
    - should
  - VP
    - V
      - send
    - NP
      - Det
        - those
      - N
        - e-mails

7.

TP
- NP
  - N
    - Children
- T'
  - T
    - –Pst
  - VP
    - V
      - are
    - AP
      - Deg
        - very
      - A
        - curious

8.

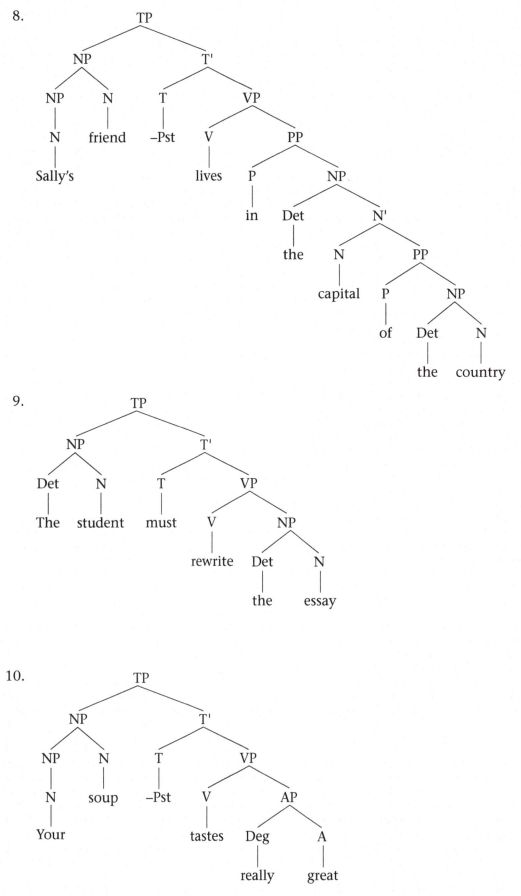

9.

10.

11.

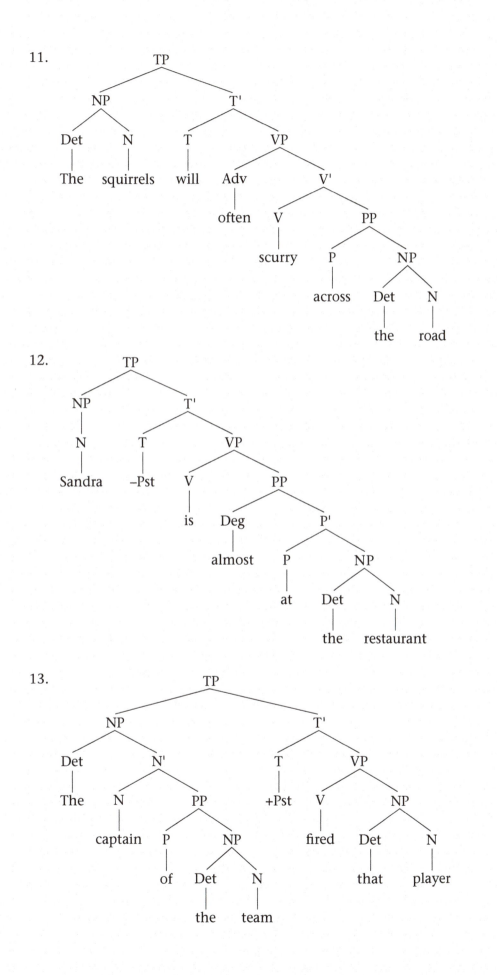

12.

13.

14.

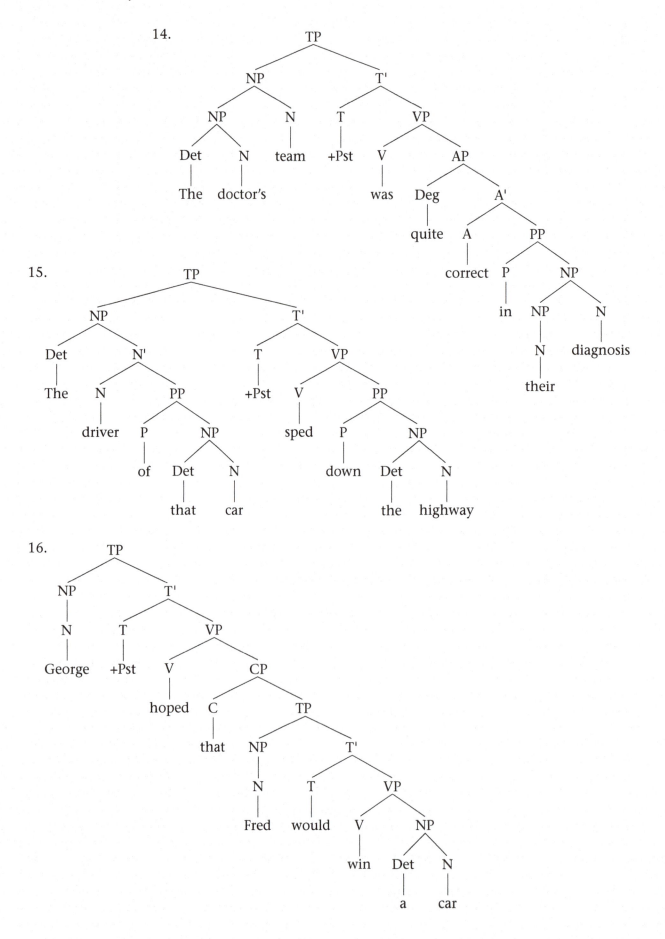

15.

16.

17.

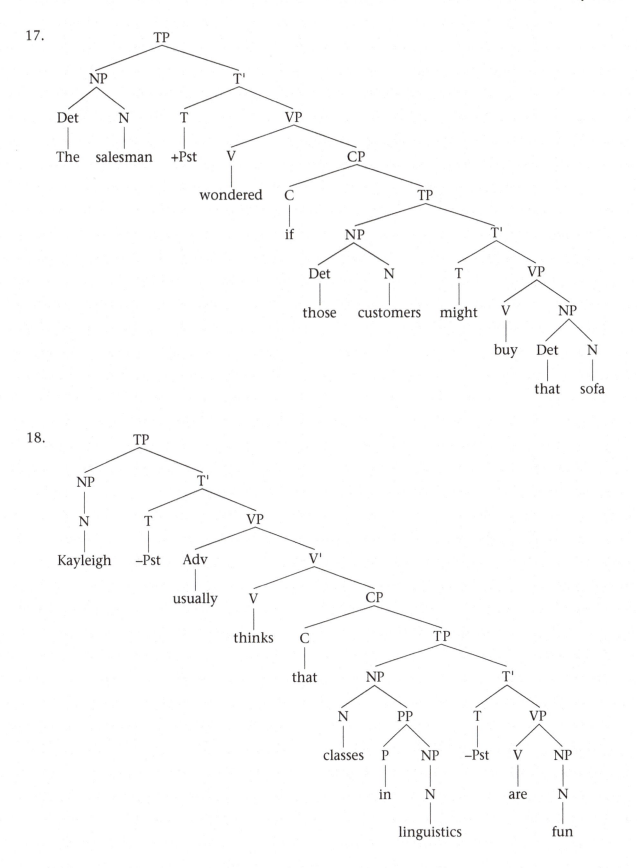

18.

19.

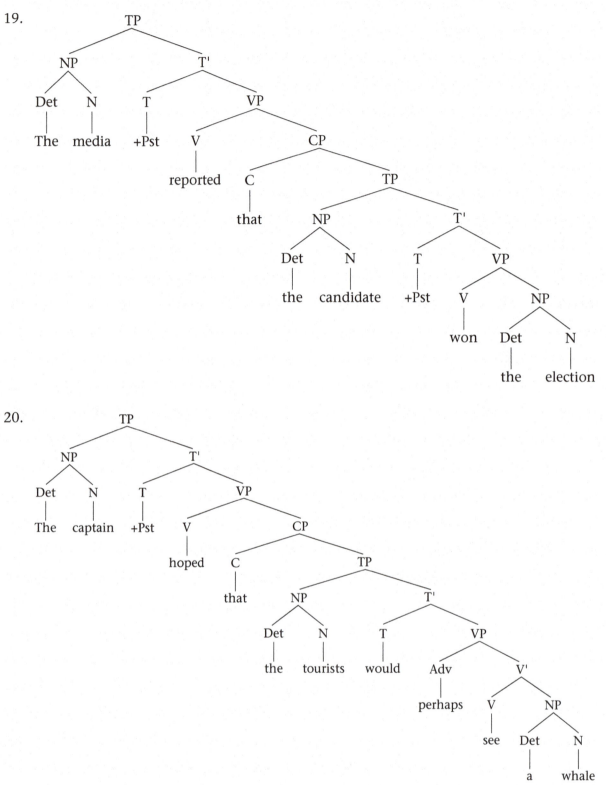

20.

Practice 5.9

1. D-structure: S-structure:

2. D-structure: S-structure:

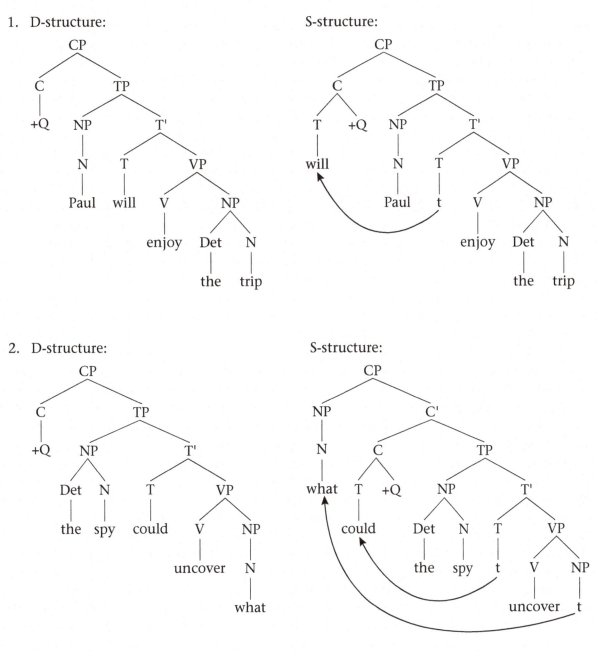

3. D-structure: S-structure:

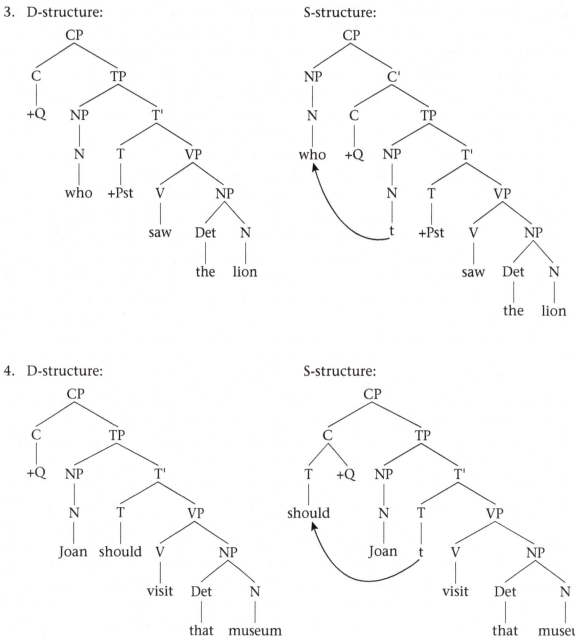

4. D-structure: S-structure:

5. D-structure: S-structure:

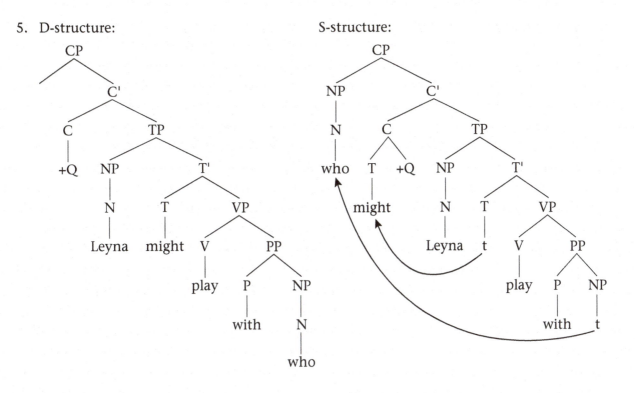

Practice 5.10

1. D-structure: S-structure:

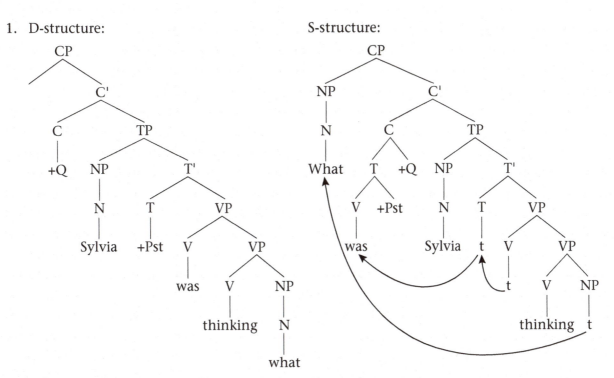

2a. D-structure: S-structure:

2b. D-structure: S-structure:

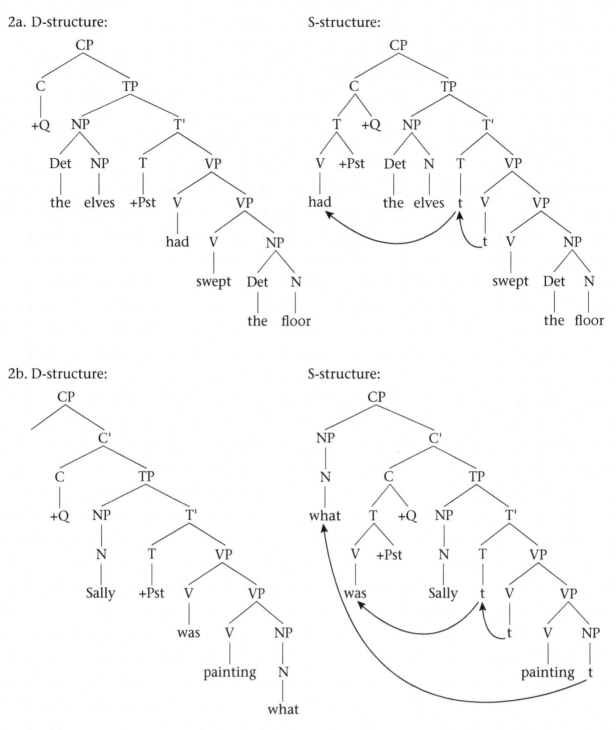

2c. D-structure: S-structure:

2d. D-structure: S-structure:

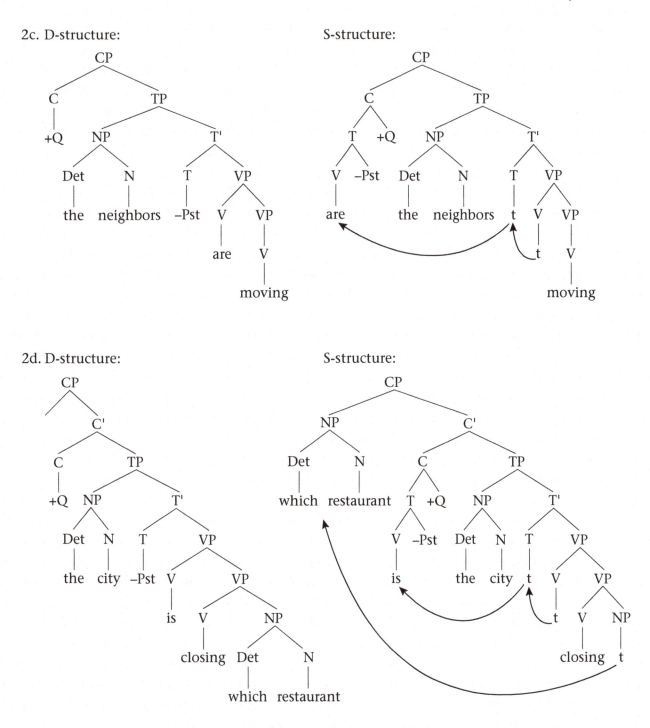

Practice 5.11 (Surface structure is shown here.)

1. Inversion

2. Inversion, *Wh* Movement

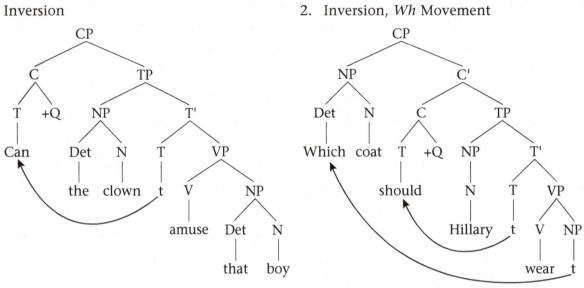

3. *Wh* Movement

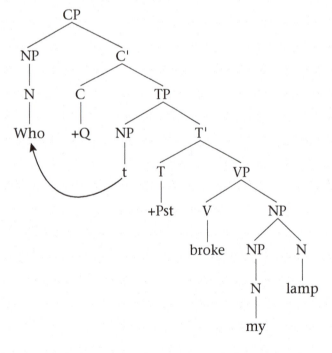

4. None

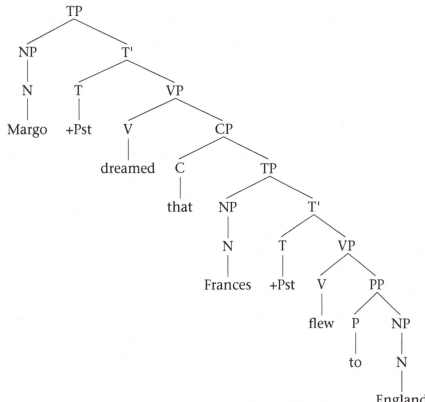

5. Verb Raising, Inversion

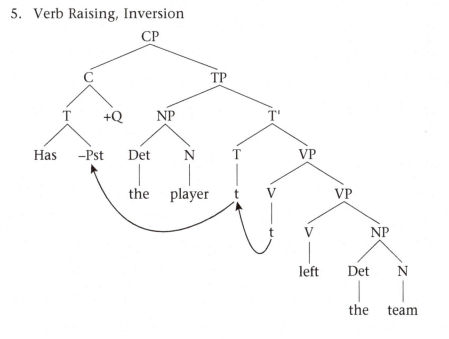

6. Verb Raising, Inversion, *Wh* Movement   7. Inversion

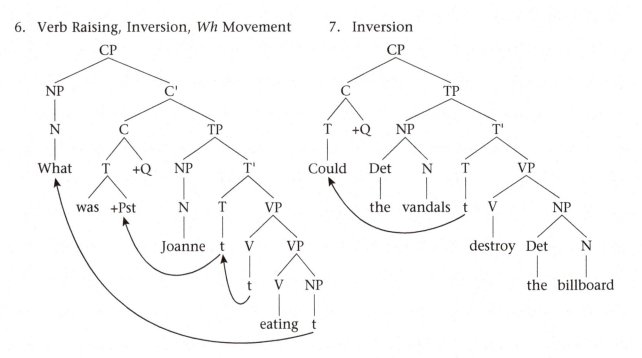

8. None

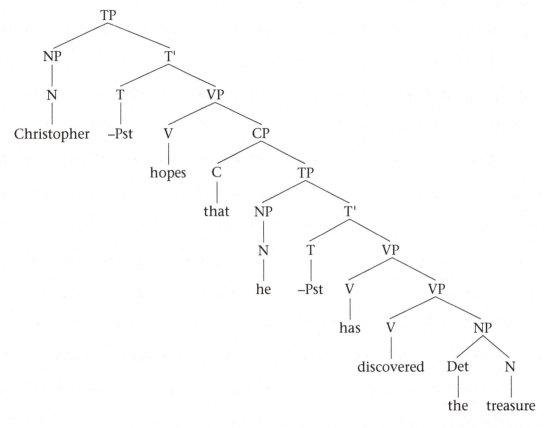

9. Inversion, *Wh* Movement

10. Verb Raising, Inversion

11. Inversion

12. Inversion, *Wh* Movement

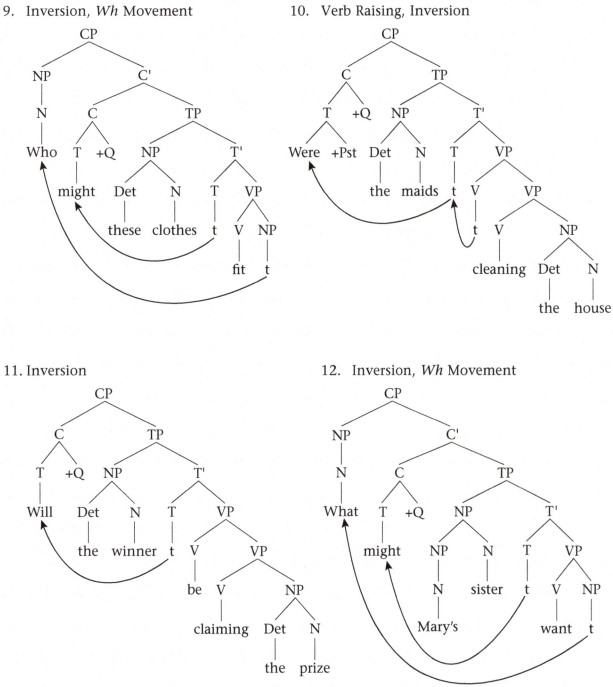

13. None

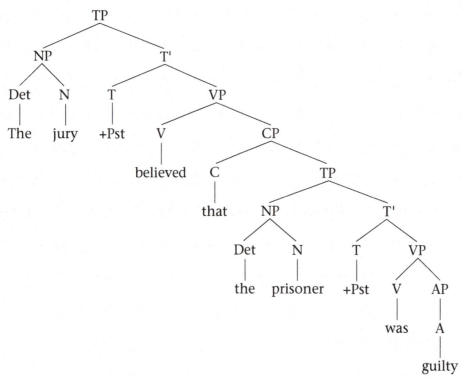

14. *Wh* Movement

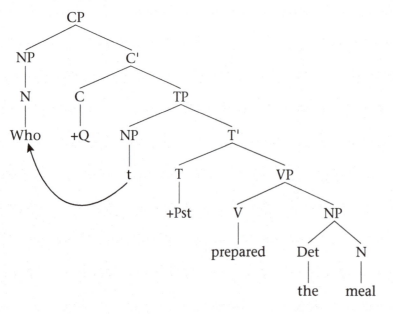

15. None

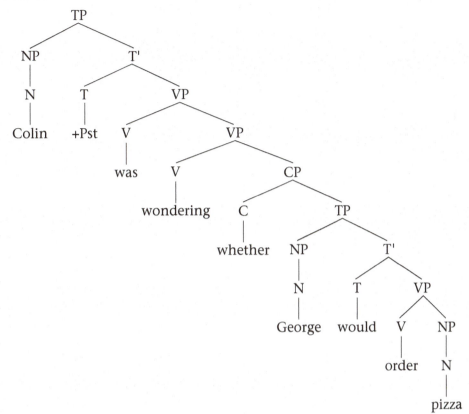

Practice 5.12

1. a. *loudly* is an AdvP that modifies the V *play*
      (Note that *often* is an Adv that is the specifier of the VP.)

   b. *really awful* is an AP that modifies the N *movie*
      top is an AP that modifies the N *prize*
      (Note that *really* is a Deg that is the specifier of the AP.)

   c. *gigantic* is an AP that modifies the N *waves*
      fiercely is an AdvP that modifies the V *pounded*

2. a. Relative clause: *which the snowplows have finished clearing*
      D-Structure: *the snowplows have finished clearing which*

   b. Relative clause: *which were plowed yesterday*
      D-Structure: *were plowed which yesterday*

   c. Relative clause: *who answered the phones*
      D-Structure: *who answered the phones*

3. a. passive. *were trained those tigers*

   b. active

   c. passive. D-Structure: *could be fixed that lamp*

Review Exercise (Surface structure is shown for all sentences.)

1.

2.

3.

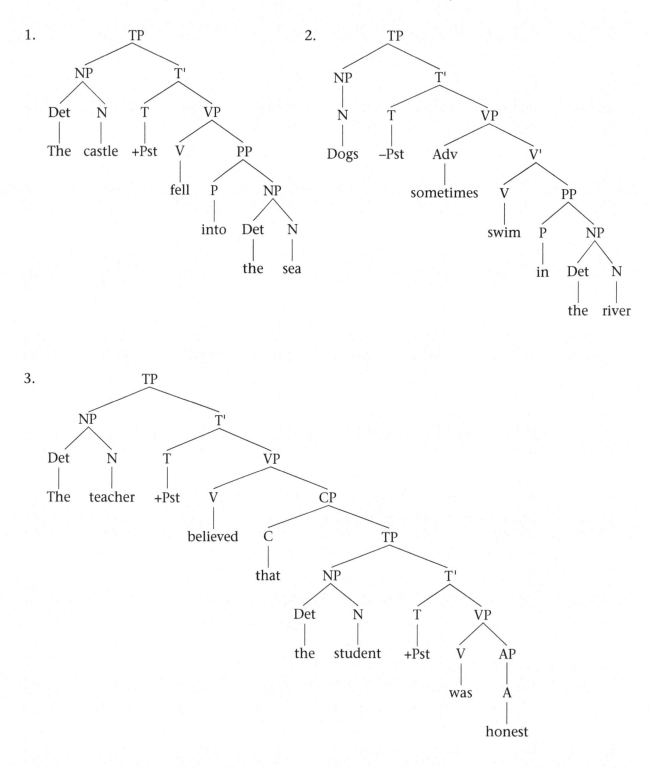

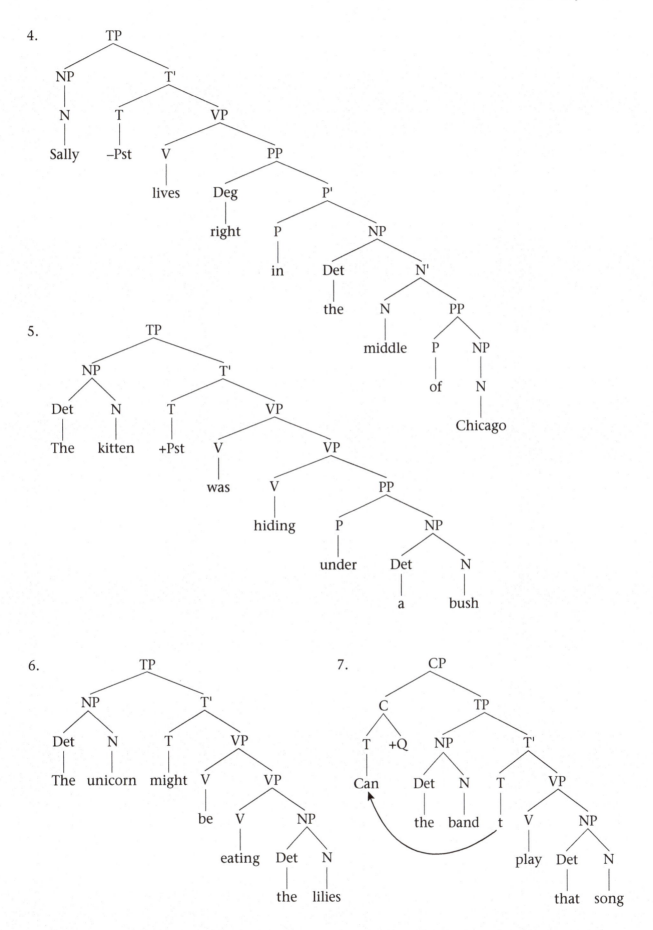

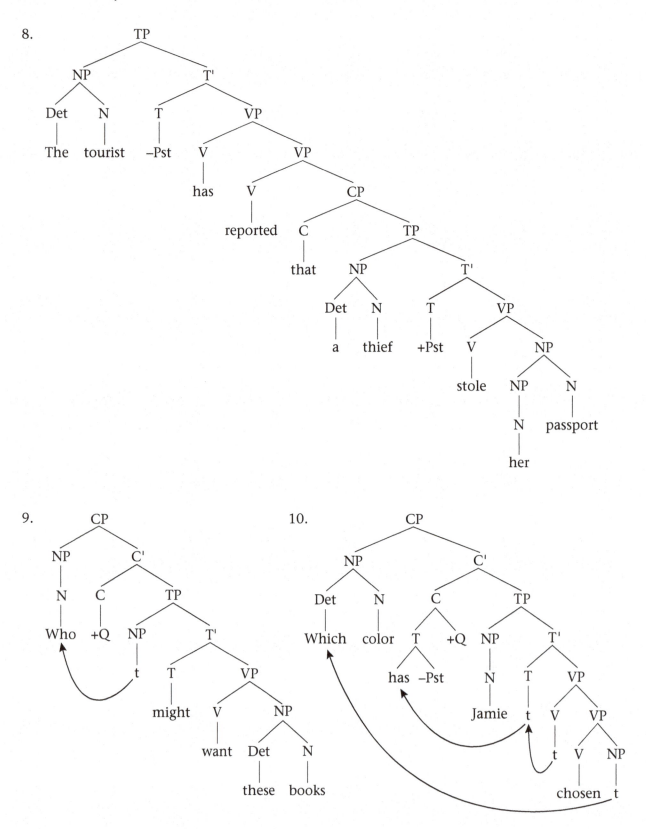

8.

9.

10.

11.

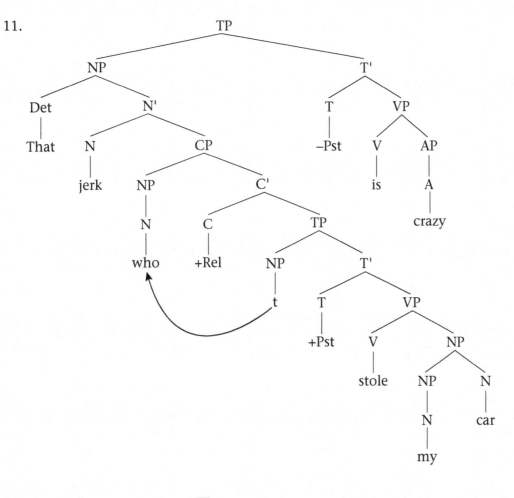

12.

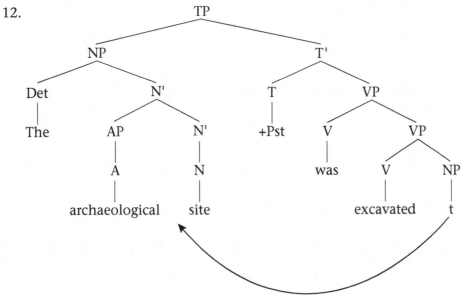

Chapter 6

Practice 6.1

1. (answer supplied in the text)
2. paraphrases
3. homophones
4. contradiction
5. entailment

6. antonyms
7. paraphrases
8. contradiction
9. synonyms
10. homophones (both are [stejk])

Practice 6.2

1. a. summer

connotation:	sunny, fun, sticky . . .
intension:	warmest season of the year
denotation:	period between summer solstice and autumnal equinox
extension:	June 21–September 20 in northern hemisphere; December 21–March 20 in southern hemisphere

    b. a linguistics instructor

connotation:	wise, funny . . .
intension:	a real or imagined person who teaches linguistics
denotation:	any person in the real world who teaches linguistics
extension:	your particular professor

    c. grass

connotation:	green, sweet-smelling, allergies . . .
intension:	green plant that grows on lawns
denotation:	narrow-leafed plant
extension:	the green stuff in my lawn that is not weeds

2. Verbs in A must have both a subject and an object. The subject will generally be animate and equipped with limbs capable of sweeping or kicking. The meanings of the verbs in A require an object to be swept or kicked, which will be expressed as an NP. The verbs in B take just a subject. It is possible that each verb may be followed by a PP of location.

3. Groups A and B are [+living, +human].
    Group A is [+female]. Group B is [–female].
    grandmother, *grandfather*, *mother*, and *father* are all [+parent].

4. | ewe | lamb | mare | filly | colt |
    |---|---|---|---|---|
    | [+animate] | [+animate] | [+animate] | [+animate] | [+animate] |
    | [+sheep] | [+sheep] | [+horse] | [+horse] | [+horse] |
    | [+adult] | [–adult] | [+adult] | [–adult] | [–adult] |
    | [+female] | | [+female] | [+female] | |

5. The problem with connotation is that different people will have different associations for words, and associations do not necessarily get at the meaning. The problem with denotation is that it cannot account for entities that exist in an imaginary realm.

Extension and intension can account for entities in an imaginary realm, but they still do not get at what meaning actually is. Componential analysis works relatively well for words that can be classed into groups according to features, but it is difficult to specify all the features that would be needed. Furthermore, it is difficult to determine smaller units of meaning for some words (e.g., what is the feature that would set the word *blue* apart from the word *yellow*?).

Practice 6.3

1. a. graded membership
   b. graded membership; fuzzy concept
   c. grammaticalized or graded membership (hour vs. lifetime)
   d. graded membership
   (Answers concerning prototypical members will vary.)

2. Menomini
   The three types of nouns are: parts of the body, kinship terms, and objects. Parts of the body and kinship terms are "inalienable." Algonquian languages, of which Menomini is one, do not allow an unpossessed form for things that must, by their very nature, belong to someone. Parts of the body and kinship terms are typically inalienable.

3. Kiswahili
   Singular [m-], plural [wa-]: used for human beings
   Singular [m-], plural [mi-]: used for features of the natural environment
   Singular [ki-], plural [vi-]: used for inanimate objects

4. German
   Dative *dem* implies a stationary place or location.
   Accusative *das* implies movement to, toward, or into a location.
   German articles contain the idea of movement, whereas English articles (*a, an, the*) contain no such meaning.

Practice 6.4

1. a. ditransitive
   b. caused motion
   c. caused motion
   d. ditransitive

2. a. Structural: a. beer that is cool plus wine (not necessarily cool)
                   b. cool beer and cool wine

   b. Lexical: a. Fred was not warm.
                   b. Fred was up-to-date and interesting.

   c. Structural: a. The woman is standing at the water cooler now. (I may have met her elsewhere.)
                   b. I met the woman while I was standing at the water cooler.

   d. Structural: a. The bill concerns dangerous drugs.
                   b. The drug bill is dangerous.

e. Structural:　a.　either George and Harry together or Fred alone

b.　George plus one of the other two (Harry or Fred)

f. Structural:　a.　The pictures are in the attic.

b.　I will be in the attic when I look at the pictures.

g. Lexical:　　key to the door, car, answers . . . ?

Practice 6.5

	NP	Thematic role	Assigned by
1.	Sarah	agent	drove
	that bus	theme	drove
	Indianapolis	source	from
	Terre Haute	goal	to
2.	children	agent	eating
	their ice cream	theme	eating
	kitchen	location	in
3.	you	agent	buy
	which shoes	theme	buy
	the store	location	at
4.	Alyssa	agent	came
	work	source	from
5.	the boys	agent	walked
	the park	goal	to
6.	Sally	agent	mailed
	a parcel	theme	mailed
	her nephew	goal	to
7.	Bill	agent	leave
	what	theme	leave
	your house	location	at
8.	the letter	theme	sent
9.	Ginger	agent	scribbled
	her address	theme	scribbled
	the paper	location	on
10.	the minister	theme	ordained
	the pulpit	location	in

Practice 6.6

1. a–b. In (a), the NP *Janice's sister* c-commands *herself* and thus can be the antecedent, according to Principle A. *Janice's* cannot be the antecedent since it does not c-command *herself*. In (b), since *Janice's sister* c-commands *her*, it cannot be the antecedent for *her*.

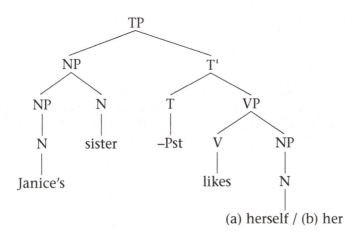

c. The NP *Fiona* c-commands *herself* and is in the same clause. Therefore, according to Principle A, *Fiona* is the antecedent. Although the NP *Janice* c-commands *herself*, it is not in the same clause and cannot be the antecedent.

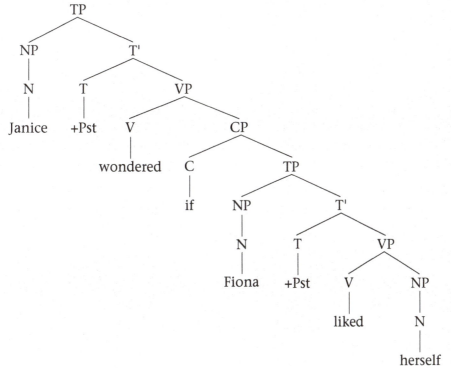

d. Although the NP *Janice* c-commands *she*, it is not in the same clause. Thus, according to Principle B, *Janice* could be the antecedent for *she*.

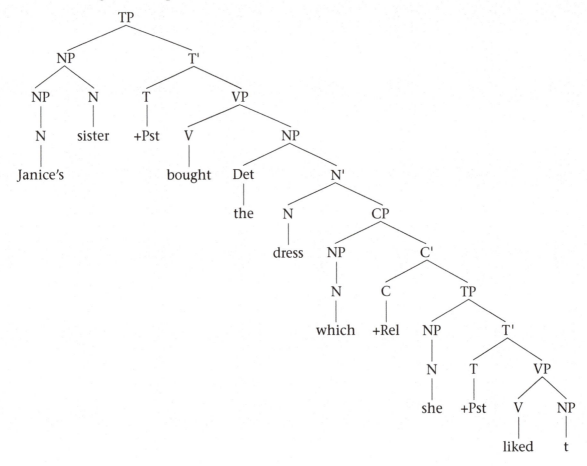

Practice 6.7

1. a. Because the bride walks down the aisle, *she* refers to the bride.
   b. Because the bride is part of the couple and we expect friends to cry at a wedding, *she* refers to every friend.

2. a. The car wreck was an accident.
   b. The car wreck was intentional with malice aforethought.

3. a. The accusation may or may not be false.
   b. The accusation is actually false.

4. a. The speaker is in China.
   b. The speaker is outside of China.

5. a. We know which hospital but not the specific priest.
   b. We know which priest but not the specific hospital.

Practice 6.8

1. Maxim of Quality
2. Maxims of Relevance, Quantity, Manner
3. Maxim of Quality
4. Maxims of Relevance, Quantity, Manner
5. No violations

Review Exercises

1. a. homophones
   b. antonyms
   c. synonyms
   d. polysems (homonyms)
   e. antonyms
   f. polysems (homonyms)
   g. homophones
   h. synonyms

2. a. entailment
   b. paraphrase
   c. contradiction
   d. paraphrase
   e. entailment

3. a. extension/intension
   b. fuzzy concept
   c. connotation/denotation
   d. lexicalization
   e. metaphor
   f. graded membership

4. The causative is grammaticized in Burmese. It is indicated by making the first consonant voiceless.

5. Answers will vary.

6. a. The witness cannot answer the question because use of *stop* presupposes that the witness has taken or is taking drugs.

   b. The implicature is not the same. The doctor is asking a genuine information question, whereas the student is making a request.

   c. The Maxims of Relevance and Quantity are being violated. As a result, the implicature of the letter is that the student does not have the necessary academic qualifications for graduate school.

Chapter 7

Practice 7.1

1. b. The statement is a universal tendency because /a/ does not occur in *all* languages and its presence has no implications for any other sounds.

   b. /a/ is unmarked since it is common in world languages.

2. c. This is in implicational universal since the presence of one implies the presence of the other.

   a. Inflectional affixes are marked because they are less common in world languages than derivational affixes.

b. Derivational affixes are unmarked because they are relatively common in world languages.

Possible or impossible?

a. possible

b. impossible: If there are inflectional affixes, there must be derivational affixes.

c. possible: Derivational affixes do not imply inflectional affixes.

Practice 7.2

1. More marked: a. nasal vowels; b. long vowels; c. rounded front vowels; d. /ɛ/

2. The language should have short vowels and oral vowels.

Practice 7.3

1. Least marked: a. fricatives; b. voiceless obstruents; c. /t/; d. voiced sonorants; e. stops

2. a. Bulgarian must have voiceless obstruents and fricatives.

   b. Based on universal tendencies we could expect it to have:

   /n/, /t/, /s/ as the most common nasal, stop, and fricative
   /r/ or /l/ since most languages have at least one liquid

Practice 7.4

1. More marked: a. VCC syllable; b. contour tones; c. five tones; d. CCVC syllable; e. CVC syllable

2. a. Syllable types: CCVCC, CVC, V, CVCC, CCV, CCVC, VCC

   b. At least two consonants are allowed in onsets and codas.

   c. It must have CV.

   d. If a language has complex onsets/codas, it must have simple onsets/codas. If a language has closed syllables, it will have open syllables.

3. a. The language has contour tones on the second word (LH) and on the third word (HL).

   b. We could predict (although it is not mandatory) that the language would have a level low tone.

Practice 7.5

1. a. impossible   d. possible   g. possible
   b. possible   e. possible   h. impossible
   c. impossible   f. possible

2. a. stop /t/; fricative /s/; nasal /n/

   b. Affricates imply stops and fricatives.

   c. voiceless obstruents

   d. At least one liquid is expected.

e. a. /i/ and /u/

   b. short vowels

   c. unmarked: The mid and high back vowels are rounded.

   d. marked: front rounded vowels

Practice 7.6

1. a. (Blackfoot) polysynthetic

   b. (Chinese) isolating (analytic)

   c. (Turkish) agglutinating

   d. (Latin) fusional (inflectional)

2. a. It must have derivational affixes since the presence of inflectional affixes implies the presence of derivational affixes.

   b. It must have derivational affixes because of the presence of inflectional affixes, but the implicational universal does not specify the presence of specific types of inflection.

   c. We cannot make a prediction. Thai may or may not have derivational affixes.

Practice 7.7

1. a. SVO   b. SOV

2. Spanish is expected to have prepositions and the PP would come after the V. Yuwaalaraay is expected to have postpositions with the PP before the V.

3. In Tinrin, the demonstrative comes after the N, but in Limbu it comes before the N.

Practice 7.8

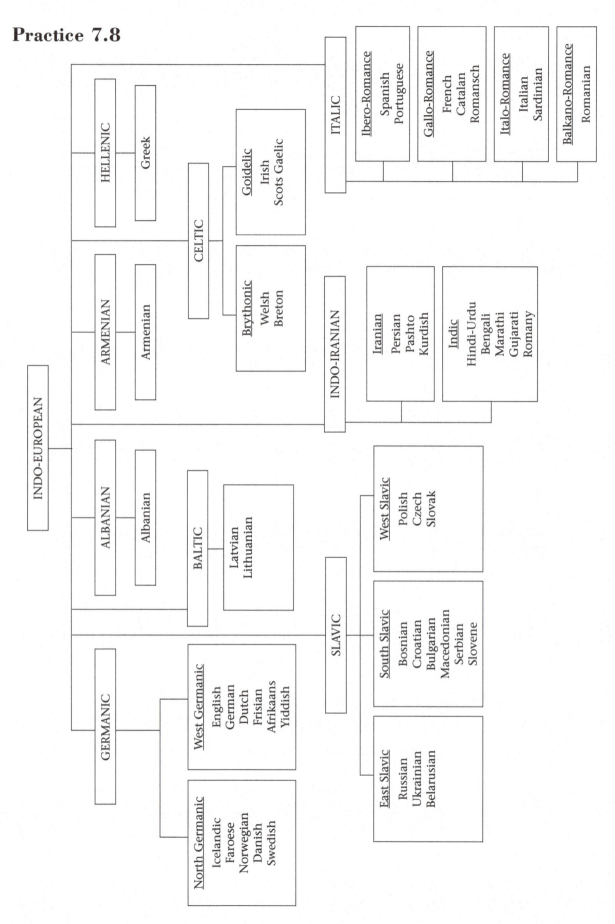

Practice 7.9

1. Sample answers are given; others are possible:

   Italian: Sardinian

   Swedish: Icelandic, Faroese

   Yiddish: German, Dutch

   Catalan: French, Romansch

   Polish: Czech, Slovak

   Russian: Ukrainian, Belarusian

   Latvian: Lithunian

   Bulgarian: Slovene, Macedonian

2. a. Greek

    b. Hungarian

    c. Persian

    d. Macedonian

    e. Albanian

    f. German

3. a. North Germanic

    b. Goidelic (Insular Celtic)

    c. Italo-Romance (Italic)

    d. Iranian

    e. Indic

    f. South Slavic

    g. South Slavic

    h. West Slavic

    i. Hellenic

    j. West Germanic

Review Exercises

1. Inventory B is real because:

   a. Unlike A, it has unmarked, expected common obstruent phonemes, e.g., stops /p, t, k/ and fricatives /s/ and /f/.

   b. Unlike A, it obeys implicational universals: affricates imply fricatives and stops; voiced obstruents imply voiceless obstruents.

   c. Unlike A, it has expected sonorants: nasals /n, m/ and at least one liquid.

2. a. Inventory A is real.

   b. Use of phonological space: the six vowels of A are spread out, so there are front and back vowels, and high, mid, and low vowels. Vowels in B are all back.

   Implicational universals: B has only nasal vowels, but the presence of nasal vowels implies the presence of oral vowels.

3. a. Hindi: SOV

   b. Warao: OSV

   c. Classical Arabic: VSO

   d. Thai: SVO

   e. Hixkaryana: OVS

   f. Toba Batak: VOS

4. Lakhota:

   d. creek along

   e. snow through he went

   f. house the around/about they stood

   Order of P and complement: NP P

   Order of Det and N: N Det

   Order of V and O: O V (because it has postpositions)

   Order of S, V, and O: SOV

Chapter 8

Practice 8.1

1. palatalization, affrication
2. consonant deletion, degemination, apocope
3. place assimilation, degemination
4. syncope, degemination, palatalization, frication, vowel weakening (iː is shortened to i).
5. nasalization, consonant deletion
6. consonant deletion word-initially, syncope, apocope
7. dissimilation (of the aspirated consonant)
8. epenthesis
9. frication
10. metathesis
11. voicing/voicing assimilation
12. consonant deletion
13. voicing, frication
14. consonant strengthening (stopping), vowel reduction, degemination, consonant deletion word-finally

Practice 8.2

1. Deaffrication

2. a. (1) Latin a ⟶ French e
   (2) Latin k ⟶ French tʃ (palatalization before a front vowel, affrication)
   (3) Latin p ⟶ French f (frication; manner assimilation between vowels)
   (4) final syllable -ut deleted
   (5) tʃ ⟶ ʃ (deaffrication)
   Note: Step (1) must come before step (2).
   Step (3) must come before step (4).
   Step (2) must come before step (5).

   b. English borrowed *chief* before step (5) had occurred. English borrowed *chef* after step (5) had occurred.

Practice 8.3

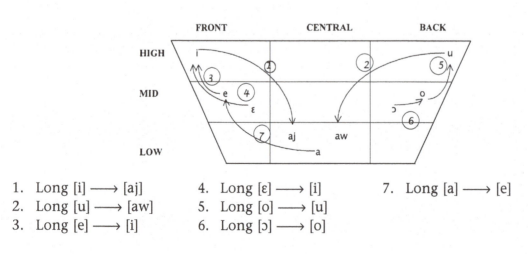

1. Long [i] ⟶ [aj]
2. Long [u] ⟶ [aw]
3. Long [e] ⟶ [i]
4. Long [ɛ] ⟶ [i]
5. Long [o] ⟶ [u]
6. Long [ɔ] ⟶ [o]
7. Long [a] ⟶ [e]

Practice 8.4

1. Reanalysis through analogy: Old English suffixes were regularized by the process of analogy, so now there is just one plural morpheme: -*s*.
2. Borrowing: Welsh borrowed plural -*s* from English.
3. Folk etymology: Unknown forms were reanalyzed (incorrectly) as English words.
4. Latin case endings were lost in Italian. Therefore, word order in the sentence becomes more important for meaning.

Practice 8.5

In these examples of early seventeenth-century English, a negative was formed by placing *not* after the verb. In the case of #2, with a pronoun as direct object, the negative is after the pronoun direct object. In contemporary English, the negative must come between an auxiliary and the main verb. If there is no auxiliary, then it is mandatory to insert the auxiliary *do*, and the negative is placed between *do* and the verb.

Practice 8.6

1. Lexical origins:
    1. Scots Gaelic; attested in the early sixteenth century.
    2. Old English; present before the twelfth century, reflecting Anglo-Saxon lifeways.
    3. Ultimately from Old Testament Hebrew, by way of Greek and Latin translations of the Old Testament. Attested in English as early as A.D. 825.
    4. From Old Norse; a case of adstratum borrowing.
    5. From French, after the Norman Conquest. Superstratum borrowing.
    6. Middle Latin, ultimately from Arabic. During the Middle Ages, Arabic was the language of science and technology.
    7. From Italian; attested in the early seventeenth century, when Italian Renaissance architecture was becoming popular in England.
    8. From Greek, via late Latin; attested in the late sixteenth century.
    9. From languages belonging to the Algonquian family, spoken by Native Americans in coastal areas from Virginia through New England during early settlement of the Northeast of America. Attested in early seventeenth century. Substratum borrowing.
    10. From Hindi and Marathi; attested in the late eighteenth century, at a time when the British were expanding into India. Substratum borrowing.
    11. Ultimately from West African languages, through Spanish/Portuguese. Attested in English in the late sixteenth century, after exploratory voyages along the African coast.
    12. This is "New Latin"—a word made from combining a Greek affix (*auto*) and Latin root *mobile*), a fairly common way of naming new technological inventions.
    13. From Tagalog *bundok* 'mountain'; attested in 1909, not long after the Spanish-American War in which the Philippines was acquired as a U.S. territory.

2. New words:

Facebook: compounding

BOGO: acronym (<u>b</u>uy <u>o</u>ne <u>g</u>et <u>o</u>ne)

tase: backformation from *taser* (itself an acronym for <u>T</u>homas <u>A</u>. <u>S</u>wift's <u>e</u>lectric <u>r</u>ifle)

LOL: initialism (for <u>l</u>augh <u>o</u>ut <u>l</u>oud)

spork: blend (<u>spo</u>on and <u>fork</u>)

app: clipping (<u>app</u>lication)

(to) friend: conversion/zero derivation

sudoku: borrowing (from Japanese)

photobomb: compounding (photo is also a clipping from <u>photo</u>graph)

dash cam: blend (<u>dash</u>board + <u>cam</u>era; dashboard is originally a compound as well)

Practice 8.7

1. broadening
2. weakening
3. amelioration
4. narrowing
5. pejoration
6. semantic shift
7. metaphor
8. semantic shift
9. metaphor
10. pejoration
11. narrowing
12. amelioration

Practice 8.8

1. Finno-Ugric

Finnish	Hungarian	Udmurt
k	h, k	k

Protoform: *k
In Hungarian, *k changed to h word-initially before a back vowel.

2. Proto-Algonquian

Fox	Ojibwa	Menomini	Evidence
ʃk	ʃk	sk	1, 6, 9
hk	kk	hk	2, 7, 10
ht	tt	ʔt	3, 4, 8
ht	tt	ht	5, 11, 12

*PA	Fox	Ojibwa	Menomini
ʔt	ht	tt	ʔt
ʃk	ʃk	ʃk	sk
hk	hk	kk	hk
ht	ht	tt	ht

3. Arabic

   a.
Position	Syrian	Iraqi	Evidence
word-initial	d, t	d, θ, ð	1, 2, 6, 7, 11, 12
word-final	d, t	t, θ, ð, d	4, 5, 6, 12
between vowels	d, t	d, θ, ð	3, 10, 14
after a consonant	d, t	t, θ, ð, d	1, 8, 9, 13

   b. Syrian has only d and t. Iraqi has d, t, θ, ð.

   c. Protoforms: *d, t, θ, ð.

   d. Proto d and ð merged to become d in Syrian, but were retained in Iraqi. Proto t and θ merged to become t in Syrian, but were retained in Iraqi.

4. Ponosakan:

   [w] was deleted between vowels: [w] → Ø / V _____ V
      (The data only shows deletion between [a] _____ [a], so that is acceptable.)
   Glottal stop was deleted word-initially: [ʔ] → Ø / # _____ (V)
   [g] became [h] after a vowel: [g] → [h] / V _____

Practice 8.9

1. Hypothetical Language Group One:
   Protoforms:

1. munto	3. pippona	5. wusa
2. fumo	4. nonka	6. fito

   Sound changes in Language A:
   - Nasalization of V before cluster of nasal + consonant
   - Vowel reduction of [o] word-finally
   - Vowel deletion of [a] word-finally in words of more than two syllables
   - Deletion of nasal before C

   Sound changes in Language B:
   - Deletion of nasal before C
   - Voicing of consonants before a vowel (i.e., word-initially and intervocalically)
   - Degemination (3)
   - Palatalization of glide before high V (5)

2. Hypothetical Language Group Two:
   Protoforms: 1. puka   2. nizudz

   Sound changes in Language A: Frication intervocalically

   Sound changes in Language B: Voicing word-initially and intervocalically; deaffrication

   Sound changes in Language C: consonant deletion word-finally (possibly preceded by deaffrication)

   Sound changes in Language D: Note that the first two changes are ordered:
   (1) Consonant deletion word-finally (possibly preceded by deaffrication);
   (2) Apocope;
   (3) Rhotacism

3. Austronesian

   *PAN. Note: Not all protoforms can be derived from data presented in the problem set. Alternative acceptable answers are given in parentheses.

   1. anak
   2. sakit
   3. hikat (probably could not be guessed from the data set; *ikat* would be an acceptable answer)
   4. uʀat (could not be guessed from the data set; *urat* or *uzat* would be an acceptable answer)

   Only changes that could be inferred from the data set are listed below.

   Changes in Malay:
   - None, or possibly rhotacism (4) (if PAN were *uzat*)

   Changes in Written Cham:
   - Vowel reduction before word-final [k] (1)
   - Substitution: Word-final stops become glottal stops
   - Substitution (or weakening through loss of place feature): Word-initial s ⟶ h
   - (Possibly rhotacism (4), if PAN were *uzat*)

   Changes in Tsat:
   - Substitution (or weakening through loss of place feature): Word-final stops become glottal stops
   - Deletion of first syllable
   - Development of tones from contact with Chinese, a tone language

4. German dialects

   Note: Protoforms are derivable from the data set given in the problem. Alternatives are given where protoforms cannot be derived with certainty from the data set.

   1. makən (or possibly: maːkən)
   2. ik
   3. slaːpən
   4. pʊnt
   5. bejtən or bajtən
   6. dat
   7. tuː

   Changes in the Northern dialect:
   - Deletion of word-final [n] in verbs
   - Possibly compensatory lengthening of vowel (1)

   Changes in the Southern dialect:
   - Frication following a vowel (1, 2, 3, 5, 6)
   - Palatalization (3)
   - Affrication of [+anterior] voiceless stops word-initially (4, 7)

Review Exercises

1. The Great English Vowel Shift

Vowel Change	Modern English word
a. oː ⟶ u	noon
b. iː ⟶ aj; ə ⟶ Ø/ __#	life
c. eː ⟶ i	sweet
d. ɔː ⟶ ow	boast
e. uː ⟶ aw	gown

2. Changes in English since Shakespeare

   a. SVO is the order in contemporary English.

   Shakespeare used primarily SVO, but the last line of 1 uses SOV.

   b. Today, *not* goes between the auxiliary and the main verb. (If there is no auxiliary, it is mandatory to insert *do*.)

   Shakespeare sometimes placed *not* after the main verb (1, 4), but also used *Do* Insertion (3). In questions with *Do* Insertion, the order could be *do* S (*not*) V or *do* (*not*) S V. This variation suggests that the change to *Do* Insertion was in process in Shakespeare's time.

   c. Word order of a *yes-no* question today is: Aux-Subject-Verb. Data in 3 and 4 show the variations Shakespeare used in *yes-no* questions. In 3, *do* is inserted, and there is Inversion. In 4, there is no *do*; we assume there was Verb Raising of the main verb since there is Inversion of subject and verb.

   d. Second-person singular pronouns *thou*, *thee*, and *thy* have fallen out of use. Along with these, the *-(e)st* suffix on verbs (*pursuest*, *didst*) has fallen out of use.

3. Sound changes in Romance

   Italian:
   - Frication: Voiced stops have become fricatives intervocalically (3).
   - Voicing: Voiceless stops have become voiced intervocalically (2).

   Spanish:
   - Epenthesis: [e] has been inserted word-initially before [s]-stop clusters.
   - Voicing + Frication: Voiceless stops became voiced stops intervocalically (2). Intervocalic voiced stops have become fricatives (2, 3).
   - Weakening: Geminate [l] weakened to [j] (2).
   - Vowel deletion (apocope): Word-final [e] has been deleted. (We can posit an intermediate stage where it was reduced to schwa before being deleted.)

   French:
   - Epenthesis + Consonant cluster simplification: [e] has been inserted word-initially before [s]-stop clusters, followed by deletion of [s].
   - Apocope: Word-final vowels in unstressed syllables have been deleted. (We may assume for 2 that degemination occurred before vowel deletion.)
   - In 2, [ut] has become a palatal glide, articulated with rounded lips.
   - In 3, the syllable [be] has been deleted with compensatory lengthening of the vowel [i].

4. Austronesian

Correspondence Table

	Tagalog	Javanese	Fijian	Samoan	Rapanui
word-final	t	t	Ø	Ø	Ø
word-final	k	ʔ	Ø	Ø	Ø
word-initial	t	—	d	t	t
word-initial	b	w	v	—	—
word-final	a	o	a	a	a
2nd syllable	o	u	u	u	u

The following reconstructions are reasonable given the data set from which you were working. They do not always correspond to the reconstructions of historical linguists specializing in Proto-Austronesian.

	Gloss	Protoform	Rationale
1.	'five'	*lima	*l → [r] in Rapanui. Word-final *a → [o] in Javanese.
2.	'bird'	*manuk	Fijian, Samoan, Rapanui lost word-final stops. The change of *k to a glottal stop in Javanese represents consonant weakening.
3.	'eye'	*mata	Word-final *a → [o] in Javanese.
4.	'ear'	*taliŋa	Tagalog seems to have deleted the word-internal *l and lengthened the vowel in compensation. The word-initial [d] in Fijian is consonant weakening, going from voiceless to voiced stop.
5.	'sky'	*laŋit	Deletion of word-final stops (see 2). *l → [r] in Rapanui.
6.	'stone'	*batu	Word-initial [b] is stronger than the fricative [v] in Fijian and than the glide [w] in Javanese. Those changes show consonant weakening. Tagalog seems to have changed [u] in the second syllable to [o] consistently.
7.	'head louse'	*kutu	Word-initial *k has weakened to a glottal stop in Samoan. The vowels are consistent with observations made in 6.